ON THE ROAD
TO
EMMAUS

ON THE ROAD TO EMMAUS

CELEBRATING 20 YEARS OF MINISTRY IN SAN DIEGO

JEONG WOO JAMES LEE

aventine press

Published by Aventine Press
55 East Emerson St.
Chula Vista CA 91911
www.aventinepress.com

ISBN: 978-1-59330-893-3
Printed in the United States of America

Contents

Introduction

It was on September 25, 1994 that we had our first Lord's Day worship service as New Life Mission Church of La Jolla. It was at the two-bedroom condo of one of our founding members (Richard Kim) in La Jolla. 15 people attended this first service—seven founding members, one visitor, and seven members from what was then New Life Mission Church of Anaheim, our sister/mother-church, at which I served for one year before I came down to San Diego to start this new church plant.

Other than one Caucasian visitor, everyone there was Korean-American. But our desire and prayer were that God would be pleased to grow this new church plant into a multi-ethnic church. As a first-generation immigrant (I came to the States when I was 15), and having grown up in Korean-American churches, I assumed that I would minister in a Korean-American church. But I came across an article which deplored the fact that the most segregated hour in America was (and quite possibly still is) 11 o'clock Sunday morning. It cut me deeply. The significance of our Lord breaking down in His flesh the dividing wall of hostility (Ephesians 2:14) between Jews and Gentiles struck me with a fresh force—especially as I was contemplating the possibility of planting a church. If Christ brought Jews and Gentiles together, whose separation was sanctioned by the Law of Moses itself, is there any justification for the current state of affairs?

This is not to say we don't need ethnic churches. Language barriers make ethnic churches necessary. After all, one of the rallying cries of the Reformation was to have the Word of God read and preached in the language that people could understand! But we also want to demonstrate the glory of the gospel of Jesus Christ, which transcends all the differences that divide people. Especially, in this nation of immigrants, where so many ethnic groups are represented, we have an amazing opportunity to have churches that reflect the church triumphant and glorified, which is made up of people from every tribe and tongue and people and nation (Revelation 5:9)!

1

Even from the beginning, being a multi-ethnic congregation was not our primary goal, however. It was understood to be only a by-product of being a Christ-centered and heavenly-minded congregation. We wanted our church to be multi-ethnic but mono-cultural—a congregation of diverse ethnic groups, all striving to cultivate one culture that is as biblical, Christian, and heavenly as it is possible—even though we will never be able to fully shake off the "American" context, in which we find ourselves. As we celebrate our 20th anniversary, we are grateful that our Lord was pleased to build us up into such a congregation.

Praying and laboring to build a multi-ethnic congregation turned out to be a great blessing, especially for me. As our congregation became more and more multi-ethnic, I began to realize how "Korean-American" I really was in my culture. Don't misunderstand me. I am grateful to be a Korean-American since it was God's will that I should be one! But this fledgling multi-ethnic church has forced me to figure out a way to preach in such a way that everyone, regardless of their ethnic or cultural background, could understand the message. It has constantly challenged me to focus on the gospel and its universal truths that are relevant to all men and women in all stages of history.

Important in this endeavor has been a conscious effort to preach Christ in all of Scripture. Although I grew up in an evangelical church, this was a "novel" idea to me, which was introduced to me when I attended Westminster Seminary in California (1987-1991). I was really struck when a professor said in class, "If you preach a sermon at a Jewish synagogue and they like it, you have not preached a 'Christian' message." Of course! What makes a message 'Christian'? Is it not its Christ-centeredness? It dawned on me that, when the Apostles preached, the text out of which they preached Christ was the Old Testament Scriptures! And what is the message God's people need to hear week in and week out? Is it not "the immeasurable riches of his grace in kindness toward us in Christ Jesus" (Ephesians 2:7)? After all, is it not Christ who is "the Way, and the Truth, and the Life" (John 14:6), the "wisdom from God, righteousness and sanctification and redemption" (1 Corinthians 1:30)? I'm grateful to Westminster Seminary and all its professors for teaching me this life- and ministry-changing truth and equipping me with the tools to preach Christ in all of Scripture!

What we have in this book are some samples from the 20 years of my preaching ministry at New Life Presbyterian Church of La Jolla, PCA[1]. They are arranged roughly in the order they were preached. To publish these sermons is quite humbling because I am rarely satisfied with my feeble efforts to preach Christ crucified. I know I have not done justice to the glory of the gospel. Yet we are publishing these sermons, more than anything, as a commemorative project—as a way to remember how this flock of Christ has been fed during the past 20 years. We also look forward to the future with the hopes that the Word of God will thrive and prosper more in the coming years. And it is our humble prayer that some would find comfort and encouragement in the messages that are contained in this book.

This book is titled, *On the Road to Emmaus*. The road to Emmaus was, of course, the setting, in which our Lord appeared *incognito* to the two disciples on their way to Emmaus from Jerusalem. There, our Lord showed them how it was "necessary that the Christ should suffer these things and enter into his glory....And beginning with Moses and all the Prophets, he interpreted to them in all the Scriptures the things concerning himself" (Luke 24:26-27). To be there to eavesdrop on our Lord's exposition of Scriptures is every theologian's dream, I'm sure! Thankfully, we are not left in the dark. As we know, this became the very pattern of the Apostolic preaching and the New Testament. I remember being so excited about learning biblical theology at Westminster and sharing that excitement with one of my roommates. We said to each other how this would make a wonderful title for a book of sermons if the Lord should allow us to write one. I guess I beat my roommate to it. My desire is that this book can help those who read it to have a little glimpse of that "on-the-road-to-Emmaus" experience.

December, 2014
La Jolla, California

---

1 "PCA" is the acronym for the Presbyterian Church in America.

Acknowledgments

I'm grateful, first of all, to the 20th Anniversary Committee (Rich Carlson, Paul Han, Richard Kim, Elizabeth Roberts, John Yi), as well as others for their suggestion and persistent "push" to have this book of sermons published. I'm grateful for their encouragement and support and patience.

I'm also thankful to Rev. Mike Kearney who edited the book. In addition to proofreading, he provided many valuable ideas and suggestions. I'm glad that I came to know a dear brother in the Lord through this process.

And I'm thankful to the congregation of New Life Presbyterian Church of La Jolla, PCA. I consider myself one of the most blessed pastors for the privilege of ministering to such a congregation! If I don't feel weary and burned out after 20 years of ministry, it is only because of God's grace in granting me a congregation like New Life, La Jolla (as we call our church)! Many of them had to sit through my growth as a pastor and preacher, making all kinds of mistakes along the way. I've said it many times because it is so true—if I'm a better preacher now in any way than when I first started, it is because of their patience with which they endured my shortcomings and all the helpful and honest comments that they have offered me in love and respect!

I also would like to thank my parents and my parents-in-law for their constant prayer and encouragement. At the beginning, they all wished that I would pastor a "big" church. Now, they are more concerned that I be a good and faithful pastor, regardless of the size of the church. I'd like to especially thank my father for the wise words he spoke to me early on in my ministry—that the people in the pews come to hear the Word of God preached, to hear why it is so good to believe in Jesus Christ, not whatever wisdom or worldly knowledge I might have!

And I'd like to thank my wife (Cassie) and children (Audrey, Connor, and Averey). With each passing day, I'm realizing more and more how undeserving I am of them, how blessed I am to have them in my life! May the Lord bless me and help me to be the kind of husband and father He wants me to be!

And what can I say about the One, because of whom I am all that I am, called to do all that I do, and have all that I have, far beyond what I deserve? My only wish is that God's grace toward me would not be in vain, that I would work faithfully and diligently for His glory and pleasure through the grace of God that is with me (1 Corinthians 15:10).

"Say You Are My Sister"

[10] Now there was a famine in the land. So Abram went down to Egypt to sojourn there, for the famine was severe in the land. [11] When he was about to enter Egypt, he said to Sarai his wife, "I know that you are a woman beautiful in appearance, [12] and when the Egyptians see you, they will say, 'This is his wife.' Then they will kill me, but they will let you live. [13] Say you are my sister, that it may go well with me because of you, and that my life may be spared for your sake." [14] When Abram entered Egypt, the Egyptians saw that the woman was very beautiful. [15] And when the princes of Pharaoh saw her, they praised her to Pharaoh. And the woman was taken into Pharaoh's house. [16] And for her sake he dealt well with Abram; and he had sheep, oxen, male donkeys, male servants, female servants, female donkeys, and camels.

[17] But the LORD afflicted Pharaoh and his house with great plagues because of Sarai, Abram's wife. [18] So Pharaoh called Abram and said, "What is this you have done to me? Why did you not tell me that she was your wife? [19] Why did you say, 'She is my sister,' so that I took her for my wife? Now then, here is your wife; take her, and go." [20] And Pharaoh gave men orders concerning him, and they sent him away with his wife and all that he had.

Genesis 12:10-20

What do you think? Was Abram right in going down to Egypt to escape the drought in Canaan? Or did Abram sin by going down? Was it an act of unbelief to leave the Promised Land and go down to Egypt?

On the one hand, what can possibly be wrong with escaping from a life-threatening danger? What's more natural than that? It is God who gave us survival instincts for our self-preservation. On the other hand, Abram was in a special situation. He was not just in any place. He was in the land of Canaan, which God promised to give him. Why did he leave his country and family and come to this foreign land in the first place? Was it not because God called him? Was it not because God promised to give him the land of Canaan, to bless him and protect him as his God? If God called him and made him His own, would He not take care of him? Shouldn't Abram have trusted God to take care of him, even in a severe drought?

What do you think Abram should have done? What would *you* have done?

This, of course, is a tough question to answer because the Bible doesn't explicitly say one way or the other. Of course, God is not confined to the laws of nature and He can perform awesome, supernatural miracles. We can readily think of Israel's exodus and the plagues that devastated Egypt. And what about the parting of the Red Sea when Israel was caught between the sea and the Egyptian chariots?

But God is not just a God of miracles. He is also a God of providence. He is the One who created the world and put in place all the physical laws in the first place. By these laws He demonstrates His wisdom and faithfulness. God delights in using and orchestrating the natural courses of events to accomplish His sovereign will, which cannot fail. That is why we do not just pray and wait for God's miraculous healing. As we pray, we take the medicine or go to the doctor because they too are the means God uses to accomplish His purpose. Even a miracle like the parting of the Red Sea—how did it happen? Did Moses just strike the sea and the waters parted instantly? No. We read in Exodus 14:21, "Moses stretched out his hand over the sea, and the LORD drove the sea back *by a strong east wind all night* and made the sea dry land, and the waters were divided."

In fact, God gave us an intelligent mind. He wants us to develop a sense of discernment and wisdom to navigate carefully the ocean of life. This cannot be done if we do not fix our eyes on the North Star of His Word, of course. But His Word does not tell us everything we must and ought to do. God desires us to use the mind He gave us to apply His Word rightly to our life instead of demanding simple yes-no answers from

Him. Common sense is a gift from God, which is to be used under the guidance of God's Word. Consider the Apostle Paul's ministry, too. At times he risked his life to preach the gospel in certain cities. At other times, he moved on to other cities when his life was threatened.

So What's The Point?

If so, maybe the main point of this account is not about whether Abram did the right thing in going down to Egypt or not. Not that the question is unimportant. But the real point may be somewhere else. Maybe Abram going down to Egypt was a matter of "adiaphora"—a matter of indifference—something that does not touch on the essential, fundamental tenets of Christianity. Paul spoke of such things—the things that are not a matter of right or wrong. One such thing at his time was the matter of eating meat which was dedicated to pagan gods. He also dealt with the matter of marriage and singlehood. In our contemporary setting, we can say that our children's schooling—whether we send them to a Christian school or a public school or homeschool them— is also a matter of adiophora (that is, as long as we are involved in our children's education in a responsible manner and do not relinquish our parental responsibility to others). We should not divide over these matters of adiaphora.

Then what is the point of this incident? We can see that God allowed it to happen in order to show Abram who he was and who God was. Why this is important, especially at this stage, is easy to see. Abram needed to learn more of this God who called him. Having grown up in an idol-worshipping household (Joshua 24:2), Abram did not know much about Him. But he also needed to learn more about himself in order to have a proper relationship with the Lord. We know what happens when we get involved in a deep, intimate relationship, such as marrying someone or having a child—not only do we grow in our understanding of the other person but also in our self-knowledge. The same is true of our relationship with God, and even more so.

But other than these existential reasons, there is another (redemptive-historical) reason for God to allow this incident to occur, I believe. But we will see what that is later.

9

Something About Abram

As they say, nothing exposes a man's true character like a crisis.

Abram was caught between a rock and a hard place. In Canaan he faced a life-threatening drought. So he decided to go down to Egypt. But Egypt was not the safest place either! Another kind of life-threatening danger existed there! His wife, Sarai, was extremely beautiful despite her old age. And he feared that the Egyptians were immoral and they would have no qualms about killing him and taking his wife away (verses 11-12). And he wasn't being irrationally paranoid about it. The Egyptians did notice how beautiful Sarai was. And the princes of Egypt spoke to Pharaoh about her. And Pharaoh wanted to take her as his wife—most likely as one of his many concubines. And he might have had no misgivings about killing an insignificant foreigner to take his beautiful wife for himself.

And, so, what did Abram do? He pleaded with his wife to lie for him: "Say you are my sister, that it may go well with me because of you, and that my life may be spared for your sake" (verse 13). Not only did he ask his wife to lie in order to save his life; in doing so, he risked his wife's chastity and let his wife end up in another man's bed! How shameful was his cowardice!

Not being in that situation, and not feeling the same fear he felt, we shouldn't be too quick to judge him. We can make all kinds of bold claims and promises now, but what would we do if something like this were to really happen? Think about what the Gospels tell us of Peter, one of the first disciples, and his bold pledge of loyalty to Christ and his denial of Jesus—not just once but three times in a matter of one night! How colossal was his failure to keep his word in that critical moment of testing! Would any of us fare better than Abram or Peter if we were in that situation? We hope we would be courageous and unflinching in our commitment to God and to our loved ones, to love and protect them. But that would not happen unless we are committed to loving them to the point of death, unless we practice dying daily in our loving service to Christ and to our loved ones, would it?

But as grave as these problems were—the Egyptians and his cowardice—I dare say they were not Abram's real problem. I don't want to psychologize too much here but I do believe that Abram was facing a crisis of sorts in his faith. This was his real problem. Why do I say that?

We already said that Abram's going down to Egypt was not necessarily a bad thing. But what matters is what motivated him to do so at a deeper level. Consider the recent, significant change in his life. He left his home country and family to follow God's call. This was incredible because he grew up in a pagan household, as Joshua told the people of Israel, 'Thus says the LORD, the God of Israel, 'Long ago, your fathers lived beyond the Euphrates, Terah, the father of Abraham and of Nahor; and they served other gods…" (Joshua 24:2). So, when Abram followed God, he was young, very young, in faith. And when he finally came to the land of Canaan, the Lord promised to give it to him and to his descendants. But what happened not too long after he entered the land? There was a severe drought. His and his family's lives were in danger. Abram might have been terribly disappointed. Was this how God rewarded him for trusting Him and following Him all this way?

We know that this was a real issue by what Abram does *not* do once the drought hits the land. Take a look at verse 7 of Genesis 12: "[When Abram came into the land of Canaan] the LORD appeared to Abram and said, 'To your offspring I will give this land.' *So he built there an altar to the LORD*, who had appeared to him." And take a look at v. 8: "From [Shechem] he moved to the hill country on the east of Bethel and pitched his tent, with Bethel on the west and Ai on the east. *And there he built an altar to the LORD and called upon the name of the LORD*." So we see that it was Abram's practice to build altars to the Lord wherever he went in the land of Canaan. This was an act of faith, Abram claiming God's promise for him and marking the territory, as it were. But this suddenly stops once the famine hits the land. We can understand why he did not build altars to the Lord in Egypt. Egypt was not the land God promised to give him. But not calling on the name of the Lord, not crying out to God for help and protection when he felt his life threatened by the Egyptians? And resorting to his cowardly scheme, sacrificing his wife to save his life?

11

Should we be surprised by Abram's cowardice when his faith was shaken like that? This is not to excuse his shameful behavior. But how tempting it is for *us* to resort to dishonorable ways when *we* feel distant from God! When our eyes are on Him, even big problems seem small. But when we lose sight of Him and His greatness, even small problems grow big and insurmountable in our eyes. Remember what the ten spies to Canaan said to the congregation of Israel? "There we saw the Nephilim…and we seemed to ourselves like grasshoppers, and so we seemed to them" (Num. 13:33)! Maybe that's exactly how Abram felt when he entered Egypt. And how his priorities got mixed up, thinking as if preserving his life, even by a shameful way, were most important!

Something About God

But even when Abram fails, God remains faithful. Abram does not call on the Lord (at least according to our passage), but the Lord intervenes on his behalf and rescues him *and* Sarai in a dramatic way. God strikes Pharaoh's household with great plagues and prevents him from violating Sarai. Pharaoh lets Abram and Sarai go. And Abram leaves Egypt safely with many gifts from Pharaoh and Sarai's chastity intact. But even more importantly, Abram leaves Egypt with a greater understanding of God—how powerful God is to subjugate Pharaoh like that. And hopefully also with a deeper confidence in God to rescue him from danger, however great and whatever it may be.

Abram would make the same error later (Genesis 20). But can we blame him? How often we make the same error over and again! But through them all Abram learned to trust his God. So, later in life, He would trust God enough to offer up his beloved son, Isaac, knowing that He would raise him up even from the dead (Hebrews 11:19).

The Redemptive-Historical Significance

But we see God doing still more—redeeming this messy situation to a greater measure. To see this, let us review the general contours of this incident. To put roughly what happened:

1. Abram comes into the land of Canaan, which God promises to give him;

2. Not too long after that, a severe famine strikes the land and Abram decides to go down to Egypt to obtain food;
3. However, Abram senses a life-threatening danger in Egypt. He fears what the Egyptians would do to him on account of Sarai's beauty and asks her to identify herself as his sister, not his wife;
4. As Abram feared, Sarai's beauty is noticed by the princes of Egypt and she ends up in Pharaoh's house;
5. Pharaoh bestows many gifts on Abram for Sarai;
6. Before she is defiled, however, God afflicts Pharaoh and his household with great plagues and Pharaoh finds out Sarai's true relation to Abram;
7. Pharaoh rebukes Abram for deceiving him and sends him away;
8. Abram leaves Egypt with his wife undefiled and with all the gifts Pharaoh gave him. (By the way, Hagar, who becomes the mother of Ishmael later on in Genesis 16, is one of the many gifts Pharaoh gave to Abram.)

Can you see the many similarities between this incident and a later incident? Yes, I'm speaking of Israel's exodus out of Egypt. This becomes clearer when we list in chronological order the highlights of that later event:

1. Jacob and his family come into the land of Canaan from Haran, the home country of Rebecca, Jacob's mother;
2. A severe famine strikes the land of Canaan and, after many turns of events, Jacob and his family come to Egypt to flee the famine in the land;
3. Though the Jews are honored in Egypt at the beginning on account of what Jacob's son Joseph has done for Egypt, when a new dynasty is established the Jews are enslaved;
4. They face the danger of extinction when Pharaoh wants to kill all the Jewish male infants;
5. God dramatically intervenes by sending Moses to Pharaoh and demands that he let the people of Israel go;
6. When Pharaoh refuses, God afflicts him and Egypt with great plagues, culminating in the Passover;
7. Pharaoh finally surrenders and sends the Jews out of Egypt;

8. The Jews plunder the Egyptians and come out with silver and gold and jewelry and clothing (Exodus 12:35).

Do you see the similarities? It seems the Lord wants us to view Abram's journey in and out of Egypt as a kind of paradigm, a prototypical pattern, for Israel's exodus. Why? Again, what's the point?

It was designed to show the *redemptive* purpose of Abram's election and calling!

Consider the context of God's calling of Abram. In Genesis 11, we have the famous story of the Tower of Babel. It tells of mankind's audacious, insolent rebellion against God, which results in the confusion of language and dispersion of nations. That story is followed by the genealogy of Shem, the line of God's promise (Genesis 9:26), which leads to God's calling of Abram. The message is clear. God is calling Abram out of fallen, rebellious humanity, in order to preserve the line of the seed of the woman and to build the city of God through him and his offspring. What is that, if not redemption? And this redemptive thrust is made clear by Abram's exodus out of Egypt.

Of course, this is in the larger context of the enmity between the seed of the woman and the seed of the serpent (Genesis 3:15), the war between the city of God and the city of man, which characterizes all of human history after the Fall. Even the promises God gave to Abram in verses 2-3 of Genesis 12 were not some generic blessings for wealth and wellness, comfort and prosperity (the kind that the Gentiles seek). This battle theme is present there—when God promises to Abram, "I will bless those who bless you, and him who dishonors you I will curse…" (verse 3). Redemption, then, is not only the people of God being delivered from their sin but also the head of the serpent being crushed by the Seed of the woman.

It is not surprising, then, some of the vocabulary used to describe the war between the seed of the woman and the seed of the serpent are used to tell the story of Abram's exodus. Consider how the descendants of Cain (the seed of the serpent) and those of Seth (the seed of the woman) are described in Genesis 4. The spirit of Cain's descendants is exemplified in Lamech, who defies God's creation order and takes two wives to himself (Genesis 4:19). And this spirit shows up again later to characterize the generation which was destroyed by the Great Flood: "When man began to multiply on the face of the land and daughters were born to them, the [so-called] sons of God saw that the daughters of man were attractive. And they took as their wives any they chose" (Genesis 6:1-2). Isn't this exactly what we see in Pharaoh in Genesis 12? He manifests the same spirit in taking as his wife whomever he chooses (and most likely as many as he desires).

But what about the descendants of Seth? We read how they began to call upon the name of the Lord (Genesis 4:26). And that is exactly how Abram is presented in Genesis 12—as someone who calls upon the name of the Lord (verse 8)!

What happened in Egypt between Pharaoh and Abram was much more than meets the eye, isn't it? It was the continuation of the battle between the seed of the serpent and the seed of the woman. So is Israel's exodus out of Egypt. It is more than just a social, ethnic, political conflict between two nations.

But we also see that Abram, though chosen by God, is not the Seed of the serpent to crush the head of the Serpent. We see his miserable failures and disgraceful shortcomings. He must be rescued by God in a dramatic fashion.

What about Moses, whom God chose to deliver Israel out of Egypt? Was he the serpent-crushing Seed of the woman? Neither was he. For he was not even allowed to enter the Promised Land.

And if Moses was not the promised Seed of the woman, Israel's exodus could not be the ultimate redemption of God, could it? It was only a shadow. As Abram's exodus was a shadow of Israel's exodus, so was Israel's exodus only a shadow of the ultimate redemption of God. We know this also on account of Abram's experience. Although he responded wrongly to the famine in Canaan, being shaken in his confidence in God's promise, he also learned an important lesson about the Promised Land. A land that is so severely afflicted by a famine could not be all that God had promised to His beloved people. And so, even his descendants, who later took possession of the land, came to experience many imperfections of the land as they experienced many afflictions and plagues in the land. In fact, they were driven out of the land. Maybe this lesson Abram learned early in his journey of faith caused him to live as a pilgrim in the land that was promised to him: "By faith [Abraham] went to live in the land of promise, as in a foreign land, living in tents with Isaac and Jacob, heirs with him of the same promise. For he was looking forward to the city that has foundations, whose designer and builder is God" (Hebrews 11:9-10).

A Greater Exodus

Both Abram's exodus and Israel's exodus all pointed to the ultimate Exodus by which God saves His people once for all. This came when, in the fullness of time, the eternal Son of God came into this world (Galatians 4:4) and was born in the Promised Land. Not too long after His birth, while in infancy, our Lord faced a life-threatening danger. Panicking at the news of the birth of the Messiah, Herod the king slew all the male children under two years old in Bethlehem and in all its environs (Matthew 2:16). Warned by an angel, Joseph and Mary took Jesus down into Egypt and escaped the murderous plot. Only after Herod died was Jesus allowed to leave Egypt and come back to the Promised Land.

The Gospel-writer Matthew sees Jesus' journey in and out of Egypt as the fulfillment of Hosea 11:1: "Out of Egypt I called my son" (Matt. 2:15). Interestingly, the Hosea passage Matthew quotes is not a prophecy. It is a historical statement referring to Israel's exodus out of Egypt. By interpreting it as a prophecy for Jesus' exodus, Matthew is saying something very important about how we interpret the Old Testament, that what is recorded in the Old Testament finds its ultimate fulfillment and meaning in the life and work of Jesus Christ. Remember? This is exactly what Jesus said about the Old Testament and Himself: "You search the Scriptures because you think that in them you have eternal life; and it is they that bear witness about me…" (John 5:39).

But our Lord's journey in and out of Egypt was *not* the ultimate Exodus, either. It was to point out that Jesus was indeed the chosen Messiah and how He must retrace all the previous exoduses in order to make it all right. So we see Jesus not only going in and out of Egypt but also being baptized at the Jordan as Israel was baptized at the Red Sea (1 Corinthians 10:1-2). And as Israel was led into the wilderness after their baptism to be tested for 40 years (Deuteronomy 8:2-3), so was Jesus led into the wilderness to be tested for 40 days after His baptism. But whereas Israel failed to learn the lesson that man does not live by bread alone but by every word that proceeds out of the mouth of the Lord (Deuteronomy 8:3), Jesus resisted Satan's temptation to make bread out of stones and showed obeying God's word is more important than filling his empty stomach—the first act of slaying the serpent. And as Moses gave the law to Israel at Mount Sinai, our Lord gave the New Law to His New Israel at a greater mountain when He preached the Sermon on the Mount (Matthew 5-7).

But even all these things were a shadow to the ultimate Exodus. So we see Jesus talking with Moses and Elijah at the Mount of Transfiguration. Talking about what? "And behold, two men were talking with him, Moses and Elijah, who appeared in glory and spoke of his departure, which he was about to accomplish at Jerusalem" (Luke 9:30-31)! The word translated as "departure" there is the Greek word for "exodus." And this exodus to be accomplished in Jerusalem was His death and resurrection and ascension into heaven, the true Promised Land for the people of God!

> Abram sacrificed his wife and risked her chastity in order to save his life. Christ, on the other hand, sacrificed *His* life for his bride, the church! But did His bride have any chastity to speak of, to be protected? No! She had to be cleansed because she was dirty. She was so full of dirty spots and wrinkles and shame and guilt that He had to give up His life to save her and cleanse her. He had to take on all her shame and guilt and punishment. He had to lay down His life to rescue us, His sinful Bride!

And what was at the center of all that Jesus accomplished for our redemption? We read in Ephesians 5:25-27: "Husbands, love your wives, as Christ loved the church and gave himself up for her, that he might sanctify her, having cleansed her by the washing of water with the word, so that he might present the church to himself in splendor, without spot or wrinkle or any such thing, that she might be holy and without blemish." Do you see the stark contrast between Abram and Christ? Abram sacrificed his wife and risked her chastity in order to save his life. Christ, on the other hand, sacrificed *His* life for his bride, the church! But did His bride have any chastity to speak of, to be protected? No! She had to be cleansed because she was dirty. She was so full of dirty spots and wrinkles and shame and guilt that He had to give up His life to save her and cleanse her. He had to take on all her shame and guilt and punishment. He had to lay down His life to rescue us, His sinful Bride! And having loved us so while we were yet sinners, He will not stop loving us until we become holy and without blemish, full of splendor and beauty! How great is our Redeemer! How great is His love for us!

Your Life, Bound Up With Jesus' Life

If you have placed your faith in Jesus Christ, your life is bound up with Jesus' life, your life's journey with His exodus. Do you realize what a blessing this is? All of our sins in the past, in the present, and even in the future are covered by the precious blood of Jesus Christ. They cannot condemn us—not now or ever! All of our shameful failures and foolish mistakes have been covered with the perfect righteousness of Jesus Christ. We cannot boast of them but even they are now testaments to our Savior's deep love for unworthy, bumbling sinners like us! Charles Wesley expressed this well when he sang,

> *Jesus, my all in all Thou art,*
> *My rest in toil, my ease in pain,*
> *The healing of my broken heart,*
> *In war my peace, in loss my gain,*
> *My smile beneath the tyrant's frown,*
> *In shame my glory and my crown.*

Let us live, then, as those whose lives have been united with the life, death, and resurrection of Jesus Christ! We have been delivered from the slavery of sin and death! Our life is a pilgrimage toward our heavenly home, the eternal Promised Land! Let us not live in fear of those who may be able to kill the body but cannot kill the soul (Matthew 10:28)! Let us trust in the Lord with unswerving confidence and live courageously for His kingdom and His righteousness!

The Burning Bush

[1] Now Moses was keeping the flock of his father-in-law, Jethro, the priest of Midian, and he led his flock to the west side of the wilderness and came to Horeb, the mountain of God. [2] And the angel of the LORD appeared to him in a flame of fire out of the midst of a bush. He looked, and behold, the bush was burning, yet it was not consumed. [3] And Moses said, "I will turn aside to see this great sight, why the bush is not burned." [4] When the LORD saw that he turned aside to see, God called to him out of the bush, "Moses, Moses!" And he said, "Here I am." [5] Then he said, "Do not come near; take your sandals off your feet, for the place on which you are standing is holy ground." [6] And he said, "I am the God of your father, the God of Abraham, the God of Isaac, and the God of Jacob." And Moses hid his face, for he was afraid to look at God.
[7] Then the LORD said, "I have surely seen the affliction of my people who are in Egypt and have heard their cry because of their taskmasters. I know their sufferings, [8] and I have come down to deliver them out of the hand of the Egyptians and to bring them up out of that land to a good and broad land, a land flowing with milk and honey, to the place of the Canaanites, the Hittites, the Amorites, the Perizzites, the Hivites, and the Jebusites. [9] And now, behold, the cry of the people of Israel has come to me, and I have also seen the oppression with which the Egyptians oppress them.
[10] Come, I will send you to Pharaoh that you may bring my people, the children of Israel, out of Egypt."
Exodus 3:1-10

What we have in today's passage is an instance of theophany. "Theophany" refers to a phenomenon by which God reveals Himself in a special, visual manner.

God reveals Himself all the time through His creation: "the heavens declare the glory of God, and the sky above proclaims his handiwork" (Psalm 19:1). This is called "general" or "natural" revelation. From time to time throughout redemptive history, however, we see God manifesting Himself in "special," supernatural ways. When He does so, God doesn't "appear" in the same way all the time. He may appear as fire (like on the Day of Pentecost in Acts 2), or as a dove (like the Holy Spirit descending on Jesus at the Jordan in Matthew 3), or even as a ladder or staircase (to Jacob in the wilderness in Genesis 28). And even when He appears as fire, it is not always in the same way. During Israel's wilderness journey later on in the book of Exodus, the Spirit appeared as a *pillar* of fire. But on the Day of Pentecost, He appears as *tongues* of fire. Why in such different ways?

Consider the reason for God's theophany. It is to communicate a specific message to His people in a specific situation. Is it surprising, then, that each theophany should be specially tailored to the particular content of His message? It is like a visual aid God uses to highlight the main point of His message. For instance, think about the Holy Spirit appearing as tongues of fire on the Day of Pentecost. Well, one reason has to be that those on whom the Spirit rested on that day as tongues of fire spoke in tongues.

What is the reason for this particular theophany to Moses? God is calling Moses to go back to Egypt and deliver the people of Israel out of Egyptian bondage. Why is God appearing to Moses in this particular way?

The Setting

The setting will begin to give us a clue.

Moses is now 80 years old. He is herding a flock of sheep in the wilderness. But this flock of sheep is not even his; it belongs to his father-in-law, Jethro, a Midianite. What a place to be at the age of 80! With nothing to show for it—not even a flock of his own! How different from his forefather, Jacob, who came away with a lot of cattle and livestock after working for his father-in-law for much fewer years! Everything about his present condition reveals a man who is dejected, resigned to the monotonous flow of life, devoid of any ambition.

Maybe we can understand why. He led a privileged life early on. While all the Hebrew male infants were thrown into the Nile to be drowned, he was rescued and adopted by Pharaoh's daughter. Though a Hebrew boy, he grew up in Pharaoh's palace, receiving all the luxuries and benefits of the royal household. But to his credit, he didn't seem to regard this simply as his personal fortune. He knew he was a Hebrew and he was mindful of the sufferings of his Hebrew brethren. He might have felt a deep sense of responsibility toward his afflicted people. There must be a reason that God placed him in such a privileged position. So, when he saw one of the Hebrew slaves being beaten by an Egyptian, he stepped in and killed the Egyptian. Yet, when he tried to mediate between two Hebrew men the next day, he was coldly rejected. And when his murder was made known to Pharaoh, he had to flee the angry Pharaoh into the wilderness of Midian. Pursued by Pharaoh and rejected by his own people, Moses must have felt abandoned by God, too. Why did God allow him to grow up in Pharaoh's palace? What a royal waste that was! Just look at his life now!

But on this particular day, Moses leads the flock to the west side of the wilderness. Probably Moses didn't know what he was doing but this is significant. Do you remember? Adam and Eve moved *eastward* after they were banished from the Garden of Eden on account of their sin. Cain moved farther *east* after he was banished on account of killing his own brother, Abel (Genesis 4:16). And after the Flood, the people moved *eastward* to (or gathered in the east, in) the plain of Shinar to build the tower of Babel (Genesis 11:2). Lot, when he split from Abram, journeyed *eastward* to the valley of Jordan (Genesis 13:11), to Sodom (which was soon destroyed by God's judgment). The easterly direction seems to represent a movement away from God's presence in these early chapters of the Bible. We know that this was not a mere coincidence. The tabernacle's main entrance was on the east side. This meant that the people, who drew near to the presence of God, had to travel from east to west, in the westerly direction, reversing the direction of banishment and sinful degeneration.

So, as Moses moves westward in the wilderness, he comes to "Horeb, the mountain of God" (verse 1). What we have here is an anachronism.

Anachronism means things are out of chronological order. In this instance, a later title is applied to an earlier event. The mountain was called "Horeb" when this event was taking place. Most likely, this incident was what caused this mountain to be called "the mountain of God" (along with a later event that took place here—namely, God's covenant with Israel at this mount, which is also called Mount Sinai). The name "Horeb" comes from the Hebrew *verb*, brex; (*charev*), which means to be dry. So the name, Horeb, means dry land, desolate region, ruins. It is in this mountain of dryness and desolation that this incident takes place. And as a result, this mountain of desolation becomes the mountain of God.

Not Your Average Bush

Without forgetting all of these circumstances, we move to the theophany itself. God appears to Moses in the form of a burning bush: "And the angel of the LORD appeared to him *in a flame of fire* out of the midst of a bush" (verse 2). You may be puzzled to find the angel of the Lord appearing instead of God Himself. Well, we read also in verse 4, "*God* called to him *out of the bush*...." Here is one of many instances in which this mysterious "angel of the Lord" is identified with God Himself. Traditionally, we understand this angel of the Lord to be the pre-incarnate appearance of the Son of God.

I guess it is possible for the bush to be the supernatural element in this theophany and the fire to be the natural one. But since fire is a most common theophanic instrument of God, I think it is more than likely that the fire was the supernatural element, which represented God. In fact, something similar happens in a much grander scale not too much later. I'm speaking of God coming down on Mount Sinai at the time of Israel's covenant with God. As we said, Mount Sinai is another name for Mount Horeb. And how did God make His presence known to Israel? "Now Mount Sinai was wrapped in smoke because the LORD had descended on it *in fire*" (Exodus 19:18).

When we consider the parallels, the bush here (like Mount Sinai) is clearly distinguished from God appearing in the form of a flame of fire.

Yet the bush is so prominent in the theophany itself. In verses 2-4, there are five references to the bush, even more than the references to the fire:

> And the angel of the LORD appeared to him in a flame of fire out of the midst of a *bush*. He looked, and behold, the *bush* was burning, yet it [the *bush*] was not consumed. And Moses said, "I will turn aside to see this great sight, why the *bush* is not burned." When the LORD saw that he turned aside to see, God called to him out of the *bush*, "Moses, Moses!" And he said, "Here I am."

The bush obviously does not refer to God. Yet it is an integral part of this theophany. In fact, we can say the wonder of this theophany depends on the presence of the bush, in the midst of which the supernatural fire was burning without consuming it. Then what is the significance of this bush? What does the bush refer to? Is it just meaningless background, something that simply happened to be there?

In order to answer this question, we must remember that this was a theophany to *Moses*. It is a prelude to God's calling of Moses. And it is also the context of the dialogue between God and Moses. Considering these facts, would it be far-fetched to conclude that the bush represents Moses and the blazing flame of fire represents God—the two parties of the dialogue, which follows?

An ordinary bush in the mountain of dryness and desolation—what an apt representation of Moses! Wilderness was his home. His days were spent wandering in the wilderness, shepherding his father-in-law's flock. Solitude was his shadow. Loneliness was his only companion, other than the baaing sheep. No one knew of him. Even his family back in Egypt did not know whether he was dead or alive. Time robbed him of his youth and vitality. The sun stole his once royal complexion and left in its place a dark, sunburned skin. The wind and the heat engraved deep, dusty wrinkles on his face. Would anyone notice him? Did his life matter at all? Did *he* matter?

But Moses' life was about to be changed radically by this encounter with God—as the ordinary bush in the mountain of desolation was radically changed into something special and amazing by the fire of God that burned in its midst.

Grace: The Encounter That Changes Everything

People change people. We influence and impact others. We inspire and affect one another in small and profound ways. What kind of doctor you meet can mean either life or death. What kind of teacher you meet can set the course for the rest of your life. What kind of friend you keep can mean a jail or a fancy boardroom. And what about the man or the woman we marry? If people can affect us in such significant ways, what about God? Can we meet God and not be changed in profound ways? Can we have an on-going relationship with God and not be changed significantly?

And could it be, then, that the ordinary bush represented not only Moses but what we *all* are apart from God, when we do not have a real, meaningful, loving relationship with God? Whatever greatness we accomplish—does it really matter in the end? We are made in the image of God. If we do not image God, we betray our own nature and purpose. When something violates its own essence, there is something grotesque about it. It would be like trying to eat through our nose.

> We are made in the image of God. If we do not image God, we betray our own nature and purpose. When something violates its own essence, there is something grotesque about it. It would be like trying to eat through our nose.

But when God *does* come into our life and takes His rightful place in our midst, nothing will be ordinary about us. It's not necessarily because we become something different, something extraordinary in ourselves. Rather, it is on account of the "strangeness" of the phenomenon—that God should choose to speak from such an ordinary and insignificant bush. It is the kind of shock we would feel if we saw the world's most expensive diamond in a cheap jewelry box. Better yet, it would be like an ordinary piece of sketch paper turned into something that costs millions of dollars because Picasso or Van Gogh or Michelangelo drew something on it. I like the second analogy because it communicates two truths about our relationship with God. There is a sense in which the paper is still what it is. By itself, it would not be any more expensive than others. But there is another sense in which the paper is forever changed once the master artist makes his mark on it. That is the dual reality of how we are transformed when God enters into covenant relationship with us. We call this God's grace. By this encounter with God at Mount Horeb, Moses the dejected shepherd of sheep is transformed into the redeemer of Israel, the shepherd of the people of God.

Consumed But Not Destroyed!

This is all the more remarkable when we consider who we truly are. Take a look at verse 5: "Then [God] said, 'Do not come near; take your sandals off your feet, for the place on which you are standing is holy ground.'" Here is a clear reminder of Moses' sinfulness—shall I say, Moses' incompatibility with a holy God—as incompatible as a bush is with a flame of fire. Later, God would give the same message to the people of Israel in a grander scale at the same mountain: "Take care not to go up into the mountain or touch the edge of it [when the Lord God descends on it in fire, verse 18]. Whoever touches the mountain shall be put to death. No hand shall touch him, but he shall be stoned or shot; whether beast or man, he shall not live" (Exodus 19:12-13). In fact, a holy God and a sinful man are far less compatible than a dry branch and a flame of fire. A sinful man would be more quickly consumed by the presence of the holy God than a dry branch by fire.

So then, we see here what is truly amazing about this theophany. It is not that this ordinary bush is not being burned by fire. No, that's just a sign that points to the true wonder of this theophanic message: Moses would be engulfed by the consuming Fire that God is and yet he would not be destroyed! Rather, he would be a sight of marvel, which would bring glory to God!

The True Burning Bush

Then, how was it that Moses just needed to take off his sandals and survive his encounter with God? Was that enough? How was it that he was allowed to enter the mountain covered with the fiery presence of God?

> If we are in Jesus Christ, the true Burning Bush, we too can have the fiery Holy Spirit dwell in us without consuming us in divine judgment.

Was it because *he* was special? No! He, too, was a sinner like the rest of us. Remember? Here in our passage, he is not allowed to come near the burning bush, from which God speaks. Then, how could he mediate between God and Israel? How could he enter the mountain of God? How could he enter the tent of meeting, the tabernacle? How could he be in the presence of God that his face should shine with the glory of God?

It is all because of this, that "all that dwell upon the earth shall worship [the beast], whose names are not written in the book of life of the Lamb *slain from the foundation of the world*" (Revelation 13:8, KJV). Did you notice that? "The Lamb slain from the foundation of the world!" Of course, this doesn't mean that the Lamb of God was actually slain at the dawn of creation. Rather, it speaks of the eternal, irrevocable decree of God that His Son should sacrifice Himself for our salvation. This was conceived in the mind of God in eternity before time was born. Because God is almighty, all-wise, and all-faithful, He cannot fail and what God wills to do is as good as done. When God willed in time immemorial that His Son should die for His people, it had absolutely no possibility of failure. It was as good as done. So, the benefit of His sacrifice for our sin could be applied to the saints of the Old Testament, who lived before the actual, historical death of Jesus Christ, who looked forward to the coming of God's anointed Savior of the world.

Now, we can see the true message of God's theophany to Moses. We said earlier it pointed to God and Moses—God the fire and Moses the bush. But for Moses not to be destroyed by the consuming Fire that God is, it depended on another condition—the incarnation of the Son of God to suffer and die and rise again for his salvation and ours. And, when you think about it, isn't that exactly what this theophany points to? After all, we read in verse 2, "the angel of the LORD appeared to him in a flame of fire out of the midst of a bush"—the angel of the Lord, who is identified as God in verse 4! In this theophany, we see a shocking union between the divine Fire and an earthly bush. This revelation came to a historical realization when the eternal Son of God (the divine fire) united Himself to human nature (the bush)—not just temporarily but for all eternity!

But there is a deep irony here, isn't there? What really happened when Jesus died on the cross for us? Did He not cry out, "I thirst" (John 19:28)? Why? Was it simply because He was dehydrated from the crucifixion? I don't think so. It was because He was being consumed by the fire of God's holiness, from which Moses was spared when he was told not to come near the burning bush. On the cross, Jesus was undergoing the punishment that we deserve for our sin—nothing less than the lake of fire, which burns eternally in the infernal pit! How amazing this is! Hanging on that cursed tree, the Son of God endured the scorching heat of God's just wrath in our place! In the fierce heat of God's wrath, the Living Water grew thirsty! And the Fountain of life was consumed by the death that sinners deserved!

And because Jesus endured the fiery judgment of God in our place, there is no condemnation for those who are in Christ Jesus (Romans 8:1)—no guilt, no judgment, no punishment, no curse—not now, not ever! When Jesus was consumed by the fire of God's wrath, God's just wrath against us was also being consumed by Christ! Therefore, if we are in Jesus Christ, the true Burning Bush, we too can have the fiery Holy Spirit dwell in us without consuming us in divine judgment. We see this literally happening on the Day of Pentecost, don't we? "And suddenly there came from heaven a sound like a mighty rushing wind, and it filled the entire house where they were sitting. And divided tongues as of fire appeared to them and rested on each one of them. And they were all filled with the Holy Spirit and began to speak in other tongues as the Spirit gave them utterance" (Acts 2:2-4). Moses was not allowed to come near the theophany of the burning bush. But the disciples on the day of Pentecost became the burning bush! And that is the reality for all those, who place their faith in Jesus Christ!

Because of Jesus Christ, the Holy Spirit is no longer the scorching heat of divine wrath and judgment. The Holy Spirit has become for us a Comforter and Advocate. He provides us with the brilliance of heavenly joy, the warmth of divine comfort, and the power of resurrection life.

What A Strange Sight We Are In Christ

A bush that is burning yet not consumed by fire—what a strange sight! But that is what we are in Jesus Christ. When people get to know us, may they be puzzled by the strangeness of our life! Not because we are obnoxious and quirky. But because the fire of Christ burns within us. We find a good example of this in Acts 4:13: "Now when [the religious leaders] saw the boldness of Peter and John, and perceived that they were uneducated, common men, they were astonished. And they recognized that they had been with Jesus." Though the first disciples were uneducated, there was something noble and inviolably regal about them and the way they defended the gospel.

About the "strangeness" of the Christian existence, the Apostle Paul put it this way in 2 Corinthians 4:7-10; 6:8-10:

> But we have this treasure in jars of clay, to show that the surpassing power belongs to God and not to us. We are afflicted in every way, but not crushed; perplexed, but not driven to despair; persecuted, but not forsaken; struck down, but not destroyed; always carrying in the body the death of Jesus, so that the life of Jesus may also be manifested in our bodies....We are treated as impostors, and yet are true; as unknown, and yet well known; as dying, and behold, we live; as punished, and yet not killed; as sorrowful, yet always rejoicing; as poor, yet making many rich; as having nothing, yet possessing everything.

These words point to the reality of life's suffering and adversity. But they also point to the triumph of the reality of the surpassing power of the kingdom of heaven! And may our Lord be pleased to burn brightly within us and enable us to do things that are impossible with us but possible only with Him! Whatever God has called you to do, He will provide you with everything you need to accomplish it! Let our testimony be, "I can do all things through him who strengthens me" (Philippians 4:13)!

In The Cleft Of The Rock

[33:12] Moses said to the LORD, "See, you say to me, 'Bring up this people,' but you have not let me know whom you will send with me. Yet you have said, 'I know you by name, and you have also found favor in my sight.' [13] Now therefore, if I have found favor in your sight, please show me now your ways, that I may know you in order to find favor in your sight. Consider too that this nation is your people." [14] And he said, "My presence will go with you, and I will give you rest." [15] And he said to him, "If your presence will not go with me, do not bring us up from here. [16] For how shall it be known that I have found favor in your sight, I and your people? Is it not in your going with us, so that we are distinct, I and your people, from every other people on the face of the earth?"

[17] And the LORD said to Moses, "This very thing that you have spoken I will do, for you have found favor in my sight, and I know you by name."

[18] Moses said, "Please show me your glory." [19] And he said, "I will make all my goodness pass before you and will proclaim before you my name 'The LORD.' And I will be gracious to whom I will be gracious, and will show mercy on whom I will show mercy. [20] But," he said, "you cannot see my face, for man shall not see me and live." [21] And the LORD said, "Behold, there is a place by me where you shall stand on the rock, [22] and while my glory passes by I will put you in a cleft of the rock, and I will cover you with my hand until I have passed by. [23] Then I will take away my hand, and you shall see my back, but my face shall not be seen."

[34:1] The LORD said to Moses, "Cut for yourself two tablets of stone like the first, and I will write on the tablets the words that were on the first tablets, which you broke. [2] Be ready by the morning, and come up in the morning to Mount Sinai, and present yourself there to me on the top of the mountain. [3] No one shall come up with you, and let no one be seen throughout all the mountain. Let no flocks or herds graze opposite that mountain." [4] So Moses cut two tablets of stone like the first. And he rose early in the morning and went up on Mount Sinai, as the LORD had commanded him, and took in his hand two tablets of stone. [5] The LORD descended in the cloud and stood with him there, and proclaimed the name of the LORD. [6] The LORD

passed before him and proclaimed, "The LORD, the LORD, a God merciful and gracious, slow to anger, and abounding in steadfast love and faithfulness, [7] keeping steadfast love for thousands, forgiving iniquity and transgression and sin, but who will by no means clear the guilty, visiting the iniquity of the fathers on the children and the children's children, to the third and the fourth generation." [8] And Moses quickly bowed his head toward the earth and worshiped. [9] And he said, "If now I have found favor in your sight, O Lord, please let the Lord go in the midst of us, for it is a stiff-necked people, and pardon our iniquity and our sin, and take us for your inheritance."
Exodus 33:12-34:9

[14] And the Word became flesh and dwelt among us, and we have seen his glory, glory as of the only Son from the Father, full of grace and truth. [15] (John bore witness about him, and cried out, "This was he of whom I said, 'He who comes after me ranks before me, because he was before me.'") [16] For from his fullness we have all received, grace upon grace. [17] For the law was given through Moses; grace and truth came through Jesus Christ. [18] No one has ever seen God; the only God, who is at the Father's side, he has made him known.

What a great offer this was! The Lord assured Moses that Israel would be able to go into the Promised Land and take possession of it. God would send an angel ahead of Israel and drive out the Canaanites for them; and according to His promise to Abraham, Isaac and Jacob, He would give to the people of Israel the Promised Land, the land flowing with milk and honey. There, they would be able to settle down in their own land and enjoy freedom as an independent nation. No Egyptian would be there to enslave them. The heavy burden of slave labor would be replaced by the hope of free enterprise. What they made and produced with their own hands, they would be able to keep for themselves. Having tasted the bitterness of slavery, what more could they ask for?

There was a caveat, however. The Lord would not go up to the Promised Land with Israel. Twice, the Lord said that He would not go up to

Canaan in the midst of Israel (Exodus 33:3, 5). Twice, the Lord stated the reason. The people of Israel were an "obstinate" (NASB) or "stiff-necked" people. Twice, the Lord warned that His holy presence would destroy the sinful people of Israel. The second time, it came with added force: "… You are a stiff-necked people; if *for a single moment* I should go up among you, I would consume you." The message was simple. If God were to spare the people of Israel, He must stay away from them.

Was this a bad deal? It must have been difficult for the people of Israel to hear how sinful they were. But could they deny it? After all, they had been constantly complaining and grumbling whenever they faced difficulties. Trusting in the Lord was not their pattern of life, no matter how many miracles they had witnessed. And to cap it all off, while Moses was up on Mount Sinai, receiving God's commands on their behalf—and this, according to their request!—they made a golden calf and worshipped it (Exodus 32). What we first read in our text from Exodus 33-34 is God's response to this horrible sin of idolatry. Even so, amazingly, God was assuring them that they would get to have all the blessings of God, except for His holy presence—which could be terrifying at times, to say the least! They would get to enjoy the Promised Land with all of its blessings, without God constantly looking over their shoulders! Wouldn't that be having the best of both worlds?

How Important Is God's Presence Anyway?

Of course, Israel was utterly dependent on God for everything. Where would Israel be without Him? Only on account of God's mighty acts in Egypt were they able to triumphantly exodus out of Egypt. God led them through the Red Sea on dry ground. It was God who gave them water out of the rock, quails out of the sky, and manna out of heaven. That was not all. How did they grow to be a mighty nation in Egypt in the first place despite Pharaoh's persecutions and evil schemes to exterminate them? Was it not because God kept His promise to Abraham, Isaac, and Jacob that their descendants would be as many as the stars in the sky? And, by the way, there's this too. Where would *you* be without God?

The only problem was that this God was good but also dangerous. One could never take Him lightly. He was no genie in Aladdin's Lamp. He was a holy God. His presence invoked profound feelings of fear and dread as well as wonder and amazement. In His presence, one could not be indifferent or lukewarm. His manifest presence aroused deep stirrings in one's heart, effecting transformations of one kind or another.

So, an offer of the Promised Land came without the presence of the Lord in Israel's midst—of just His good gifts without His dangerous presence! A tempting offer, perhaps hard to refuse?

Protesting and Petitioning

"When the people heard this disastrous word, they mourned, and no one put on his ornaments....Therefore the people of Israel stripped themselves of their ornaments, from Mount Horeb onward" (verses 4, 6). Even the people of Israel knew better, that this was not good, not good at all! Moses knew this better than anyone, of course. For Moses *alone* was given the privilege to enter the tent of meeting outside the camp (verse 8). There the Lord spoke with Moses (verse 9). He spoke with Moses "face to face, as a man speaks to his friend" (verse 11). Moses experienced the awesome blessing of being in the presence of God. Oh to hear God speak to him directly and share with him His divine wisdom and purpose! And had he not just spent 40 days and nights up on Mount Sinai, without eating bread or drinking water (Deuteronomy 9:9)? So energizing, so filling, so satisfying, so life-giving was the presence of God that Moses did not need any food for those 40 days! And being in God's presence would make Moses' face so shine that people would be afraid of coming near him (Exodus 34:30)!

> A heart that is touched by the goodness of the Lord cannot be satisfied with God's gifts. He must have God Himself.

Moses was completely devastated when he heard this "disastrous word" from God. He immediately responded with protest and petition. The force of Moses' protest is felt by his repeated usage of the second personal pronoun in his words in reference to God. You see, in Hebrew, a verb can stand on its own without any pronoun because the gender and the number of its subject is implied in the verb itself. So, when the personal pronoun is spelled out, it is done for the purpose of emphasis. And that is what you have in Moses' initial response to the Lord's devastating declaration. "See, *You Yourself* say to me, 'Bring up this people,' but *You Yourself* have not let me know whom You will send with me. Yet *You Yourself* have said, 'I know you by name, and you have also found favor in My sight'" (verse 12, author's amplified rendering).

Then, Moses moves right on to an urgent petition: "Now therefore, if I have found favor in Your sight, please show me now your ways, that I may know You in order to find favor in Your sight. Consider too that this nation is Your people" (verse 13). Here, Moses does not directly address the issue at hand—whether or not the Lord would go up in the midst of Israel to Canaan. Could it be that Moses, at this point, does not know how to handle the situation? He too must have been convinced of the irreconcilable tension between Israel's desperate need of God's presence and the detrimental effect of God's presence in the midst of sinful Israel. All he could do was pitifully petition the Lord to enlighten him regarding what He really had in mind. All he could do was remind God that Israel was still His people!

Interestingly, it is God who redirects the conversation back to the issue at hand. Moses has pleaded, "Please show me Your ways!" And the Lord responds, "My presence will go with you, and I will give you rest" (verse 14). Moses is delighted to hear this but he wants to make sure: "If Your presence will not go with me, do not bring us up from here. For how shall it be known that I have found favor in Your sight, I and Your people? Is it not in Your going *with us*, so that we are distinct, I and Your people, from every other people on the face of the earth?" (verses 15-16).

A Daring Request

The Lord grants what Moses pleads for—readily and graciously, as if He had been waiting for Moses to utter those very words—as if He were more anxious (than Moses) to go in the midst of His people: "This very thing that you have spoken I will do, for you have found favor in My sight, and I know you by name" (verse 17). It seems God was testing

Moses to remind him of an important truth—without God, the Promised Land is nothing! And Moses seems to understand it very clearly. In fact, Moses doesn't stop there. He petitions God further and says, "Please show me your glory" (verse 18)!

How daring was this request! No sinner can see the glory of a holy God and live! Those to whom God appeared were struck with fear that they would surely die! When they did not die, they could only marvel at their fortune! But what Moses was asking here was so much more than what others had experienced. He asked to see the glory of God, not just a veiled appearance of God!

Quite possibly he is asking this as the assurance of the promise God just made. The gracious revelation of God's glory would be a sealing affirmation of God's promise to be present in the midst of Israel. Or, maybe this is something that he has always desired in his heart. Though God spoke to him face to face as a friend, God still "merely" spoke to him. The favor of God he experienced through His words, Moses now wants to see with his eyes. Emboldened by God's gracious answer to his prayer for Israel, he musters up the courage to ask this great favor from God. A heart that is touched by the goodness of the Lord cannot be satisfied with God's gifts. He must have God Himself. And God is not offended by this request. He graciously grants Moses' wish.

God designated a specific place for Moses to witness His glory: "Behold, there is a place by Me where you shall stand on the rock" (verse 21). Moses was to stand on the rock—more precisely in the cleft of the rock—to witness the glory of the Lord. Notice how the Lord referred to the place: "*the* rock," not just "*a* rock." Why this specific designation with the definite article, "the"? The Lord seems to suggest that this rock is something that Moses should already know, something that we have seen before.

The Rock

Regarding the identity of this rock, an important clue is found in Exodus 17. At Rephidim, their last stop before coming to Mount Sinai, the people of Israel complained about the lack of water. When Moses cried

36

out to the Lord because of the hostility with which Israel complained, the Lord responded, "Pass on before the people, taking with you some of the elders of Israel, and take in your hand the staff with which you struck the Nile, and go. Behold, I will stand before you there *on the rock at Horeb*, and you shall strike the rock, and water shall come out of it, and the people will drink" (verses 5-6). You see, we are told that this rock was at Horeb. As you may remember, Horeb is another name for Sinai and Mount Sinai is where this later interaction between God and Moses is taking place! It is more than likely that the rock, which Moses struck with his staff to bring forth water, was the same rock in the cleft of which God placed Moses. It is also possible that the cleft of the rock was made by Moses' striking.

When Moses struck the rock with the staff, the Lord was standing on it: "Behold, I will stand before you there *on the rock at Horeb*, and you shall strike the rock, and water shall come out of it, and the people will drink." As unbelievable as it may seem, it was the Lord who was struck with the staff of judgment—the Lord! But who was the guilty that deserved the striking? Was it not Israel who complained and grumbled against the Lord and His servant? Should the people sin and their Judge be punished? For the treason of the people, should the King Himself be penalized? But such was the case. Through God's suffering came the water to restore life to the people and silence their grumbling.

Now, Moses stood in the cleft of the same rock, safely tucked away while the glory of the Lord passed by him. What a remarkable picture! The site of judgment had become a refuge. Where the staff of judgment once struck, there was formed the cleft of safety and protection—like the blackened, sooty ground already once consumed by fire is no longer under the threat of fire.

Not only that, but the Lord laid His hand gently over him to shield him from the awesome glory of the Lord. What a moving picture of God's tenderness toward Moses! This anthropomorphic (that is, human-like) image is used of God to show, in a palpable way, God's tender care for Moses.

What Moses Saw

But what is it that Moses actually saw? God said, "You cannot see my face, for man shall not see me and live.... I will cover you with my hand until I have passed by. Then I will take away my hand, and you shall see my back, but my face shall not be seen" (Exodus 33:20, 22-23). Of course, God is a Spirit and He doesn't have a body like we do. In fact, the Hebrew word that is used for God's "back" is never used "for the back of a person's anatomy.... The word... means 'back' in the sense of direction [in the sense of behind]." What Moses saw was "the...afterglow behind the Lord as he passed by."[2] So, then, what Moses saw was not God's back as opposed to His face. What Moses saw was the trace of God's passage—like the trail of ripples lingering behind a cruise ship.

Here, we sense the inherent tension in Moses' experience. The favored position that he enjoyed before God is contrasted with the limited nature of his encounter with the Lord. While the Lord passed by in His glory, Moses had to hide himself in the cleft of the rock, covered with the hand of the Lord. This moment of glory was clouded by a real threat of death, lurking outside the cleft of the rock. God allowed him to see the traces of His passage left behind, but he was not allowed to see the face-presence of the Lord.

Interestingly, what dominates Moses' encounter with God's glory is not his *visual* experience; rather, it is his *auditory* experience. Though God permitted Moses to see His back, what happens when God actually passes by? "The LORD passed before him and proclaimed, 'The LORD, the LORD, a God merciful and gracious, slow to anger, and abounding in steadfast love and faithfulness, keeping steadfast love for thousands, forgiving iniquity and transgression and sin, but who will by no means clear the guilty, visiting the iniquity of the fathers on the children and the children's children, to the third and the fourth generation.' And Moses quickly bowed his head toward the earth and worshiped" (Exodus 34:6-8). He could *hear* the words of God but not really *see* the glory of God.

---

2 R. Laird Harris, "*achor*," *Theological Wordbook of the Old Testament* (Chicago: Moody 1980), 1:33.

Yet what glorious words! They came and enveloped Moses, who was ducking in the cleft of the rock. And oh how Moses bathed in those words! Though he could not quite see the glory of the Lord, he heard it and he felt it. For these words proclaimed the glorious character of God's divine being. With what power the words came to him! These were the very words that brought life out of nothing at the beginning of time. At the touch of these words, the dusty, lifeless earth bubbled up with all kinds of animals and insects, birds and beasts. With the same force, the words of the Lord touched Moses to the core of his being. What ecstasy! What glory he experienced! What more could he ask for?

What We Now See

But hold your breath and hear the words of the Apostle John found in the New Testament:

> And the Word *became flesh* and [tabernacled] among us, and we *have seen His glory*, glory as of the only Son from the Father, full of grace and truth.... For the Law was given through Moses; grace and truth *came* [not just proclaimed but came, being realized] through Jesus Christ. No one has seen God [not even Moses!]; the only God, who is at the Father's side, He has made Him known. (John 1:14, 17-18)

John uses the language of Exodus 33 and 34 to show the surpassing greatness of God's grace to New Testament believers. What Moses caught only a glimpse of, what Moses only heard of, John and the disciples *saw* in Jesus Christ. Indeed, John refers to it in a similar way in 1 John 1:1: "That which was from the beginning, which we have heard, which we have seen with our eyes, which we looked upon and have touched with our hands, concerning the Word of Life...."

Of course, we do not see the Lord Jesus as the disciples saw him. We will not see Him until we enter into glory in heaven. Until then, we must live by faith in the Word of God. But what we read and hear of in the Scripture is no longer just the Word of the invisible God. We read and hear of the Word of God made flesh! The Word Moses only heard became flesh in Jesus Christ! And the incarnate Word of God lived, suffered, died and rose again in the flesh in order to accomplish and fulfill grace *and* truth—the Greek translation of the very Hebrew words used in Exodus 34:6 to describe God's character, "steadfast love and faithfulness."

Yes, in Jesus Christ, the grace and truth of God were realized, once and for all. For the sin of man, the Son of God offered Himself as the atonement. The guilty man was spared and the righteous God was punished. *He* was struck for *our* transgression. And from His riven side flowed water and blood to cleanse us from the guilt and power of sin. Most unexpectedly, the glory of the Lord shone most brilliantly in the sacrificial death of the Son of God in the darkness that covered the hill called Calvary. As the song written by Michael Card and popularized by Amy Grant says, "The most awesome work [of God] was done through the frailty of His Son."

Jesus is truly the Rock cleft for us. Isn't that exactly what we read in the words of the Apostle Paul, in 1 Corinthians 10:1-4? "For I want you to know, brothers, that our fathers were all under the cloud, and all passed through the sea, and all were baptized into Moses in the cloud and in the sea, and all ate the same spiritual food, and all drank the same spiritual drink. For they drank from the spiritual Rock which followed them, and the Rock was Christ." The rock that was struck to give water to thirsty Israel, the rock in the cleft of which Moses saw the passing glory of God, was the same rock which pointed to Jesus Christ our Savior!

And now *we* are safe in the cleft of the Rock, Jesus Christ. And now *we* can boldly behold the glory of the Lord, face to face. As Paul also says, "And we all, with unveiled face, beholding the glory of the Lord, are being transformed into the same image from one degree of glory to another. For this comes from the Lord who is the Spirit" (2 Corinthians 3:18)! After all, what covers us in the cleft of the Rock? Just the almighty hand of God? No. More than that, it is none other than the nail-pierced hands of Christ, which testify to the perfect and complete atonement for our sin in his death and resurrection!

"Marrying" For Love, Not Money

How important is God's presence to us?

Moses rejected the blessings of the Promised Land—if they were going to come without God's presence. How about us? The land of Canaan was only a physical representation of heaven and a very faint one at that. The Promised Land, cleared of the Canaanites, flowing with milk and honey, pointed to heaven, free of sin and sinners, and overflowing with the glorious riches of heavenly treasures. As the last book of the Bible states, "There shall no longer be any death; there shall no longer be any mourning, or crying, or pain" (Revelation 21:4). All the sufferings of this life will be replaced with the comfort and plentitude of heaven.

So what if we could have heaven without God?

What is one of the worst things that can happen in a relationship? When people become a means to an end. When the giver is ignored for the gift he gives. When people get married for money or for convenience. There is no doubt, when someone loves us and does good to us, it's so much easier to love him or her. But true love goes beyond being grateful for the good someone else shows us. True love is ultimately tied to the person, not just to the good she does for us or the gifts he gives us. True love does not stop when the gifts stop coming. If it does, then it's not true love. Instead, it's the activity of just a fair-weather friend.

So, then, to desire heaven without God's presence is to marry for the money, not for love. And what good is a feasting table if we have to eat alone? What good is a multi-million-dollar mansion if we have to come to an empty house every night with no one waiting for us? And even if we had good companions to live and eat with in a fancy house, would we be truly satisfied? Is man no different from animals and beasts? If we are indeed made in the image of God, as the Word of God declares to us, our hearts will remain restless until they find rest in God—as Saint Augustine has so aptly put it.

If so, can there be heaven without God? True religion is not the pursuit of heaven. It is rather the pursuit of God and His presence as He offers Himself to us in Jesus Christ. If we lose Christ, we lose everything! Can there be eternal life—let alone any life—without Christ, who *is* the Life and the Resurrection? Can there be joy in heaven without Christ, who is the Fountain of joy and the River of delight? Indeed, there will be no light in heaven without Christ, for He is the Light. There will be no lasting treasure in heaven without Christ, for Christ Himself is the true, everlasting Treasure. Likewise, Christ is the living Water, the Bread of heaven, and the Tree of life.

Our redemption, then, is not about "going to a better place." The true essence of our redemption is none other than our union with God. Has not our Lord made it unmistakably clear? Why did He abandon the glories of heaven and come into this fallen world, fully knowing all that He had to suffer and endure for our sake? Wasn't it because, to quote another Michael Card song (*Could It Be?*), He would "really rather die than live without us"? In the Incarnation of the Son of God, we see that Moses' longing to see the glory of God was nothing compared to God's longing to be with us through all eternity. For that, He was willing to pay any price, even the price of His Son's own precious life!

How is it that the all-sufficient God desired us so, even while we were yet sinners and rebels against Him? Not because He needed anything from us. Only because He desired that we know Him to whom belong all glory, majesty, dominion, and authority in infinite blessedness forever more!

May all that we do and say and think—may all the decisions we make with our time and efforts and resources—show the supreme value of our awesome God!

The Father Of Mercies And God Of All Comfort

[3] Blessed be the God and Father of our Lord Jesus Christ, the Father of mercies and God of all comfort, [4] who comforts us in all our affliction, so that we may be able to comfort those who are in any affliction, with the comfort with which we ourselves are comforted by God. [5] For as we share abundantly in Christ's sufferings, so through Christ we share abundantly in comfort too.
2 Corinthians 1:3-5

Imagine this. Some of you don't have to go too far down memory lane to do this. Someone who should know better—because you care for him so much and have made numerous sacrifices for him—does something terrible to you. What hurts you the most is that he questions your motive and character in doing so. You are hurt to the core because you have loved him so dearly. You feel utterly betrayed. And now you need to write a letter to confront him and resolve the issue. This is by far the most difficult letter you have had to write. How would you start the letter when all you want to say is, "How could you do this to me?"

Paul the Apostle was in that kind of situation when he wrote this letter. He loved the Corinthians dearly and deeply. He preached to them the gospel of Jesus Christ in the midst of much affliction (Acts 18:1ff). He could say with all sincerity that he considered them as "my beloved children. For though you have countless guides in Christ, you do not have many fathers. For I became your father in Christ Jesus through the gospel" (1 Corinthians 4:14-15). Yet, when some false teachers came and stirred them up, they were quick to question the integrity of Paul's character as well as the legitimacy of his apostleship. Paul must have been anxious to address those issues—not just because he was personally offended but also because questioning his apostleship could lead to a distorted understanding of the gospel. So what should he say? And how should he begin this difficult letter?

Blessing God—More Than A Mere Formality

What do we find at the beginning of this letter? His benediction of God: "Blessed be the God and Father of our Lord Jesus Christ, the Father of mercies and God of all comfort..." (2 Corinthians 1:3).

Was this merely a formality? In the Greco-Roman culture of that time, it was common to begin a letter with some formulaic benediction of god(s). Does this mean that such a benediction was just a formality mindlessly performed? It depended on how pious and religious the writer was. Especially if the writer recently experienced unusual fortune or was in an urgent, deep need of divine assistance, the benediction could not have been a mere formality. This was especially so in the case of Paul.

For Paul, there were no simple, arbitrary, pragmatic solutions to the problems he faced. For Paul, the true, effective solutions could come only from a clear vision of the one and only true God in His surpassing glory and majesty. Reflecting on the glory of God puts everything in its proper perspective. However grave and enormous our problems may seem, when viewed against the background of God's glory, they are but a flickering candlelight before the morning sun on its way to its zenith. No obstacle can thwart, no problem can spoil the eternal plan of God. What joy, what peace will be ours if we can only remember and bless the Lord in times of trouble! Wisely Paul begins his letter with an outburst of praise: "Blessed be the God and Father of our Lord Jesus Christ, the Father of mercies and God of all comfort..." (verse 3).

Of course, Paul could have chosen many different attributes of God to praise Him. The Old Testament abounds with different titles of God—El Shadai ("God Almighty"), Jehovah-jireh ("The Lord Will Provide"), Jehovah-nissi ("The Lord is My Banner"), Jehovah-sabbaoth ("The Lord of Hosts"), etc. These titles all reflect something of God's divine attributes. Sometimes, the title of God appears in conjunction with a direct reference to one of His attributes: God of faithfulness (Deuteronomy 32:4); God of forgiveness (Nehemiah 9:17), etc.

God's True Comfort

In this introductory benediction, Paul highlights God's mercies and comfort. And even between the two, Paul's focus seems to be on the comfort God gives us, as we read in the immediately following verses: "who comforts us in all our affliction, so that we may be able to comfort those who are in any affliction, with the comfort with which we ourselves are comforted by God. For as we share abundantly in Christ's sufferings, so through Christ we share abundantly in comfort too" (verses 4-5). God's mercies in view here are the kind of mercies with which God comforts us. He comforts us out of His merciful disposition toward us.

What a marvelous blessing this is—that the almighty God should be the Father of mercies and God of all comfort to us! Have you ever felt really desperate, so utterly alone in the world? Not because you didn't have a supportive family. Not because you didn't have caring friends. You just felt like no one could understand what you were going through at that time—not even your closest friends, not even your flesh and blood. And even if anyone did, you knew he couldn't get you out of the abyss you were in. Like when you are fighting a terminal disease. Not that you don't appreciate every sympathetic look, every word of comfort they give. You cannot be grateful enough. But at the end of the day, you are the one who is sick unto death, who must face your mortality all alone. Or you get into some trouble because you've made some foolish choices and not-so-honorable mistakes. You are too ashamed to let others know. You are dying on the inside, sinking deeper and deeper into the quicksand of despair no matter how hard you try. Other people

Other people notice your distress and ask how things are going. You give a vague, general answer, how you are going through some difficulties. And they cheerfully tell you not to worry, how things will turn out okay. You smile back, thanking them, but their words only drive you deeper into your sense of isolation and aloneness.

But what if God should be your comforter? He knows the depth of your trouble unlike any mortals that surround you. And He has the power and wisdom to sustain you in the face of your trouble, no matter how deep or how great.

notice your distress and ask how things are going. You give a vague, general answer, how you are going through some difficulties. And they cheerfully tell you not to worry, how things will turn out okay. You smile back, thanking them, but their words only drive you deeper into your sense of isolation and aloneness.

But what if God should be your comforter? He knows the depth of your trouble unlike any mortals that surround you. And He has the power and wisdom to sustain you in the face of your trouble, no matter how deep or how great. What if He should say to you, "Fear not, for I have redeemed you; I have called you by name, you are mine. When you pass through the waters, I will be with you; and through the rivers, they shall not overwhelm you; when you walk through fire you shall not be burned, and the flame shall not consume you" (Isaiah 43:1-3)? "Can a woman forget her nursing child, that she should have no compassion on the son of her womb? Even these may forget, yet I will not forget you. Behold, I have engraved you on the palms of my hands; your walls are continually before me" (Isaiah 49:15-16).

Is it any wonder that God should be the God of *all* comfort? As the almighty God, He is able to comfort us in all things—in all our afflictions pertaining to our body and soul, both in life and death (Heidelberg Catechism, Question #1)! When we are sick, we can look to Him as our Healer. When we are lost, we can look to Him as our Guide. When we are in need, we can look to Him as our Provider. When we feel abandoned, we can look to Him as our ever-present Companion. When we are afraid, we can look to Him as our Refuge, our Shield and Fortress. When we are weary, we can look to Him as our Strength. When we are sad, we can drink from the river of His delights!

Comfort From The Father Of Mercies

But there is more to the comfort that is found in God! God offers His comfort to us as the Father of mercies. This is important because not all the comfort is the same. A person's comfort can come in an awkward way. Or it can come in a rather exaggerated, artificial way. Or it can come in a cold, businesslike way. But we can all agree that true comfort comes from a sympathetic, merciful heart. And that is exactly what we are told here. Not only does God's comfort come to us with His almighty, divine power; it also flows out of His merciful heart! God wraps the force of His omnipotent power with the warmth and tenderness of His mercies! How marvelous is God's comfort!

But we are still not done yet! We are further told that the God of all comfort is also the *Father* of mercies! It is not merely as an almighty God that He is merciful toward helpless, needy creatures, out of pity. Think about that! Who can look at a little baby that is mortally sick, or a little child that is starving, and not feel heartbroken and sympathetic? But can it compare to how his own mother or father would feel? And we are told God is merciful toward us as a Father is toward His dearest children, out of His fatherly love! And His mercy is so great that it is not enough to address Him as the Father of mercy (singular)! He must be addressed as the Father of merc*ies* (plural)!

How wonderful it is that the almighty God comforts us as our merciful Father! We must recapture again and again this glorious vision of God's love for us! Keep in mind that many religions cannot even imagine something even remotely close to what the gospel offers to us. They may recognize their need for God's comfort, His manifold mercies. But they have no idea how closely and intimately God draws near to us.

Because He Is "The God And Father Of Our Lord Jesus Christ"

But is this a universal state of affairs? No, it has not always been like this. We have to remember that, if Paul can speak of God's relationship with us in this way, it is only because the Old Testament had already happened, and all that is recorded in the Gospels has already transpired as well. There was a brief time of bliss between God and man in the Garden of Eden. But everything changed after Adam and Eve disobeyed God and listened to the Serpent. The result? We read in Genesis 6:5, "The LORD saw that the wickedness of man was great in the earth, and that every intention of the thoughts of his heart was only evil continually." Paul says elsewhere that we were all dead in trespasses and sins (Ephesians 2:1), that we were by nature children of wrath (Ephesians 2:3).

How, then, can a holy God be to sinners like us "the Father of mercies and God of all comfort"? The answer is given in the same verse. He can be "the Father of mercies and God of all comfort" only because He is first "the God and Father of our Lord Jesus Christ"!

Notice something fascinating here. In this benediction, God is called not only the Father but also the *God* of our Lord Jesus Christ. How can this be? If God is called the God of Jesus Christ, can Jesus still be divine?

We know that, as far as His being is concerned, Jesus is the second Person of the Trinity. He is the eternal Son of God and God is the eternal Father of Jesus. But something amazing happened when the eternal Son of God entered this world through incarnation. He was born of woman, born under the law (Galatians 4:4). Thus the eternal Son of God took upon Himself our human nature—both a body and a reasonable soul—and identified Himself with us completely (except for sin). Thus He took our place—as our Representative and Substitute—to suffer and die and rise again from the dead for us (again, in our place). And it is in His identification with us, as our Representative, that Jesus calls His eternal Father His God. Jesus said to Mary Magdalene in John 20:17, "Do not cling to Me, for I have not yet ascended to the Father; but go to My brothers and say to them, 'I am ascending to *My Father and your Father, to My God and your God.*'" What a remarkable truth this is! Because Jesus addresses *our* God as *His* God, we can address *His* Father as *our* Father!

Sonship With God

Do you realize how completely we are allowed to come into the presence of God, into His fellowship? This is beautifully expressed in Galatians 4:4-5: "But when the fullness of time had come, God sent forth His Son, born of woman, born under the law, to redeem those who were under the law, so that we might receive adoption as sons." We are told that we are not just God's creatures. We are God's beloved children, His kinsmen (without being divine ourselves). This, because the Son of God came and took our place under the law. Thus He redeemed us from being crushed under the curse and punishment of the law!

But that was not all that He did. By uniting Himself with us, not only did He take away our guilt and punishment, but He also gave us adoption as God's sons, sharing with us the privilege and blessing of His sonship to God. (And, ladies, don't be offended that Paul here speaks only of our "adoption as *sons*" and not as "sons *and daughters*." He is highlighting "sons" here because, at that time, it was normally the sons who received the family inheritance. He wants us to know that we are *all* co-heirs with Christ, whether we are men or women, boys or girls! So he goes on to say in verse 7, "So you are no longer a slave, but a son, and if a son, then an heir through God.")

What we are speaking of here is a beautiful instance of the dual aspect of our "union with Christ." This idea of "union with Christ" (which is often expressed in the familiar phrase, "in Christ") is central to our salvation. So, when we picture our salvation, we should not think of it merely as something Jesus *gives* us. Jesus is more than Someone who *gives* us salvation. Jesus *is* our salvation. He is the Way and the Truth and the Life (John 14:6). "Christ Jesus…became to us wisdom from God, righteousness and sanctification and redemption" (1 Corinthians 1:30). "For all the promises of God find their Yes in him" (2 Corinthians 1:20). We should not be surprised by this idea of union. Is it not the very essence of what covenant is—our union with God, for God to be our God and for us to be His people in an intimate, unbreakable relationship? What is surprising is, of course, how intimate this union really is, which God designed for our salvation!

Intimacy Taken To A New Height

This becomes all the more striking when we view what Paul is doing in this benediction against the background of the Old Testament. In the Old Testament, the phrase, "God of…" is used most frequently in conjunction with the name of Israel (thus "the God of Israel") or with the name(s) of the three Patriarchs (thus "the God of Abraham, Isaac, and Jacob"). The name of God was invoked in conjunction with the Patriarchs' names because God's covenant with them was the foundation and fountain of Israel's relationship with God. In times of trouble, the people of Israel addressed God as the God of Abraham, Isaac, and Jacob, and appealed to His covenant with the Patriarchs as the basis of God's mercy. Even when they were utterly without any merit but full of guilt and sin, the people could plead for God's mercy, but only on the basis of God's gracious promise unto Abraham, Isaac, and Jacob.

Invoking the God of Abraham, Isaac, and Jacob also had a nostalgic dimension as well. God's relationship with the Patriarchs was tender, intimate, gentle, and loving. God even spoke of Abraham as His friend! By calling upon God as the God of Abraham, Isaac, and Jacob, they expressed their desire to share in the intimate fellowship the Patriarchs enjoyed with God.

Now, here in 2 Corinthians 1, those prominent, cherished divine titles of the Old Testament are replaced with a new one. The New Testament believers no longer call upon the God of Abraham, Isaac, and Jacob. With Paul, we call upon "the God and Father of our Lord Jesus Christ." Can it be otherwise? Glorious and marvelous was the name of God as the God of Abraham, Isaac, and Jacob, the God of Israel! But oh how its glory fades in the surpassing glory of the name of God as the God and Father of our Lord Jesus Christ! Intimate might have been the Patriarchs' fellowship with God. But what was that compared to the intimate communion between God the Father and God the Son? How can the Patriarchs' intimacy with their *God* measure up to Jesus' intimacy with His own heavenly *Father*? In fact, the Patriarchs' communion with God was possible only on account of Jesus Christ. How could sinful men and women back then have such an intimate communion with God on their own? It was only because they looked forward to their coming Savior, Jesus Christ, and found themselves in His saving, refreshing shade.

And by blessing God as the God and Father of our Lord Jesus Christ, Paul is rejoicing in the privilege given to New Testament believers—for those who are in Christ Jesus, even for those that were once Gentiles in the flesh. The Patriarchs do not represent the height of man's covenant relationship with God. Through the earth-shattering, epoch-shifting arrival of God's redemption in Jesus Christ, a new height that far surpasses the height of the Patriarchal period has been established. It is to that new height that we have been invited. That is why Paul blesses God as the God and Father of our Lord Jesus Christ!

Comfort For Sufferers, Comfort For Sinners

Are you in need of comfort today? Maybe you are growing weary of doing the right thing. Never mind that people don't notice all the efforts you are putting in, all the sacrifices you are making for them. They have actually turned on you and are paying the good you have done with evil. You feel deeply hurt. You feel like giving up, maybe. Here is someone who knew where you are coming from, who knew exactly what you are going through. And he spoke from the painful place you are standing in. He said, "Blessed be the God and Father of our Lord Jesus Christ, the Father of mercies and God of all comfort!" He was able to say this with all sincerity because he knew Jesus Christ. Paul knew he suffered no injustice that Jesus had not suffered. He knew that the injustice he suffered, no matter how great, was nothing compared to the injustice suffered by the eternal Son of God at the hands of sinful men—for him!

But Paul's comfort was not that Someone else suffered more than himself. That's how we often comfort ourselves, isn't it? "I shouldn't complain because there is this person or that person who is suffering so much more than I am." No, that's not the kind of comfort Paul experienced. It was what Christ accomplished through His suffering, and what God did for Jesus Christ. God raised His Son from the dead unto peerless glory, "far above all rule and authority and power and dominion, and above every name that is named, not only in this age but also in the one to come" (Ephesians 1:21)! So he is able to say in 2 Corinthians 1:5, "For as we share abundantly in Christ's sufferings, so through Christ we share abundantly in comfort too." This is what kept him going, even through unbearable afflictions. "We do not want you to be ignorant, brothers, of the affliction we experienced in Asia. For we were so utterly burdened beyond our strength that we despaired of life itself. Indeed, we felt that we had received the sentence of death. But that was to make us rely not on ourselves but on God who raises the dead" (vv. 8-9).

But maybe that's not where you are—suffering for doing good. Maybe the affliction you are experiencing is due to your mistakes, or your failures, or even your sins. You know you deserve every bit of it. Can there be any comfort for you? That is the amazing thing about the gospel of Jesus Christ, isn't it? The comfort of God in Jesus Christ is available even for sinners, especially for sinners who are full of guilt and shame, fully deserving of all the terrible consequences of their sin! Jesus said, "Those who are well have no need of a physician, but those who are sick. I came not to call the righteous, but sinners" (Mark 2:17). (Not that anyone is actually righteous before God. Jesus was speaking of those who are blind to their sickness because of their pride.)

What is the comfort that is offered to sinners, even those writhing in pain, in the bitter consequences of their sins? It is the most marvelous truth that Jesus came into this world to save sinners. He came to save us precisely because we cannot save ourselves. And because Jesus died for the penalty of our sin once for all, there is no condemnation for those who are in Christ Jesus (Romans 8:1). We may suffer the direct consequences of our sin. But it is no longer a *judicial* penalty for our sin. For those who are in Jesus Christ by faith, even the affliction we suffer for our sin is God's *fatherly* discipline—not to punish us for our sin but to help us become more like Him in goodness and love! Because of Jesus Christ our Savior, God's will toward us is for good, not for evil, now and forever!

Afflicted To Know His Comfort, To Give His Comfort

As we conclude, maybe we can address a burning question you may be asking. If God loves and cherishes us so much in Jesus Christ, why does He allow us to be in a situation where we need His comfort and mercies? Sometimes the afflictions we go through in our lives are so disorienting, so painful, so exhausting that we have a hard time wondering why God would allow it—if He loves us so much!

Before we go further, we must affirm that our Father of mercies and God of all comfort will bring us to that place where there will be no affliction or hardship. There "He will wipe away every tear from [our] eyes, and death shall be no more, neither shall there be any mourning, nor crying, nor pain anymore, for the former things have passed away" (Revelation 21:4). Indeed, we shall walk through the pearly gates and stroll along the golden streets. All the heavenly riches will be ours to enjoy. But, in our glorified state, the glorious things of heaven cannot and will not distract us. As wonderful as they may be, as good as they are, as enjoyable as they are, even so, even the things of heaven will be to us nothing but rubbish next to the surpassing greatness of God, our true Inheritance.

But we are not there yet. We live in a fallen world, a world of change and decay. This is not heaven. Misery and death cannot be avoided in this world. So, as we journey through this fallen world, God promises His manifold mercies and all comfort in Jesus Christ. Sometimes, out of His mercy and pity, He removes our afflictions and trials. But, also out of His mercy, He sometimes keeps us there. Instead of removing our afflictions, He makes us strong through them! He gives us the strength to walk through fire so we can emerge on the other side much stronger, much more refined and purified.

And why should we be strengthened and refined this way? The Father of mercies and God of all comfort "comforts us in all our affliction, so that we may be able to comfort those who are in any affliction, with the comfort with which we ourselves are comforted by God" (verse 4). We may suffer for a while. But our suffering will not be wasted. God will mold us and build us into instruments of blessing—to be able to comfort others with the comfort we have received from Him. We all know how a widow can minister to a widow in a unique way, or how a cancer-survivor can minister to a cancer patient in a powerful way. May our hearts desire more than anything to be used of God to be a comfort and blessing to others!

"Are They Hebrews?"

[16] I repeat, let no one think me foolish. But even if you do, accept me as a fool, so that I too may boast a little. [17] What I am saying with this boastful confidence, I say not as the Lord would but as a fool. [18] Since many boast according to the flesh, I too will boast. [19] For you gladly bear with fools, being wise yourselves! [20] For you bear it if someone makes slaves of you, or devours you, or takes advantage of you, or puts on airs, or strikes you in the face. [21] To my shame, I must say, we were too weak for that! But whatever anyone else dares to boast of—I am speaking as a fool—I also dare to boast of that. [22] Are they Hebrews? So am I. Are they Israelites? So am I. Are they offspring of Abraham? So am I. [23] Are they servants of Christ? I am a better one—I am talking like a madman—with far greater labors, far more imprisonments, with countless beatings, and often near death. [24] Five times I received at the hands of the Jews the forty lashes less one. [25] Three times I was beaten with rods. Once I was stoned. Three times I was shipwrecked; a night and a day I was adrift at sea; [26] on frequent journeys, in danger from rivers, danger from robbers, danger from my own people, danger from Gentiles, danger in the city, danger in the wilderness, danger at sea, danger from false brothers; [27] in toil and hardship, through many a sleepless night, in hunger and thirst, often without food, in cold and exposure. [28] And, apart from other things, there is the daily pressure on me of my anxiety for all the churches. [29] Who is weak, and I am not weak? Who is made to fall, and I am not indignant?

[30] If I must boast, I will boast of the things that show my weakness. [31] The God and Father of the Lord Jesus, he who is blessed forever, knows that I am not lying. [32] At Damascus, the governor under King Aretas was guarding the city of Damascus in order to seize me, [33] but I was let down in a basket through a window in the wall and escaped his hands.

2 Corinthians 11:16-33

There are times we face sufferings because of our own foolish mistakes and even sins. How do you feel, then? Do you feel like you are being punished by God and you have disqualified yourself from sharing the gospel? What about when unexpected sufferings come your way for no apparent reason? Do you feel distant from God and doubt His love for you? When you feel like that, sharing the gospel would be the last thing on your mind, right? So when would you feel right about sharing the gospel? When everything is going well in your life? But what if the people around you are richer and higher in position than you, better educated and more accomplished than you? I dare say that all these attitudes stem from misunderstanding the gospel in one way or the other. The Apostle Paul's response to the false teachers in the Corinthian church reminds us of the truth of the gospel and provides us with an antidote to many misperceptions of the gospel. I hope it will enable us to be bold, winsome witnesses of Jesus Christ.

Not too long after Paul left Corinth, some false teachers came into the Corinthian church and incited the members to question Paul's apostleship and ministry. Who were these false teachers? And what did they teach?

The Judaizers

We can get a sense of who they were from verses 22-23: "Are they Hebrews? So am I. Are they Israelites? So am I. Are they offspring of Abraham? So am I. Are they servants of Christ? I am a better one." We can learn two things about these false teachers: 1) they were Hebrews like Paul (verse 22); 2) they considered themselves servants of Christ (verse 23). But we do not call them Jewish Christians. We call them Judaizers. What's the difference? Well, Jewish Christians would be those Christians who happened to be Jews ethnically. They would be Christians first and foremost. Their ethnicity would be of only incidental importance, if any importance at all. It would have no significant bearing on their Christian faith or their standing in the church of Jesus Christ. Does it matter whether one is an African, or an Anglo, or an Asian, or a Hispanic in the new covenant community? Neither should it matter whether one is a Jew or not. Even for Jewish Christians, what is essential to their identity must be Christianity, not their ethnic background. However, to these false teachers, their Jewishness was more than ethnic identity.

We can see why. Under the old covenant, being a Jew meant much more than mere ethnic identity. God chose Abraham and his descendants as His special people. It was with the Jews that God entered into covenant at Mount Sinai, setting them apart from the rest of the world. So Paul was justified in saying, "Then what advantage has the Jew? Or what is the value of circumcision? Much in every way. To begin with, the Jews were entrusted with the oracles of God" (Romans 3:1-2).

So we are not surprised to find out that Judaizers demanded Gentile converts to be circumcised according to the Mosaic covenant (Galatians 5:2ff). We also know they required Gentile converts to keep the Jewish dietary laws and feasts (Colossians 2:16). But, at Corinth, what they promoted was not so much certain external rituals. It was more subtle. They were promoting a certain spirit and attitude—what we call "triumphalism."

Triumphalism

Triumphalism views suffering and pain as incompatible with Christian faith and living. This belief is closely associated with what theologians call "over-realized eschatology." Eschatology is the study of the end times. But in its broader definition, it includes the age to come, which follows the end times. Over-realized eschatology sees the present era as the age in which all of God's promises and blessings can be fully experienced. One aspect of this belief is defining and expecting God's blessings in earthly terms. This is what is behind the modern day health-and-wealth gospels. You know what they say. "If you have enough faith, you won't get sick and, if you do, you can be healed. After all, 'with his stripes we are healed' (Isaiah 53:6). As Jesus died so we don't have to die for our sin, Jesus suffered so we don't have to suffer! After all, if God loves you so much, would He want you to starve and suffer in poverty? You are a prince and a princess—a child of God the King of the universe! So you deserve all the best this world has to offer, now!"

Triumphalism is a manifestation of this over-realized eschatology. The problem with triumphalism is that it sees Christian life *only* in terms of triumph and defines Christian triumph in earthly terms. For sure, we are more than conquerors in Christ (Romans 8:37). But Christian victory in this day and age is mainly spiritual, not necessarily physical. While we reign with Christ in the heavenly places (Ephesians 2:6; cf. 1:20f), we suffer tribulation and persecution in this world (Romans 8:18, Philippians 1:29, etc.). Jesus Himself spoke of this duality in John 16:33: "In the world you have tribulation, but take courage; I have overcome the world."

You see, what characterizes our Christian life in this age is this tension between our spiritual victory and our physical suffering. Theologians refer to it as "semi-realized eschatology." What this doctrine teaches is most clearly expressed in the phrase, "already and not yet". According to this view, the kingdom of God has *already* come in the death and resurrection of Jesus Christ but is *not yet* fully here. It will be consummated only at the Second Coming of Christ. When Christ returns, this present evil age will be replaced by the age to come—that is, the first creation will be replaced by the new creation.

But triumphalists can't wait that long. They must have their victory—both spiritual and physical—*now*! According to their theology, there is a directly proportional relationship between their spiritual maturity and physical blessings. The greater one's faith, the greater God's material blessings. The reward for their faith is not just their spiritual well-being but also material abundance, financial security, power and influence over the world, and success in whatever they do. They won't allow the world to persecute them or even look down on them. By having more than the people of the world, they want to command their admiration and envy. Their evangelistic slogan is, "Do you see all that I have in this world? If you want what I have, believe in Jesus Christ as I do!"

There was something in Judaism that fostered such an outlook and attitude in these Judaizers. We do not have to look any further than Deuteronomy 28, in which God lists the blessings and curses of the covenant. The Lord says in verse 2, "And all these blessings shall come upon you and overtake you, if you obey voice of the LORD your God." Then God lists a catalogue of His blessings:

"Blessed *shall* you *be* in the city, and blessed *shall* you *be* in the field. Blessed *shall be* the fruit of your womb and the fruit of your ground and the fruit of your cattle, the increase of your herds and the young of your flock. Blessed *shall be* your basket and your kneading bowl. Blessed *shall* you *be* when you come in, and blessed *shall* you *be* when you go out…" (verses 3-6).

You get the idea. The blessings listed here are earthly, material in nature, such as fertility, abundant harvest, victory over enemies, etc. And the blessings would be found everywhere in the land—in the city as well as in the country, etc. The same was true of the curses God promised for disobedience:

"But if you will not obey the voice of the LORD your God or be careful to do all His commandments and His statutes that I command you today, then all these curses shall come upon you and overtake you. Cursed *shall* you *be* in the city, and cursed *shall* you *be* in the field. Cursed *shall be* your basket and your kneading bowl. Cursed *shall be* the fruit of your womb and the fruit of your ground, the increase of your herds and the young of your flock. Cursed *shall* you *be* when you come in, and cursed *shall* you *be* when you go out" (verses 15-19).

The list goes on and on through the end of the chapter. What is striking, again, is the physical, material nature of God's curses: drought, famine, pestilence, defeat, exile, etc. And these curses would be found everywhere in the Promised Land as well.

A Resume' Revealing A Reversal

Steeped in the Mosaic covenant, the Judaizers still expected the blessings and curses of the old covenant for their religious conduct. That is why they boasted of their Jewish pedigree, oratorical skills, social connections and (relatively) trouble-free life. That is why they viewed Paul with suspicion and questioned the legitimacy of his apostleship. Why would he suffer so much if he obeyed God? Why would God allow His servant to go through so much affliction if he served God faithfully?

How does Paul defend his apostleship? By listing his sufferings and afflictions! In so doing, Paul declares that a new age has arrived! The old covenant has been replaced with a new covenant! The people of God have been brought into a new environment! What we have in Paul's apostolic resumé is a complete reversal of the old covenant administration!

Please pay attention to the language of Paul's resumé, particularly in verses 26-27: "[I have been] on frequent journeys, in danger from rivers, danger from robbers, danger from my own people, danger from Gentiles, *danger in the city, danger in the wilderness, danger at sea*, danger from false brothers; in toil and hardship, through many a sleepless night, in hunger and thirst, often without food, in cold and exposure." Paul's sufferings are ubiquitous. Paul experiences hardships everywhere and from everyone. Isn't this a picture of a cursed man according to Deuteronomy 28?

Can this great redemptive-historical reversal be any clearer? It is as if Paul were saying, "Five times I received at the hands of the Jews forty lashes less one. Three times I was beaten with rods. Once I was stoned. Three times I was shipwrecked; a night and a day I was adrift at sea" (verses 24-25)—but oh how blessed I am to be considered worthy to suffer for Jesus' sake! Blessed am I when I am on frequent journeys! Blessed am I when I face danger from rivers, danger from robbers! Blessed am I when I face danger from my own people, danger from the Gentiles! Blessed am I when I face danger in the city; blessed am I when I face danger in the wilderness and blessed am I when I face danger at sea! Blessed am I when I face danger from false brothers! Blessed am I when I am in toil and hardship, through many a sleepless night, in hunger and thirst, often without food, in cold and exposure! In this world of change and decay, nobody is immune to suffering. But how blessed am I to suffer for the sake of Christ, for an eternal reward!" The covenant curses of the Mosaic Law are now listed in Paul's resumé as his beatitudes, his blessings—in fact, as a proof of his apostolic calling!

The Arrival Of The New, The Ultimate

This reversal does not imply contradiction between the old covenant and the new covenant. This reversal is designed to unmistakably mark the arrival of what was foreshadowed from the beginning. This reversal signals that the time of shadows is past and now the time of true substance has finally arrived. For even under the husk of the old covenant, the kernel of the new covenant is found— hidden, yet present. You see, even the old covenant did not present the earthly blessings and curses as the ultimate goal of It is as if Paul were saying, "....But oh how blessed I am to be considered worthy to suffer for Jesus' sake! ....In this world of change and decay, nobody is immune to suffering. But how blessed am I to suffer for the sake of Christ, for an eternal reward!" The covenant curses of the Mosaic Law are now listed in Paul's resume' as his beatitudes, his blessings—in fact, as a proof of his apostolic calling!

the covenant. The blessings in the land were but incentives; the curses in the land were but preventative measures. As such, they could not be the ultimate goal; they were there to help achieve the goal. Parents might promise certain gifts to their children if they do well in school. But the parents certainly don't want their children to think of the gifts as the goal; the goal is to work hard and do well in school.

In the same way, the ultimate goal of Israel's covenant with God was not the blessings in the land. Rather, it was Israel's covenant union with Yahweh (the covenant name of God) itself. That is why, even under the old covenant administration, the Levites were not given the inheritance in the land. Regarding their inheritance, the Lord said of the Levites, "You shall have no inheritance in their land, neither shall you have any portion among them. I am your portion and your inheritance among the people of Israel" (Numbers 18:20). Do you see? The Levites were chosen to serve Him at the sanctuary! How could He be so cruel as to withhold from them the blessings of the Promised Land—unless Israel's ultimate inheritance was God Himself, not a piece of real estate! That is why Habakkuk, too, was able to say,

> Though the fig tree should not blossom, nor fruit be on the vines, the produce of the olive fail and the fields yield no food, the flock be cut off from the fold and there be no herd in the stalls, yet I will rejoice in the LORD; I will take joy in the God of my salvation. GOD, the Lord, is my strength; he makes

my feet like the deer's; he makes me tread on my high places. (Habakkuk 3:17-19)

Habakkuk saw the vision of God's coming judgment on Judah. Judah would be deprived of all the blessings of the land. Yet he was able to rejoice! How? For what?

We are distracted by so many things. We think we have to do all these things and we have to have all these things in order to have a good life. And we fret, worry, and agonize about all these things. We feel like we are always behind, needing to catch up, desperately trying not to drown. And something big happens—like a major illness—and our life comes to a screeching halt. We cannot tend to everything we used to. We cannot do everything we used to. And as we are forced to stop everything, we are able to see life more clearly—what is truly important and what is not.

It was precisely when all the blessings of the Promised Land were taken away all around him that Habakkuk was enabled to see how utterly temporary and fragile and vulnerable these things were. And, in his disappointment and despair, he was compelled to look up. And when he lifted up his eyes toward heaven, he was able to see, with a greater clarity and appreciation than ever before, the Giver behind all the gifts, who is greater than all the gifts. He who will be with us even when all the gifts are destroyed and perish away. He who is not just the Fount of every blessing but also the greatest blessing Himself. He who is able to satisfy us and delight us above all things, even when all things are taken away from us. Of whom we can say, "Your steadfast love is better than life" (Psalm 63:3); "a day in your courts is better than a thousand elsewhere. I would rather be a doorkeeper in the house of my God than dwell in the tents of wickedness" (Psalm 84:10)!

A Kingdom Unlike All The Others

With the coming of Jesus Christ, this kernel of truth is brought out into the open, out of the husk of the old covenant. He came *not* to restore the kingdom of David but to usher in the kingdom of heaven! He made this clear from the outset of His public ministry. "Repent, for the kingdom of *heaven* is at hand" (Matthew 4:17)! Obviously, the kingdom of heaven is not of this world; it is of heaven! But how can this heavenly nature of His kingdom be made clear to all? By the power of swords and spears? By the riches and wisdom of this world? No. Such a kingdom would be just like the other kingdoms of this world—even if it were far more powerful than all other nations. The nation of Israel in the Old Testament was a good example of this.

There was a good reason for that, too. In the ancient world, conflicts between nations were seen as contests between their gods. A nation's victory was an evidence of the superior power of its god over the other. God demonstrated His supremacy over all other gods through Israel's victory. The 10 plagues He sent to Egypt were designed to show that He was the Lord of all nature, not the gods that the Egyptians worshipped. Israel's conquest of the Canaanite nations also showed the same thing— as did Israel's golden age under David's and Solomon's reign.

But do you see the limitation of this arrangement? Heaven was being defined in earthly terms. The spiritual was being defined in physical terms. The power of heaven was brought down to bring about a relief and rescue on earth—and it could be done only temporarily. But what if it should be the other way round? Isn't that how it is with a sign and what it signifies? A sign does not exist for itself; it exists to direct our attention to the thing it represents! How foolish it would be for us to be so attached to our family photo that we neglect spending time with our family! Israel was an earthly representation of heaven. Its role was to point people to heaven, not to itself.

God made this clear even from the beginning. In establishing Israel as a nation, God's goal was not to make it the most powerful and prosperous nation in the world. It was to make Israel into "a kingdom of priests and a holy nation" (Exodus 19:5)! Doesn't this suggest how unusual, how utterly other-worldly, how heavenly Israel was to be among all the nations of the world? How can there be a nation just of priests? How can a nation of priests survive in this world? Consider also how this promise was made right before God entered into covenant with Israel at Mount Sinai and formally established Israel as a nation. According to this covenant, Israel could not be a nation of priests. Because it was that very covenant which set aside the Levites as the priestly tribe! Only they were allowed to serve at the temple! This showed that the nation of Israel was merely a temporary arrangement. For God's purpose to be realized, God's people would have to be under a different covenant, in a different kind of commonwealth—and ultimately, in the kingdom of heaven itself!

The Way Of Jesus Christ

That's why Jesus had to come the way He did, live the way He did, suffer as He did, and die as He did! Even though He was David's greater Son, Jesus the Son of God was born, not in a palace, but in a manger because there was no room for Him anywhere! Though He is Most High God, Possessor of heaven and earth, while He lived in this world, He had no place to lay His head when even the foxes have holes and the birds of the air have nests. He had a great following but He did not organize a political party or a military band. And what kind of people did Jesus befriend? The people of high position and influence, of wealth and power? No. He was laughed at and despised by the Jewish leaders for being a Friend of sinners! And how did He speak of His impending execution by crucifixion? The hour of His glory! When asked by Pilate whether He was the King of the Jews, Jesus replied, "My kingdom is not of this world. If my kingdom were of this world, my servants would have been fighting, that I might not be delivered over to the Jews. But my kingdom is not from the world" (John 18:36).

But of course all this would only make Jesus a radical philosopher or activist, were it not for the fact that Jesus did not go the way of all mankind and end His short life in death. Jesus rose again from the dead, conquering death and sin once for all! What demonstrates the reality of the kingdom of heaven more than His resurrection? For this world of change and decay cannot escape from the grip of death.

What does all this mean? We can now see the radical ramifications of the life, death, and resurrection of Jesus Christ, can't we? The kingdom of heaven has come in Him in a purer and fuller form than ever before! How is the reality of the kingdom of heaven to be shown? When Christians overpower others with spears and swords? When Christians become wealthier and healthier than others? When Christians become more influential and enjoy greater comfort and ease in the world than others? No.

I must hasten to add, this is not to say that Christians cannot enjoy the material blessings of the Lord. We are so blessed to live in this country and, materialistically speaking, we are better off than most of the people in the world, by far. But does this mean we are better Christians than our brothers and sisters in the rest of the world? How ridiculous! We must not think that the earthly blessings we enjoy in this country is the sole, full measure of God's favor. After all, we often hear how some of the Christians in developing countries worry about us and pray for us! They worry about so many distractions we have in our lives because of our material wealth. They worry about us placing our trust in our earthly blessings and not leaning on the Lord. They worry that we are too busy keeping up with the Joneses rather than seeking first God's kingdom and His righteousness.

We must be mindful of what our Lord Himself said: "I tell you, it is easier for a camel to go through the eye of a needle than for a rich person to enter the kingdom of God" (Matthew 19:24). As John Piper has said, there is nothing wrong with making a lot of money. The trouble begins when we want to keep it for ourselves.

Suffering Not Without Purpose, Not Without Confidence

Why does God allow sufferings in our lives—if God so loves us? In fact, didn't Jesus suffer and die in our place so we don't have to? That is true. Because Jesus suffered and died in our place, there will come a time when we will live eternally in the kingdom of heaven where there is no suffering, no death. But until then, we suffer in this world and this is not news to anyone. Then is there any benefit for us now in this present age? Of course! Through His suffering and death in our place, Christ has taken the sting away from our suffering and death. When we

65

suffer, even as a direct consequence of our own foolish mistakes and sins, we do not suffer God's judicial punishment. To those who are in Christ, God is no longer our Judge. He is our heavenly Father. And the sufferings He allows in our life, even as a direct consequence of our sin, are not punitive but redemptive in purpose—in order to make us hate sin and grow in our love for God and His righteousness. Yes, even after the death and resurrection of Christ, we die. But our death is not God's punishment for our sin, the wages of sin we have to pay. Christ has paid it all! Our death, then, is our farewell to this world of change and decay, to our sin and sinfulness, as we enter the kingdom of eternal life and glory!

And there is another dimension to our suffering. Jesus did not suffer only to pay for the penalty of our sin. He suffered because He was not of this world. He was of heaven, a stranger and alien to this world. He was despised and persecuted by the people of this world because He was not one of them. And He told us in advance that, if the world hated Him, it would also hate His disciples. We should expect to suffer, then, because we too are not of this world, because we are strangers and aliens in this world, heavenly pilgrims. To this category of suffering belong the sufferings we suffer without any apparent reason, such as certain sicknesses and accidents. These are designed to show us that this world is not our home, that the treasures and blessings we enjoy in this life are not our true wealth. As those whose hopes are firmly anchored in heaven, what is important is not whether we suffer or not in this world. Rather, it is how we respond. As Augustine said, God stirs up the pot of our life with the big spoon of affliction in this world—both Christians and non-Christians. The question is what comes out of our heart—a foul stench of bitterness and resentment or a sweet fragrance of unswerving trust in God and thanksgiving to Him? For, if heaven is so much better than this world, and if God loves us, He cannot allow us to settle for less, for this world that is perishing away.

What is our source of confidence? What is our boasting? What is our hope? Why is the gospel of our risen Savior good news? Do we not say, "Nothing!" to the question, "What does it profit a man to gain the whole world and forfeit his soul?" (Mark 8:36)? And if we have obtained eternal life in Jesus Christ, the treasures of this world cannot be the basis of our happiness and self-worth, much less the basis of our witness to the gospel, can they? Should we be blessed with the blessings of this world, let us be grateful but not become complacent and arrogant. Should God allow us to suffer for Christ's sake, let us not be ashamed of the gospel! Rather, let us remind ourselves what we put our hope in when we follow Christ and persevere in faith. As we do so, may the Lord be pleased to let the light of heaven shine through us, even in our afflictions!

But all we have been saying pertains to this present age. For the day will come when Christ shall return, not as the suffering Servant but as the Judge of the living and the dead. With Him will come the kingdom of heaven in fullness to destroy every rebel and judge every sin! Then the time of God's grace will come to an end, even of God's common grace. Oh, how diligent we ought to be in bearing witness to Christ with a greater sense of urgency!

"Behold, Your Son; Behold, Your Mother!"
Preached On Good Friday, 2013

.... [25] but standing by the cross of Jesus were his mother and his mother's sister, Mary the wife of Clopas, and Mary Magdalene. [26] When Jesus saw his mother and the disciple whom he loved standing nearby, he said to his mother, "Woman, behold, your son!" [27] Then he said to the disciple, "Behold, your mother!" And from that hour the disciple took her to his own home.
John 19:25-27

Introduction: The Seven Words Of Jesus On The Cross

We have in this passage one of the Seven Words of Jesus on the cross. The Seven Words are:

"Father, forgive them, for they know not what they do." (Luke 23:34)

"Truly, I say to you, today you will be with me in Paradise." (Luke 23:43)

He said to his mother, "Woman, behold, your son!" Then he said to the disciple, "Behold, your mother!" (John 19:26-27)

"My God, my God, why have you forsaken me?" (Matthew 27:46, Mark 15:34)

"I thirst." (John 19:28)

When Jesus had received the sour wine, he said, "It is finished," and he bowed his head and gave up his spirit. (John 19:30)

Then Jesus, calling out in a loud voice, said, "Father, into your hands I commit my spirit!" (Luke 23:46)

It is not hard to imagine the enormous significance of one's last words, especially when he knows that his final moments are upon him. With a sense of urgency, he would say and do only what he considers to be most important. And what he considers most important will speak volumes about what kind of person he truly is. What do Jesus' last words tell us about Him?

The first three Words show the magnitude of Jesus' love. His love was directed not only to those who were close to Him—namely, His mother and His beloved disciple. His mercy was extended to one of the criminals as well. Judging from the fact that he was being crucified, this criminal must have been guilty of a heinous crime or many such crimes. But when he expressed his remorse and clung to Jesus for mercy, Jesus readily promised him forgiveness and eternal life in Paradise. But Jesus' mercy extended even to those who were crucifying Him on the cross. Even in the midst of the pain which they inflicted on Him, He did not curse them; rather, He prayed for their forgiveness!

His Words in the middle show the intensity of His pain—the pain of being forsaken by His heavenly Father for the sins of His people; the pain of thirst because He was enduring the hellish heat of God's wrath against sinners. These words, too, express the unimaginable magnitude of His love for His people. The pain He suffered, He suffered for the sins of His people. The horrific death He died, He died to pay the penalty of our sin!

His last Words show the successful completion of His work of redemption. "It is finished!" They also show His confident trust in God's justice to vindicate Him, even to the very last moment of His earthly life—"Father, into your hands I commit my spirit!"

The Third Word

Now, we come back to Jesus' Third Word—His words to His mother, Mary, and to His beloved disciple, John. Seeing the two together, Jesus said to Mary, "Woman, behold, your son!" Then, to John, "Behold, your mother!" Among all the Seven Words of Jesus on the cross, the Third is the most curious of all. Jesus came to save the world, to give eternal life to those who believe in His name. Different aspects of His redemptive work are clearly reflected in all the words of Jesus on the cross—except this Third Word. The Third Word seems to be concerned with a mundane matter—that of making some kind of earthly provision for His mother, Mary.

We may feel very much encouraged by this perspective. Jesus was not just concerned about our spiritual well-being, after all! We may feel relieved that He is also concerned about our physical well-being. After all, it is He who made us both body and soul! He knows *all* of our needs, *both* physical and spiritual! Throughout His ministry, He healed the sick and cast out demons and fed the hungry! How wonderful it is to know that our wonderful Shepherd takes care of *all* our needs, both physical and spiritual! And the beloved Disciple did take her to his own home and took care of her (verse 27).

More Than Earthly Provision

We must not deny God's concern for all of our being, not just one or some aspects. But the question we must ask is whether that is all Jesus was doing, addressing Mary's physical well-being.

Let us not forget the redemptive character of all Seven Words of our Lord—His prayer for forgiveness; His grant of admission into Paradise; His suffering for our sin; His successful completion of His redemptive mission, etc. We should not think that this Third Word was an exception.

And we have a nagging suspicion that this was more than just for Mary's earthly provision. After all, Mary was not alone. She might have been widowed by this time. But Jesus was not the only Child she had. Joseph did not have relations with her when she was pregnant with Jesus by the Holy Spirit. But the two had children of their own. When Jesus was ministering to people, His disciples notified Him, "Your mother and your brothers are outside, seeking you" (Mark 3:32). We know for certain that Jesus had half-brothers. We know of four, for sure—James (the author of the New Testament letter of James) and Joseph and Simon and Judas (Matthew 13:55). It seems He had half-sisters as well (Matthew 13:56). It is hard to imagine that Mary was being neglected by *all* of her sons (and daughters) so as to be homeless, especially in that Ancient Near Eastern culture!

A New And Different Kind Of Family

So, then, Jesus was doing much more than making an earthly provision for Mary. If that were all that He was doing, why specifically use these familial titles? "Woman, behold, *your son!*" "Behold, *your mother!*" He could have just told John to take care of Mary. Could it be, then, that Jesus was actually establishing a new and different kind of family?

Should this be surprising? Jesus said, "If anyone comes to me and does not hate his own father and mother and wife and children and brothers and sisters, yes, and even his own life, he cannot be my disciple" (Luke 14:26). With these words, our Lord hinted that His bond with His disciples would be deeper and stronger than family ties. Also consider how, when His mother and brothers came looking for Him earlier, Jesus, "looking about at those who sat around him," "said, 'Here are my mother and my brothers! For whoever does the will of God, he is my brother and sister and mother" (Mark 3:34-35). Jesus was indeed speaking of a new kind of family!

> ...Jesus was doing much more than making an earthly provision for Mary. If that were all that He was doing, why specifically use these familial titles? "Woman, behold, *your son!*" "Behold, *your mother!*" He could have just told John to take care of Mary. Could it be, then, that Jesus was actually establishing a new and different kind of family?

Throughout the Gospel according to John, Jesus' redemption is presented as a new creation. That is why the Prologue begins by identifying Jesus Christ as the Word who is coeternal with God the Father, who created all things: "In the beginning was the Word, and the Word was with God, and the Word was God. He was in the beginning with God. All things were made through him, and without him was not any thing made that was made" (John 1:1-3). This was important to point out from the outset. If redemption is a new creation, who can bring it about except the Creator God Himself?

It is also no accident that John included only seven miracles of Jesus. Of course, Jesus performed many more miracles than seven, as is evident from the accounts in the other (Synoptic) Gospels. Indeed, John tells us, "Now Jesus did many other signs in the presence of the disciples, which are not written in this book; but these are written so that you may believe that Jesus is the Christ, the Son of God, and that by believing you may have life in his name" (John 20:30-31). The number seven obviously corresponds to the week of creation. The first creation was God making all things out of nothing, from the primordial formlessness and void. The new creation is our Lord Jesus Christ making all things anew from our brokenness and sin, from death and hell.

With these words to Mary and John, the beloved Disciple, Jesus was creating a new family! Why did He? The first human family was defiled by sin on account of Adam and Eve and their Fall. Of course, even with the Fall, human family is by far the best there is in this fallen world. But whatever wonderful things we may enjoy in our families, they are overshadowed by the reality of sin—especially by the fact that family (as it is perpetuated by "ordinary generation") is the very conduit through which sin is transmitted from one generation to the next! No matter how much we love our children, we cannot help but hand down the Original Sin from Adam and Eve—like a bad, genetic illness.

New Family, New Family Ties

This vicious link has to be broken for our redemption. And that is why Jesus is creating a new family. This new family is not bound together by flesh and blood, by human ancestry connected all the way to Adam and Eve. This new family is born at the foot of the cross, in the death of Jesus Christ, the Son of God, the last Adam! It is born of the blood and the water, which from Jesus' riven side flowed. It is born of the greatest birth pang in history—the suffering our Lord suffered under the curse of the law for our forgiveness; the death our Lord died under the infinite wrath of God for our life. This new family is born of the greatest and deepest love—a love that is infinitely greater than any human love—the sacrificial love of a holy God for wretched sinners like us! This new family is bound by the precious blood of Jesus Christ, grounded in the common faith in Jesus Christ, sustained by the power of the Holy Spirit. The bond of this heavenly family transcends all earthly bonds *and* all earthly divisions. How glorious is this new family, to which we belong! Horatius Bonar remarks:

> It was God's purpose from the beginning, not merely to redeem for Himself a people out of a world of sinners, but to bring that people

into a peculiar relationship to Himself…. To carry out this purpose was the Word made flesh…. Being "made of a woman," He has become partaker of our lowly humanity, so as to be bone of our bone, and flesh of our flesh; and we being "born of God" are made partakers of the divine nature, becoming "members of his body, of his flesh, and of his bones." Thus the saints are the nearest kinsman of the Son of God [as much as it is humanly possible without being made divine ourselves]; and if of the Son, then of the Father also…. We are elevated to creation's highest level. We are brought into the inner circle of the Father's love—nearer his throne, nearer his heart than angels, for we are the Body of Christ, and members in particular—"the fullness of him that filleth all in all."[3]

Bonar also says,

Thus a new relationship was established, such as till then could never have been conceived of as even possible. The tie of creation, though not dissolved, was now to be lost in the closer, dearer tie of kindred [with God]….[4]

How awesome is this privilege to belong to the family of God! Should we be envious of the Rockefellers and the Vanderbilts when we have inherited the family name of God? To this new family belong the glory and majesty of God! "All that is beautiful in human relationship, or tender in human affection, or gentle in human intercourse; all that is lovable and precious in the movements of a human heart from its lowest depth to its uppermost surface."[5] These are what we long for in our earthly families but never quite obtain! But all these are fulfilled and perfected in this new family of God!

It is easy to see how this new family of God transcends all our earthly families. Our earthly families are of this world of change and decay. This new family is of heaven, everlasting and indestructible. Our family relations here are temporary—we won't be in heaven what we are to

---

3 Horatius Bonar, *Night of Weeping and Morning of Joy,* (Pensacola: Mount Zion Publications), pp. 13-14.

4 Horatius Bonar, *Night of Weeping and Morning of Joy*, p. 13.

5 Horatius Bonar, *Night of Weeping and Morning of Joy*, p. 16.

one another here on earth. The relations of this new family are eternal. Our earthly family, apart from Christ, is the conduit for the Original Sin, passing it down from generation to generation. This new family is the Storehouse of all the blessings of God. Our security is found in the almighty power of God who created the heavens and the earth out of nothing, who raised Jesus from the dead! Our safety is found in the full acceptance of God—pardoning all our sins on account of the perfect sacrifice of Jesus Christ, declaring us righteous and pleasing in His sight on account of Christ's perfect righteousness. All the riches of heaven are ours because we are co-heirs with Christ (Romans 8:17), because we are Christ's and Christ is God's (1 Corinthians 3:23)!

How Much More Should We Love One Another

We treasure our earthly families because the bond of flesh and blood is the strongest of all earthly ties. But we are bound by something far more powerful and lasting in the family of God—by the precious blood of Jesus Christ, the blood of God's eternal covenant. The tie that binds us together, therefore, is unbreakable. Nothing in this world and in the world to come can sever it. Not even death can destroy it. For our bond is established by our risen Lord who conquered death!

Behold your mothers and fathers in the Lord! Behold your sons and daughters in the household of God! Behold your brothers and sisters in the family of God! If we should honor our parents and love our siblings because of our earthly ties, how much more should we love those that are our new fathers and mothers, brothers and sisters, sons and daughters (for now, until we are all brothers and sisters in heaven) on account of the precious blood of Jesus Christ! We now share a new family name—that of God and our Lord Jesus Christ! We share all the blessings and privileges of the sons and daughters of God! We have God as our Father and Jesus Christ as our Brother! Oh, how we ought to love and treasure one another as those that are cherished by God! Let us love one another as Christ has loved us and laid down His life for us! Let the world know that we are His siblings, God's beloved sons and daughters by the way we love one another—not just in words but also in deeds!

75

Elizabeth Heard The Greeting Of Mary
Preached At Advent, 2005

*[39] In those days Mary arose and went with haste into the hill country, to
a town in Judah, [40] and she entered the house of Zechariah and greeted
Elizabeth. [41] And when Elizabeth heard the greeting of Mary, the baby
leaped in her womb. And Elizabeth was filled with the Holy Spirit, [42] and
she exclaimed with a loud cry, "Blessed are you among women, and blessed
is the fruit of your womb! [43] And why is this granted to me that the mother
of my Lord should come to me? [44] For behold, when the sound of your
greeting came to my ears, the baby in my womb leaped for joy. [45] And
blessed is she who believed that there would be a fulfillment of what was
spoken to her from the Lord."*
Luke 1:39-45

John the Baptist is not the protagonist of Luke's Gospel. Jesus Christ
is. Yet Luke begins the birth narrative of Jesus with the story of John's
birth. Why?

What Luke does with the birth narrative of John is what Matthew does
with the genealogy of Jesus Christ in his Gospel . With precision and
economy Matthew uses the genealogy to summarize what the entire Old
Testament was about—the anticipation of the appearance of the promised
Seed of David and Abraham. Luke uses Zechariah and Elizabeth and
the birth of their son John as the summary of the Old Testament. For
the birth of Christ did not take place in a vacuum. It happened in the
continuum of redemptive history. And His birth marked the beginning
of the decisive, climactic juncture in redemptive history, ending the old
and bringing in the new. Like a sequel that begins with a brief summary
of the prequel, so is Luke's Gospel. Under the inspiration of the Holy
Spirit, Luke artfully presents the birth story of John as a brief, accurate
summary of the Old Testament.

Darkness In Israel

The new era in redemptive history starts here. But it was dark in Israel at that time. Israel had lost its independence long ago and it was now occupied by Rome. And on its throne sat Herod the Great. But who was this Herod? Was he from the line of David, to whose descendant God promised, "I will establish the throne of his kingdom forever" (2 Samuel 7:13)? No! Was he from the tribe of Judah, from which "the scepter shall not depart" (Genesis 49:10)? No. Herod was not even from the line of Jacob. For he was an Idumean—a descendant of Esau, not of Jacob. Yet he sat upon the throne over Israel as its king.

What kind of king was he? He was called Herod the Great because he was a shrewd politician. But he was great also in his infamy. He came upon the throne by slaying all his enemies, including the whole Sanhedrin Council, except for two.[6] He was a man of insatiable cruelty, killing not only his enemies but also his own wife and sons. He began rebuilding the temple of Jerusalem, but only as a political maneuver to win the favor of the Jews. He was no worshipper of "Yahweh," the God of Israel. His building projects also included many temples dedicated to pagan gods and Roman emperors. Such was the man who reigned upon the land of Israel. It was dark. And if the darkness of God's chosen nation was this great, how much greater is the darkness of the fallen world under the tyranny of Satan and sin!

Introducing Zechariah And Elizabeth

Zechariah and Elizabeth lived in that dark period of Israel's history. Through their life we shall see that the darkness that covered Israel was not just from the wicked, atrocious reign of Herod. We don't know much about the couple. But what little information Luke 1 gives us is very significant. Zachariah was a priest, belonging to the division of Abijah. His wife, Elizabeth, too, belonged to the priestly family of Aaron. We know that God set apart the people of Israel from the world as His chosen people, as His own special possession. But even among

---

6 A.R. Fausset, *Fausset's Bible Dictionary*, "Herod." (http://www.bible-history.com/faussets/H/Herod/)

the Jews, the priests were a chosen lot. They were set apart from the rest of the Jews to serve the Lord at the sanctuary.

But this arrangement was not meant to be a permanent one. Even from the beginning the Lord said, "[I]f you will indeed obey my voice and keep my covenant, …you shall be to me *a kingdom of priests* and a holy nation" (Exodus 19:5-6). The priests represented, then, what the rest of Israel was meant to be someday. The priests were an expression of the ideal Jew. And Zechariah was a priest and his wife came from a priestly family.

And we are told that Zechariah and Elizabeth were "righteous before God, walking blamelessly in all the commandments and statutes of the Lord" (Luke 1:6). Zechariah was not just a priest in status and position only; his calling as a priest was more than just a job to him. He did not just perform his duties; he lived out his calling. He did not just hold on to a form of godliness; he displayed in his life the liveliness and vigor of godliness. So did his wife, Elizabeth. What more could one ask of these Jews?

Childless, Old, And Symbolic

"But they had no child, because Elizabeth was barren, and both were advanced in years" (verse 7). A dark cloud hung even over the life of this godly couple. They were childless and they were old. What a hopeless combination! This was certainly no small matter, especially to Elizabeth. She referred to her childlessness as "my reproach" (verse 25). Even in our modern, post-modern culture, even after the rise of feminism and woman's liberation, a woman's sense of worth is often closely associated with bearing children. Imagine how it must have been in the olden days! In Israel, childbearing for women was not merely a psychological issue. There was also the issue of inheritance. As we studied in Numbers, ordinarily a Jewish woman was not entitled to any inheritance except through her husband and her son(s). To be childless, therefore, was a devastating double-blow to a Jewish woman. That was Elizabeth's lot. Every time she celebrated the birth of her relatives' and neighbors' children, whenever she saw a tender interaction of a mother with her child(ren), she must have felt the brunt of this painful blow again and again.

But the childlessness of this godly, priestly couple was more than just an individual problem. What did we note at the outset? The story of Zechariah and Elizabeth in Luke's gospel is the transition from the old covenant to the new covenant. They are more than just two individuals. I daresay that they represent the Old Testament. More specifically, Zechariah and Elizabeth symbolically embodied the epitome of Old Testament piety, of the ideal Jew.

Take a look at the descriptions of this couple again. They were righteous before God, walking blamelessly in all the commandments and statutes of the Lord (verse 6). Do these words remind you of anything? "Enoch *walked with God*" (Genesis 5:22, 24). "Noah was *a righteous man, blameless* in his generation. Noah *walked with God*" (Genesis 6:9). "Then the LORD said to Noah, 'Go into the ark, you and all your household, for I have seen that *you are righteous before Me* in this generation" (Genesis 7:1). And regarding Job, the Lord said, "[T]here is none like him on the earth, *a blameless and upright man*, who fears God and turns away from evil" (Job 1:8; 2:3). Not only that, but God told Abram, "I am God Almighty; *walk before Me*, and be *blameless*" (Genesis 17:1). And the Lord told the nation of Israel, "You shall be *blameless before the LORD* your God" (Deuteronomy 18:13). Do you see? In the descriptions of Zechariah and Elizabeth, we have echoes of the Old Testament heroes and giants of faith!

"But they had no child because Elizabeth was barren…" (Luke 1:7).

What a telling picture of the limitations of the old covenant! As Zechariah and Elizabeth could not bear children, the old covenant could not bring forth life. "For by works of the law no human being will be justified in His sight, since through the law comes knowledge of sin" (Romans 3:20). The Apostle Paul also referred to the old covenant as a covenant of the letter that kills, not of the Spirit that gives life (2 Corinthians 3:6). The old covenant in Moses was "the ministry of death, carved in letters on stone"; it was "the ministry of condemnation" (2 Corinthians 3:7, 9).

The Light Of Heaven Breaks Through

You see? The darkness was deep in the land of Israel. It had been so for 400 years. Ever since Malachi, the last of the Old Testament prophets, no light of heaven broke through the darkness of the land...until now!

An angel comes down from heaven and delivers a message of gladness: "Do not be afraid, Zechariah, for your prayer has been heard, and your wife Elizabeth will bear you a son, and you shall call his name John. And you will have joy and gladness, and many will rejoice at his birth..." (verses 13-14)!

"But they had no child because Elizabeth was barren..." (Luke 1:7)....

What a telling picture of the limitations of the old covenant! As Zechariah and Elizabeth could not bear children, the old covenant could not bring forth life.

Here, we see a meeting between heaven and earth. And what a stark contrast we see! On the one hand we see a fear-stricken man of earth and on the other we see a glorious angel of heaven; the barren womb of Elizabeth and the life-giving power of heaven; the bleakness of a childless marriage and the joyful news of a supernatural conception; the dark reality of foreign occupation and the bright hope of the coming of the Lord (verse 17). Oh, how this world of darkness needs the bright light of heaven! The barrenness of our existence and work here needs the life and fruitfulness of heaven. Our tear-filled petitions and longings cry out for the power of heaven and its abundance! Our rebellious hearts, our sinful wills, and our earth-bound minds need the Spirit of heaven to turn us back to the Lord our God. Yes, we who live in this fallen world need the God of heaven! And when heaven broke through, the reproach of Elizabeth among people (verse 25) was replaced with the joy and gladness of many (verse 13)!

John Giving Way To Jesus, The Greater One

So John the Baptist was born, whose name means "Yahweh's Gift." He was special, destined to be "great before the Lord" (verse 15). He was born to do great things. But he was not the long-awaited Messiah. Someone far greater than he was coming. For John was born into the household of Aaron, of the tribe of Levi. But the Messiah must come from the tribe of Judah, from the line of David. The Messiah would be mightier than John, and John would not be worthy to untie the strap of His sandals (Luke 3:16). John would be great but his greatness would come from his mission to prepare the way of the Lord (Luke 1:17), "the Son of the Most High" (verse 32), the long-expected Messiah. And the Messiah's name would be Jesus—"Yahweh Saves." For He is the Lord who came to save His people.

There are many parallels between the two births:

- Both births are pre-announced by the angel Gabriel.
- Both were supernaturally conceived: John by an old, childless couple who were way past their childbearing age; Jesus by a virgin.
- Their births were in fulfillment of Biblical prophecies.
- Their names were given by God through the agency of the angel Gabriel.

But even these parallels show the supremacy of Jesus over John:

- Zechariah, John's father, was rebuked for lack of faith when the announcement was made. Mary, on the other hand, was free from such rebuke.
- Both conceptions were supernatural but that of Jesus was far superior. John was born between a father and mother, though old and barren. There had been other supernatural conceptions like John's. We can think of Sarah's conception of Isaac and Hannah's conception of Samuel, etc. God used these supernatural conceptions to tell us how our salvation must be of God, not of men—that what is impossible with men is possible only with God (verse 37). But Jesus' conception was unique even among all the supernatural conceptions in biblical history. Jesus was conceived by the Holy Spirit of a virgin. But why a virgin conception? Every descendant of Adam conceived by the natural means shared in the original guilt of the Father, Adam. The cruel tyranny of Adam's sin reigned over all men from generation to generation—until the Son of God was conceived by the Holy Spirit of the Virgin Mary. This most supernatural, most extraordinary

conception was necessary to break the chain of Original Sin. Though a human being was involved in bringing the Son of God into the world, the guilt of that human being was overcome by the holiness of God: "And the angel answered [Mary], 'The Holy Spirit will come upon you, and the power of the Most High will *overshadow* you; therefore the child to be born will be called holy—the Son of God" (verse 35).

Jesus thus conceived was much greater than John. John was "the *prophet* of the Most High" (1:76); Jesus was "the *Son* of the Most High" (verse 32). John was to prepare the way of the Lord (1:76); Jesus was the Lord coming to save His people. Again, John was not fit to untie the strap of Jesus' sandal (3:16).

Yet Jesus Himself said of John, "I tell you, among those born of women none is greater than John" (7:28a). Why? John was more than a great prophet; he was the *greatest* of all the prophets because he was allowed to see in person, with his very own eyes, Jesus Christ, the glorious Fulfillment of all the prophecies, the Object of all the prophets' yearning. But Jesus went on to say, "Yet the one who is least in the kingdom of God is greater than he" (Luke 7:28b). So much greater was Jesus than John. So much greater was the kingdom Jesus brought than the nation of Israel.

Elizabeth's Greater Longing

And how wonderfully this is demonstrated in Mary's encounter with Elizabeth! Upon seeing Mary, Elizabeth blesses her, "Blessed are you among women, and blessed is the fruit of your womb!" (1:42) Elizabeth blesses Mary not as Mary's superior but as a humble admirer. Elizabeth herself was a blessed woman, blessed in her old age with a child, and not just with an ordinary child but with a child destined to be great before God. But she blesses Mary as the most blessed among all women. Why? Because Mary was chosen by God to be that woman through whom the Seed of the Woman would come to crush the head of the serpent and save His people from sin and death (Genesis 3:15). Elizabeth was so amazed and so humbled that the mother of her Lord should come to her (Luke 1:43).

Compare this to Elizabeth's reaction to her own pregnancy. She seemed to have spoken to no one. For we are told that she kept herself hidden for five months (verse 24). Her only words, maybe to herself, were: "Thus the Lord has done for me in the days when he looked on me, to take away my reproach among people" (verse 25). Do you sense gratitude? Yes. Do you sense great jubilation? Not really. Danker suggests that there might even be an element of fear (as suggested by her seclusion).[7] For she had seen how her husband was struck with muteness.

But there was no holding back when Mary came to her. What wonder and joy filled her heart! And Mary's greeting made the baby John leap in her womb. Mary's greeting filled her with the Holy Spirit! So abundant was the filling of the Holy Spirit, so uncontainable was the jubilation of her heart, that she could not help but cry out with a loud voice, blessing Mary and the Fruit of her womb.

How could this be? Wasn't her barrenness, wasn't her childlessness, the cause of the darkness in her godly life? Her miraculous pregnancy should have removed that darkness. Yet, her own pregnancy had not filled her with the kind of jubilation that filled her heart now. At that moment of encountering Mary, everything became clear. The greatest longing of her heart was not having a child of her own. The greatest longing of her heart was not having her reproach removed from her. For what does it profit a woman to have a son, to be adored and envied by people, and forfeit her soul? Her *physical* barrenness was cured by her miraculous pregnancy. But what about the barrenness of her *soul*? Her reproach *among men* was removed by her pregnancy. But what about her reproach *before the God* of the living and the dead? Was she perfect in her righteousness so as not to need a Redeemer? Hadn't she sinned and fallen short of the glory of God?

In Mary's greeting, Elizabeth heard the gospel of Jesus Christ—that her Lord, her God, her Savior came to seek and save her! Her son, her precious son, her long-awaited son could not water that barren soul of hers. But now her Lord came to her, her God and her Savior, who alone

---

7 Frederick W. Danker, *Jesus and the New Age*, (Philadelphia: Fortress Press, 1988), p. 34.

could fill her barren soul with the Holy Spirit, with the kind of joy she had never felt before. Her son, now growing in her womb, was able to remove only her reproach among men. But now the Son of the Most High came to her and honored her as one of the first recipients of the gospel in the dawning of a new age! Her joy of having a son of her own grew pale in comparison to

In Mary's greeting, Elizabeth heard the gospel of Jesus Christ—that her Lord, her God, her Savior came to seek and save her! Her son, her precious son, her long-awaited son could not water that barren soul of hers. But now her Lord came to her, her God and her Savior, who alone could fill her barren soul with the Holy Spirit, with the kind of joy she had never felt before.

a greater joy of receiving the Son of the Most High coming to her to save her soul from sin, death and the serpent of old. The true Son of David had finally come to take the throne of David and to establish a kingdom, which would have no end (verse 33), which would never be overcast with the dark clouds of sin, death and Satan.

Fulfillment In Jesus Christ
But don't you see? The joy that Elizabeth felt was not her individual joy. Did we not say what Zechariah and Elizabeth represented? The priesthood of the old covenant. The best of Old Testament piety. In Elizabeth's adoration of Jesus Christ, the priesthood of the old covenant found its satisfaction; the piety of the Old Testament found its true fulfillment. With Elizabeth the entire Old Testament humbly bows down before Jesus Christ, the object of its ultimate hunger. As the earth-bound, crawling caterpillar gladly sheds its cocoon to become a beautiful butterfly with wings to fly; as the seed gladly dies in the ground to give way to the earth-breaking seedling to grow into flower-bearing plants and fruit-bearing trees, so must the old covenant give up all of its limitation--and even its best!--and give way to the arrival of its fulfillment in the eternal Son of God.

Again, don't you see? Don't you see in the story of Elizabeth and Zechariah that true satisfaction cannot be found apart from Jesus Christ, the Son of the Most High, the Savior of our souls? Do you not see that even the good and precious things of this world cannot give you the true joy and gladness that only the kingdom of heaven can give you? The first chapters of Luke's Gospel are replete with the words "joy" and "gladness" and "rejoicing." For the kingdom which Jesus Christ brings is a kingdom of true joy, abounding gladness, and everlasting jubilation. It is to that kingdom you belong if you have received Jesus Christ. Whatever season of the year or of life you find yourself in, won't you hold on to this gospel truth? Won't you repent of obsessing over the things that cannot truly satisfy? Won't you now humbly bow before Christ and confess, being filled with the Spirit and joy of heaven, that Christ is your all? So, gladly, deny yourself and take up the cross and find your true life in Christ—until that day when you shall be transported into heaven and experience fullness of joy through all eternity in the presence of your God!

On The Road To Emmaus—A Resurrection Message

Preached On Easter Sunday, 2001

[13] That very day two of them were going to a village named Emmaus, about seven miles from Jerusalem, [14] and they were talking with each other about all these things that had happened. [15] While they were talking and discussing together, Jesus himself drew near and went with them. [16] But their eyes were kept from recognizing him. [17] And he said to them, "What is this conversation that you are holding with each other as you walk?" And they stood still, looking sad. [18] Then one of them, named Cleopas, answered him, "Are you the only visitor to Jerusalem who does not know the things that have happened there in these days?" [19] And he said to them, "What things?" And they said to him, "Concerning Jesus of Nazareth, a man who was a prophet mighty in deed and word before God and all the people, [20] and how our chief priests and rulers delivered him up to be condemned to death, and crucified him. [21] But we had hoped that he was the one to redeem Israel. Yes, and besides all this, it is now the third day since these things happened. [22] Moreover, some women of our company amazed us. They were at the tomb early in the morning, [23] and when they did not find his body, they came back saying that they had even seen a vision of angels, who said that he was alive. [24] Some of those who were with us went to the tomb and found it just as the women had said, but him they did not see." [25] And he said to them, "O foolish ones, and slow of heart to believe all that the prophets have spoken! [26] Was it not necessary that the Christ should suffer these things and enter into his glory?" [27] And beginning with Moses and all the Prophets, he interpreted to them in all the Scriptures the things concerning himself.

[28] So they drew near to the village to which they were going. He acted as if he were going farther, [29] but they urged him strongly, saying, "Stay with us, for it is toward evening and the day is now far spent." So he went in to stay with them. [30] When he was at table with them, he took the bread and blessed and broke it and gave it to them. [31] And their eyes were opened, and they recognized him. And he vanished from their sight. [32] They said to

each other, "Did not our hearts burn within us while he talked to us on the road, while he opened to us the Scriptures?" [33] And they rose that same hour and returned to Jerusalem. And they found the eleven and those who were with them gathered together, [34] saying, "The Lord has risen indeed, and has appeared to Simon!" [35] Then they told what had happened on the road, and how he was known to them in the breaking of the bread.
Luke 24:13-35

The Sad Journey Back Home

Have you ever wanted something really, really badly? And have you ever been so close to getting it that you thought you could almost touch it and taste it? And have you been so close to it, only to have the realization of your hope dashed to pieces at the last minute?

Then you will know what it was like for the two disciples to walk on the road to Emmaus. The road to Emmaus was a journey of broken hearts, lost dreams, dashed hopes. It was only seven miles long. But how do you measure the distance of such a journey simply in mileage? How do you weigh the burden of disappointments pressing down on the two disciples? How do you account for their pain as they treaded on the broken pieces of their lost dreams and shattered hopes?

Walking on the road to Emmaus was more than a journey from one city to another. It signified a change of monumental proportion for the two disciples. Their whole world had just collapsed. But how bad could it have been? After all, they were coming home! They were coming back to where they grew up. They were coming back to all that they were familiar with and accustomed to.

But that was precisely the problem. They were coming back to how things used to be before they had left. And coming back to how things used to be meant coming back to the same old drudgery of life—to the uneventful, mundane cycle of commonplace existence from day to day.

And that was why they had left Emmaus in the first place. Not that they were necessarily unhappy with their lives there. They lived where their fathers used to live, doing what their fathers used to do, content only if they could leave behind for their children a bit more than what they themselves had received from their fathers. They knew every street, every corner of their village. Their neighbors, they knew them one and all—who lived where and how they lived. Nothing much had changed in that village of Emmaus for many generations. The only life they knew about was what they had seen and experienced in that village of Emmaus. What they had seen and experienced in that village was what they had expected their future to be. And they knew, when their time would come, they too would have to follow their fathers before them in the way of all men—death.

Why The Two Disciples Had Earlier Left

But one day, something happened that changed everything. It was like a huge volcanic eruption that suddenly and radically transformed the dull, flat landscape of their lives. They finally saw their lives as they truly were. Theirs was a life where hope was anchored in hopelessness; where dreams were chained to the monotony of daily routine; where happiness was built on shifting desert dunes of fluctuating fortunes. Theirs was a life where one found contentment only in low expectations.

But something tremendous had happened. And, after that, what once seemed normal became insufferably intolerable. That which was once acceptable became unacceptable; that which was once satisfactory became terribly unsatisfying. What they had once enjoyed with contentment, they viewed with contemptuous disgust. Their lives suddenly seemed unbearable in the light of something new and different. And the single force that brought about this radical change was Jesus of Nazareth—a man, of all places, from Nazareth! "Can anything good come out of Nazareth" (John 1:46)?

"The time is fulfilled, and the kingdom of God is at hand; repent and believe in the gospel," declared Jesus (Mark 1:15; cf. Luke 4:43). With those words, Jesus burst onto the center stage of Israel's public consciousness. In an unprecedented manner, He announced the arrival of the kingdom of God. He demonstrated the presence of the kingdom of God through His powerful preaching and teaching, miracles and healing.

His message swept across the dry land of Palestine like a gushing flood. The dormant seed of the prophetic promises of God began to sprout into saplings of hope and expectation. The barren hearts of men were plowed into new furrows of excitement and anticipation. What wondrous wisdom flowed out of His lips every time He opened His mouth! How simple and yet how profound were His parables! How penetrating was His preaching! How insightful was His teaching! And with what ease He put the challenges and objections of the Pharisees and scribes to silence! Something new and different was taking place in the land of Palestine and everyone felt it in the air.

The two disciples in Emmaus felt it as well. Yes, the kingdom of God was at hand! The promises of God were not in vain, after all. The time of humiliation for Israel was finally passing away. The formal glory of David and Solomon would return once again back to the Promised Land. Oh, they felt it in their souls. They saw it in the person of Jesus. They heard it in the voice of Jesus. They sensed it in the presence of Jesus. Chills went down their spines as they saw Jesus healing the sick and casting out demons. When Jesus preached and taught about the kingdom of God, their blood boiled with expectation and hope!

But He was not just an inspiring teacher, mighty in words. He was mighty in deeds as well. Wherever Jesus went, remarkable things happened. The sick and crippled were healed. Yes, those who once were blind now saw. The deaf began to hear. The lame started to walk. The demon-possessed were set free and the lepers' repulsive skin became as soft and healthy as a newborn babe's skin. When the disciples thought they were confronted with an impossible situation, Jesus did something that far exceeded their wildest expectations. He fed the 5,000 with just five loaves and bread and two fish. He calmed the raging sea simply by rebuking it—as if it were His submissive pet! And just when they thought that they had seen the pinnacle of Jesus' incredible powers, did He not exceed their expectation yet again by raising from the dead a widow's son at Nain (Luke 7)? The Hope for the downtrodden, a Friend of the outcasts was Jesus—a great prophet sent by God.

With His powerful teaching and mighty deeds, Jesus aroused irrepressible hopes in you. He made things seem possible, no matter how challenging. What you could not dare to hope for, you dared to when Jesus was around. How could you not? In His presence, their laments were turned into joyful singing, their sighs of sorrow into laughter of gladness. The disciples had no doubt that this was the promised prophet mighty in deed and word in the sight of God and all the people (Luke 24:19). He would end the centuries of Israel's humiliation. He would restore the former glories of King David. He would cleanse the temple, bring people to repentance and Israel would become a mighty and holy nation, the envy of all peoples!

How Their Hope Died

But how quickly, how suddenly this hope vanished! In just a few days after His triumphal entry into Jerusalem, hailed by all as King, Jesus was dead—crucified like a criminal, hanging on a tree, cursed!

Not that Jesus had never talked about His suffering and death at the hands of the religious leaders! Yes, He even said something about being raised from the dead on the third day, too. But they dismissed such sayings as nonsense. What could the religious leaders do to Jesus? Their Master was endowed with supernatural powers—even the winds and storms obeyed Him! He even knew the thoughts of men, and if anyone dared to plot against Him He would surely know! And the public was fully

But how quickly, how suddenly this hope vanished! In just a few days after His triumphal entry into Jerusalem, hailed by all as King, Jesus was dead—crucified like a criminal, hanging on a tree, cursed! .... That's why the two disciples were on the road to Emmaus. This was a sad, pitiful homecoming—a truly tragic conclusion to unfulfilled dreams and failed endeavors. This was a journey back to their old life, now made worse because of the hope they tasted up until a few days ago. The two disciples were on this journey of shattered dreams and broken hearts.

91

behind Jesus. Just a few days ago, did the disciples not witness Jesus' triumphal entry into Jerusalem? If the multitudes had their way, if the disciples had their way, they would have crowned Him their king right there and then—as they symbolically did by laying down their garments and waving palm branches! The religious leaders tried many times but they could not touch Him because of such a public, unrestrained display of affection by the people. How could they dare kill Him—mighty in deed and word, loved by the people? But what they thought impossible happened. Jesus their Master died at the peak of His career, crucified like a condemned criminal. With the death of Jesus, their new world of hope collapsed completely.

That's why the two disciples were on the road to Emmaus. This was a sad, pitiful homecoming—a truly tragic conclusion to unfulfilled dreams and failed endeavors. This was a journey back to their old life, now made worse because of the hope they tasted up until a few days ago. The two disciples were on this journey of shattered dreams and broken hearts.

What Happened On The Way Home

But how strange it was that they should be on such a journey still— that they should remain sad (Luke 24:17) on this first day of the week, when the resurrected Jesus walked right alongside them! Was Jesus not raised from the dead according to His promise? Was He not there, right next to them? How could they not recognize Him? Was He changed so much by the resurrection that His own disciples could not identify Him? He was certainly changed—He was now clothed with a glorified body. He was changed, but not beyond recognition. His disciples later on recognized Him. Until then, their eyes were temporarily prevented from recognizing Him (verse 16). Why?

You see, the resurrection of Jesus Christ changed everything. Jesus did not come back to life just to pick up where He left off when He died. His resurrection was different from all others in redemptive history. All others were brought back to life to breathe again as they did before. They came back to how things used to be—to the same people, the same environment, the same situation—to the same life of suffering and pain, syncopated only by temporary relief and gratification. Their coming back to life was but a prolonging of what used to be. Sure, this second chance might have given them a deeper appreciation for life and those around them. With this renewed appreciation, they might have tried to make something better of their life. But then what? Once again, Death inevitably awaited them with its ghastly, insatiable mouth wide open. The widow's son at Nain went back to his mother, his house, his village after he was raised from the dead—only to die again later.

Jesus' resurrection, on the other hand, was more than simply being brought back to the same old life as it used to be. When Jesus was raised from the dead, He did not go back to His old life as the widow's son went back to his mother, his old occupation, his old village—or as Lazarus went back to Mary and Martha (John 11). Jesus was raised to a new life—a life that is radically different and immeasurably better than the mortal life we have here. Such was the resurrection, in which Jesus was raised. Jesus did not just come back to life. He was raised from the dead to enter into eternal glory (Luke 24:26). True—Jesus remained on earth for 40 days following His resurrection, but this world could no longer be the primary residence for His resurrection life. He remained on earth only to prove His resurrection to His disciples through His appearances. But it was inevitable that His resurrection be followed by His ascension to heaven. That is why the 40 days of Jesus' post-resurrection life on earth were radically different from the days of His life prior to His death. He appeared to His disciples but He did not stay with them. He no longer lived as the people of this world lived. He no longer lived as His disciples lived. Where did Jesus stay? What did He do when He did not appear to His disciples? Did He sleep in the wilderness, or did He sleep in the streets? You see, though He interacted with His disciples, He lived in a different order of existence.

This also meant that the mode of Jesus' fellowship with His disciples had to be changed forever as well. Do you see? After the resurrection of Jesus, the disciples had to commune with Christ in a different way. Once they saw Jesus with their eyes and touched Him with their hands (I John 1:1). But not after He was raised from the dead. Though He was raised in a tangible body, He had to ascend to the right hand of the Father. He would no longer be with them in physical presence as before. The proof of His presence would no longer be His physical body, which they could behold and handle. How, then, would they come to know their Savior and His presence with them?

Fellowship With Christ By Faith

Isn't it interesting that Jesus *spoke* to the two disciples on the road to Emmaus while their *eyes* were kept from recognizing Him (Luke 24:16)? This was so because the resurrection of Christ ushered in a new era. The disciples were no longer to fellowship with Christ by sight. They were to fellowship with Christ by faith—the faith which came by the *hearing* of the word of Christ.

The effect that the words of Christ produced, the two disciples describe in the following way: "Did not our hearts burn within us while He talked to us on the road, while He opened to us the Scriptures?" Only the strongest emotions and their movements are described as burning. Even sadness is too weak and passive an emotion to be described as such. But our passions burn! Our anger and our jealousy burn! Our hatred burns! Our lust burns! And only the deepest and strongest love is said to burn. Here, the disciples' hearts are said to be burning at the hearing of Jesus' words. What did they hear? What did they feel? Oh, how we wish that we were there on the road to Emmaus!

The Scriptures, All About Christ Our Savior

We do not know the exact words that Jesus uttered on the road to Emmaus. But we know what His words were about. They were about Jesus Himself! "And beginning with Moses and all the prophets, He interpreted in all the Scriptures the things concerning Himself" (verse 27). He must have shown how the grand plan of God for the redemption of His people was revealed in all of Scripture and how God's glorious redemption was fulfilled in the death and resurrection of the promised Messiah, Jesus Himself. The promised Seed of the woman was Jesus, who did come and crush the serpent's head through His death and resurrection. The Seed of Abraham, through whom all the families of the earth should be blessed, was Jesus. When God, in the form of a burning torch, passed between the halved carcasses of the animals in an oath of self-malediction, it pointed to the cursed death of the Second Person of the Trinity on the cross. When God commanded Abraham to sacrifice his only son, Isaac, He was talking about the sacrifice of His only begotten Son, Jesus Christ. When God spared Isaac's life by providing a ram caught in the thicket by its horn, He showed how He would spare His people by the substitutionary atonement offered by the only begotten Son of God. He did the same when He passed over the Jewish households, whose doorposts and lentils were painted with the blood of the paschal lamb, when He commanded Moses to build the tabernacle and institute the Levitical sacrificial system. It all pointed to Jesus the Lamb of God who, throught His once for all sacrifice obtained our eternal redemption. And when the Lord established the Levitical priesthood and Davidic kingship, when the Lord promised a prophet like Moses, He was pointing to His beloved Son—the true, heavenly Priest in the order of Melchizedek; the eternal King far greater than David and Solomon; the final Prophet infinitely greater than Moses and all other prophets that followed him.

As Jesus spoke, the Scriptures opened up before their eyes in a grand panoramic splendor. God's eternal plan of salvation was revealed in a crystal clear way. Jesus' words gave them a glimpse into the very mind of God. And their hearts burned with joy inexpressible as their minds were allowed to peek into the infinite wisdom of God.

And to know that this grand, eternal plan of God was for us! The two disciples on the road to Emmaus felt their hearts burn within them as this incredible reality hit them. Jesus' death was not a tragic, unexpected end to the heroic, yet deficient efforts of an ambitious revolutionary. Jesus' death was necessary. It was made necessary by God's eternal decree and unalterable predestination. "And there is salvation in no one else, for there is no other name under heaven that has been given among men by which we must be saved" (Acts 4:12). It was made necessary by the gravity of our sin itself. A sin committed against the infinite honor of God deserves an infinite punishment. Only God, who is of infinite value, can therefore make the atonement for our sins. And that was exactly what took place on the cross. Jesus did not die because of any crime or sin He committed. He was holy and righteous, completely and perfectly. Yet, He died as a cursed man, hung on the cross, for the sins of His people.

He Could Not Stay Dead

But Jesus could not be condemned to suffer forever! Infinite was the gravity of our sins, having offended the infinite honor of God, and eternal was the punishment we deserved! Countless is the number of my sins—past, present and future! And innumerable is the number of God's people, for whom Christ laid down His life! Indeed, infinite is the wrath of God that each of our sins deserves! And infinite upon infinite is the wrath of God that our Substitute must endure! Who can bear such a burden, except the eternal God the Son Himself? And He did bear the punishment of all our sins upon the cross. The infinite wrath of God was unleashed upon Him, all at once, without any restraint! So great was the punishment that the eternal Son of God had to cry out, out of the depth of His infinite pain, infinite agony, "My God, My God, why have You forsaken Me" (Matthew 27:46; Mark 15:34)? Infinite upon infinite was the gravity of all our sins. Infinite upon infinite was the wrath of God against our sins. But praise the Lord! Infinite upon infinite, too, was the eternal Son of God, who bore away our sins—all our sins!

Oh, this Jesus could not remain dead forever! No condemnation could hold Him down in the grave forever! With His one-time death, with His one-time sacrifice on the cross, He paid for it all—all of our sins, all of our guilt, all of our punishment! Our sins, one and all, have been removed—as far as the east is from the west, never to be brought against us, forever erased! Scarlet they were but now they are as white as snow! They were red like crimson but now they are like the purest wool (Isaiah 1:18)! So complete, so perfect was Jesus' atonement for our sins on the cross. Yes, Jesus remained in the grave for three days. That was not because it took Him three days to pay for our sins. The infinite God-man didn't have to take three days to do it. He remained in the tomb for three days to demonstrate that He was indeed dead—that he did not just faint.

And the resurrection of Jesus Christ proved that all our sins have been fully, completely, totally, entirely paid for. For the wages of sin is death.

Jesus the sinless, the perfectly righteous One, did not have to die, for He had no sin. If He died, it was to die *our* death to bear away *our* sins. So, when Jesus was raised from the dead, it meant that all of our sins were fully, completely taken care of. If not, Jesus would still remain in the grave, still paying for our sins. When all of our sins were paid for, death could no longer hold Him down. And when He was raised from the dead, He was raised for us—for our justification (Romans 4:25)! And when He was raised, He was not simply resuscitated but raised to life eternal on our behalf!

From Broken Dreams To The Renewed Hope Of Heaven

Think about it, friends! After all that Jesus accomplished by His death, would He resume His earthly life? After all that Jesus accomplished by His death, would we live the same kind of life on earth? God forbid! Through His incarnation and death, Jesus identified with our fallen condition. But through His resurrection, Jesus was raised to eternal life on our behalf. On our behalf, He was raised to a heavenly life—a life in the presence of God in heaven—a life free from suffering and pain, sin and death—a life of infinite joy and endless bliss!

Do you see why the disciples could no longer hold on to the way they used to commune with Christ? Do you see why they were not allowed to recognize Him by sight (at first) until Jesus spoke to them and broke the bread? The death and resurrection of Jesus Christ changed everything and nothing could remain the same! They were called to live—not by sight, but by faith. Their hope could no longer be attached to earthly things—not even to the nation of Israel with all of its sacrificial system and earthly inheritance! For the life they received from Christ was not of this world but of the kingdom of heaven. They were to view their lives and this world with the eyes of faith fixed on heaven. Faith is by nature *heavenly*. "Now faith is the assurance of *things hoped for*, the conviction of *things not seen*" (Hebrews 11:1). The genuineness of this Christian faith is not demonstrated by how well things work out for us in this world. It is rather demonstrated by how much we experience and enjoy the reality of heaven, even in the midst of the most extreme tribulations in the here and now.

A journey of broken earthly dreams on the road to Emmaus was transformed into a journey of the renewed hope of heaven when Jesus joined the two disciples on the road to Emmaus. Are you on the road to Emmaus as well—on a journey destined for broken dreams and dashed hopes? Do not despair! Does not Christ come to you as his word is proclaimed? In church, do we not also break the bread and drink the cup? May your hearts burn within as you hear the word of life and partake of the Lord's Table! And may you turn around and embark on a new journey—a journey to heaven! And may you live, truly live, in the reality of your resurrection life in Christ, in the hope of your eternal life in heaven—no longer chained to the status, treasures and pressures of this world! May you never forget what you have in Jesus Christ—a life that is indestructible, justification that is irrevocable and fellowship with God that is unbreakable! What more can you ask for in life? What can temporary tribulations do to us to break our spirit? Oh, as long as you live in this world, may you declare the glory of the resurrection of Jesus Christ, our Lord!

"I Will; Be Clean!"

[40] And a leper came to him, imploring him, and kneeling said to him, "If you will, you can make me clean." [41] Moved with pity, he stretched out his hand and touched him and said to him, "I will; be clean." [42] And immediately the leprosy left him, and he was made clean. [43] And Jesus sternly charged him and sent him away at once, [44] and said to him, "See that you say nothing to anyone, but go, show yourself to the priest and offer for your cleansing what Moses commanded, for a proof to them." [45] But he went out and began to talk freely about it, and to spread the news, so that Jesus could no longer openly enter a town, but was out in desolate places, and people were coming to him from every quarter.
Mark 1:40-45

This is a very short story, consisting merely of six verses and 95 words. But it is a story of profound transformation. The story begins with a leper coming to Jesus. Then we see the man healed. Though brief, it is a powerful story about an amazing event which changed the man's life in a radical way.

But that's not all. Did you notice? The story does not end with the man being healed. The healing takes place in the middle of the story and the story goes on. What does this tell us? That the healing is not the main point of this incident, as important and amazing as it is! This should not surprise us. Last week we saw the priority of Jesus' words over His miracles. We have something similar going on here. What I hope to do today is like what a docent at a museum does. I want to show you why this story—Mark's inspired telling of this historical incident—is a masterpiece. I want to show you how Jesus redeems us in a most wonderful (and surprising) way. And, by doing so, I want to exalt Christ and help you trust in Him and even boast of Him.

A Leper Comes To Jesus

Mark simply begins this account by saying, "And a leper came to Him" (verse 40). The leper appears out of nowhere. Mark does not tell us what his name is, where he is coming from, what he looks like, etc. The only thing we know about him is that he is a leper. Mark seems to be saying that is all we need to know about him. Why? Because, when one was struck with leprosy, only one thing mattered—the leprosy. It did not matter what his name was, what he was capable of, what he had and what he had accomplished. Now there was only one thing. It alone defined him, and that was his disease. His disease swallowed whole whatever identity he had, along with all of his prior relationships. As a leper, he was cast out of the covenant community. As a leper, he was shunned by everyone—his friends and neighbors, including his family. As a leper, he lived as a social outcast, in isolation, away from human society. His life was a living death, as one cursed by God and abandoned by men. Do you feel sorry for him? We all should. Because he is our mirror, a physical reflection of our spiritual condition as sinners without Christ--the living dead: "you were dead in the trespasses and sins in which you once walked, following the course of this world, following the prince of the power of the air, the spirit that is now at work in the sons of disobedience—among whom we all once lived in the passions of our flesh, carrying out the desires of the body and the mind, and were by nature children of wrath, like the rest of mankind (Ephesians 2:1-3).

This leper came to Jesus. Throughout our life, we meet a lot of people. But we know that not all meetings are the same. Most of our encounters are ordinary and forgettable. Some are downright unpleasant and even infuriating. But there are others that are memorable in a positive way. And there are a few fateful encounters that change our lives radically. It can be a teacher or a mentor. It can be our future spouse. It can be a friend whose friendship and loyalty stay with us lifelong. And what about our very first, fateful encounter with our children when they are born?

A Ray Of Hope

This leper must have had quite a few encounters in his lifetime. Even after the leprosy, he must have sought help from others to get healed.

Obviously, no one could do anything for him. Time after time, whatever hope he was able to muster was snuffed out by the utter helplessness of the so-called healers. Then he began to hear about Jesus—how He healed the sick and cast out demons. The news about Jesus came as a bright ray of hope to his cold, dark existence. He could not sit in that darkness anymore. His heart began to beat with hope again. He had to see Jesus.

You see, everything was about to change because he came to Jesus! It was Jesus who would make all the difference in the world. Going to someone for help—it is something he must

Now there was only one thing. It alone defined him, and that was his disease. His disease swallowed whole whatever identity he had, along with all of his prior relationships. As a leper, he was cast out of the covenant community. As a leper, he was shunned by everyone—his friends and neighbors, including his family. As a leper, he lived as a social outcast, in isolation, away from human society. His life was a living death, as one cursed by God and abandoned by men. Do you feel sorry for him? We all should. Because he is our mirror, a physical reflection of our spiritual condition as sinners without Christ.

have done many, many times in his life. And this time would have been no different from others were it not for the fact that he came to Jesus. He came to Jesus because Jesus had been preaching in the synagogues of Galilee and casting out demons (Mark 1:39). Before the leper came to Jesus, the news about Jesus came to him first. What welcome news to a man whose soul and future were covered with the leprosy of thick, dark despair! Jesus was his only ray of hope and he followed the ray all the way to see Him in person. Should we complain when all the neon lights of our superficial hopes are turned down if that compels us to see the light of Christ clearly?

The God Who Is Both Willing And Able

When the leper sees Jesus, he implores Him on his knees. He has nothing to offer to Him. He cannot give any reason that Jesus should heal him. All he can do is throw his leprous self at His mercy. Although Mark does not describe in detail how desperately he pleaded, we can imagine the intensity of his plea from Jesus' response. Jesus was moved with pity (verse 41).

The account Mark gives is extremely brief. Just take a look at how short the exchange is between the leper and Jesus. The leper says, "If you will, you can make me clean." Jesus replies, "I will; be clean" (verses 40-41)! But there is something quite striking about this dialogue apart from its brevity and simplicity. Notice it! The leper says, "If you will...." And Jesus says, "I will." The leper says, "You can make me clean." Jesus says, "Be clean." The vocabulary is the same! Jesus takes on the leper's words: our merciful Lord takes upon His lips the words that the leper spoke out of his brokenness. But observe how the words are transformed as Jesus echoes the words back to the leper! The leper's words came in a mixture of uncertainty and hope. He was confident about Jesus' ability to heal him ("You can make me clean"), but he was not sure whether Jesus should care for him and use His power for him ("If you will..."). After all, who is he that Jesus should pay attention to him?

Can you not identify with this leper? What is so difficult about praying? It's not that we don't believe in God's power to do what we ask for, is it? No, it is rather our uncertainty as to whether God wills it or not. For we know that, if God should will it so, it will be done. Nothing in heaven and earth can thwart His sovereign, omnipotent will in any way! So, how should we pray, especially concerning the things to which the Bible does not give explicit directives—such as, whether to marry or not to marry, whom to marry, where to go to school or for work, etc. Well, we have a wonderful model for our prayer in this leper's petition, don't we? We can pray, "If You will, Lord, You can...." We should ask with all sincerity. We should do it passionately. We should do it with a sense of urgency. And we should wait with expectation and hope that our gracious Lord will do what is best for us.

Observe how Jesus responds to the leper's pitiful plea. Jesus returns the leper's uncertainty with an unquestionable assurance—"I will!" Jesus responds to the leper's hope for healing with an immediate healing—"Be clean!" How striking! Contrast this response to that of Israel's king in 2 Kings 5. There, Naaman, an Aramean leper and general, comes to the king of Israel with a letter from his own king, requesting his cure. How does the king of Israel respond? We read in 2 Kings 5:7, "And when the king of Israel read the letter, he tore his clothes and said, 'Am I God, to kill and to make alive, that this man sends word to me to cure a man of his leprosy? Only consider, and see how he is seeking a quarrel with me.'" His words make it obvious how curing leprosy was way up there on the list of divine prerogatives, right up there with the power to resurrect the dead! But Jesus is not daunted by this leper's request at all. Jesus simply says, "I will; be clean." He does not pray! He does not chant some magic incantations. He simply says, "I will; be clean!"

Quite often we hear, "I will!" But we have been disappointed too many times (and we have disappointed others, too). So when we hear those words, we automatically translate them into "maybe" (at best!) and that is often what we get. Our will often lacks the resolve to uphold our promise, to control our appetite and laziness, let alone control our circumstances and events (contrary to the wishful thinking of the New Age optimism about human potential). But there is a world of difference when Jesus says, "I will." Here we are talking about the eternal, unchangeable, irrevocable will of the Son of God, accompanied by His divine omnipotence and, in this case, His infinite mercy! So, when the Son of God wills, it cannot not be done. How precious those words are! What a blessing to hear Jesus say, "I will!" Moved with pity, Jesus speaks these words to this pathetic, helpless leper!

The God Who Is Moved

Isn't it amazing that Jesus can be moved like that? He is the omniscient God. If so, nothing can surprise Him, right? If nothing can surprise Him, how can He be so deeply moved by anything? He knows us. He knows our condition perfectly. Nothing we say or do can further His knowledge of our condition. But that is the amazing thing about our God and how He deals with us! Maybe a human analogy will help. We have all seen, I am sure, how grandparents respond to the things that their grandchildren do. Usually, things that a child does cannot be too extraordinary. But have you seen how grandparents respond? They exclaim, "He is amazing! He is a genius!" In a very imperfect way, that shows how the omnipotent God can be moved with pity. It is not based on any merit or value of our petition, however ardent it may be; it is only on account of His deep, sympathetic love, that He is moved to pity. What comfort it gives us to see the leper's most desperate plea reciprocated by Jesus most heartfelt pity. Isn't it wonderful that Jesus hears our petitions with such a deep, powerful pity? He is no idol which cannot feel or hear or say anything. In Jesus Christ we have the most sympathetic High Priest. All we have to do is present our petitions to him with all sincerity and wait with confidence.

But another possible rendering of verse 41 is that Jesus was "moved with *indignation*...." Why would Jesus be indignant? Jesus looks at the miserable condition of the leper and gets indignant at the horrible effects of the Fall. So this is actually just another aspect of Jesus being moved with pity for the leper.

The God Who Touches The Untouchable

How remarkable is this exchange between the leper and Jesus-- the exchange of words and the exchange of deep emotions! But this exchange becomes even more poignant when we consider what Jesus does, not just what He says and feels. Between this exchange of words, what does Jesus do? We read in v. 41, "Moved with pity, he stretched out his hand and *touched* him...." So deeply moved, Jesus stretches out His hand and touches him. Why does Jesus do this? Can Jesus not heal him without touching him? Of course He can! But do you see Jesus' tender love for the leper? He knows how utterly isolated the leper has been. He knows how his life has been so utterly devoid of human touch ever since the disease struck him. So Jesus touches him. How surprised the leper must have been! A human touch—it is the last thing the leper expects, at least until he is made clean. Even his family members feared touching him!

But we cannot see this act of Jesus merely as an unexpected gesture of kindness. Many of you already know the deep religious meaning of His act. Think about it. The leper dared not touch Jesus, as desperate as he was. Why? Because he knew of the Law of Moses: "The leprous person who has the disease shall wear torn clothes and let the hair of his head hang loose, and he shall cover his upper lip and cry out, 'Unclean, unclean.' He shall remain unclean as long as he has the disease. He is unclean. He shall live alone. His dwelling shall be outside the camp" (Leviticus 13:45-46). The regulations of the rabbis were even stricter because they wanted to ensure the observance of the law: "If an unclean man [afflicted with leprosy] stood under a tree and a clean man passed by, the latter becomes unclean. If a clean man stood under a tree and an unclean one passed by, the former remains clean. If the latter stood still, the former becomes unclean."[8] The leper knew that he was unclean. He also knew that whatever, and whomever, he touched would become unclean. That is why he dared not touch Jesus. That is why he simply asked Jesus to make him clean.

The Clean Prevails Over The Unclean

Notice also what the leper actually says. The leper asks to be clean rather than be healed. Why? For the leper, it was not simply about getting well, you see. The leper had a two-fold problem. He was sick with disease; but he was also ceremonially unclean according to the Mosaic Law. Just getting well physically would not solve all of his problems. Technically speaking, even as a healthy Jew, he could still be made unclean by many things. And to be ceremonially unclean was to be ostracized—not only from the society of men but more importantly from the worship of God at the temple. If he was a proper Jew, he would not consider himself whole again until he could worship God at His temple. So he asked to be made clean, not just to be healed. And Jesus touches him, a leper, an unclean man! Can you imagine the shock on the part of the man—not being touched like that by another person in who knows how many years? And what about Jesus? Doesn't He know the religious consequence of His action?

We cannot ignore the Mosaic Law when we read this passage. The leper desired to be clean, not just healed, because of the Mosaic Law. And Jesus' instruction to the leper to go and show himself to the priest was according to the prescription of the Mosaic Law. The Mosaic Law

---

8 M. Nega'im XIII. 7, as quoted by William L. Lane, *The Gospel According to Mark*. NICNT 2 (Grand Rapids: Eerdmans, 1974), p. 85.

dominates the background to this incident and it clearly delineated the principle—when the clean and the unclean come into contact, it was the unclean, which prevailed. The clean became unclean, not the other way around. So, according to the Mosaic Law, Jesus would have become unclean when He touched the leper.

But something truly extraordinary is taking place here! Mark does not mention anything about Jesus becoming unclean. He does not say anything about Jesus spending a day in isolation to be clean again. What is going on? Is Jesus ignoring the Mosaic Law? No. He tells the leper to show himself to the priest according to the Mosaic Law! But something greater than the Mosaic Law is here! Jesus is not violating the Law. You see, there was an exception to the Law. It was not clearly stated in the Law but certain Old Testament incidents showed that there was an exception. The prophet Elijah revived the son of a widow at Zarephath by stretching himself on his dead body three times. Elisha did something similar to revive the son of a Shunammite widow. In both cases, we hear neither of them becoming unclean. Though the silence does not necessarily prove it so, we can see how this can be the case. For throughout the Bible, there is one consistent exception to the rule, in which the clean prevails over the unclean: when God, or His agent by His power, touches the unclean, or the common, it becomes clean and holy. So the places of His appearance were considered sacred, including Mount Sinai. So when Jesus, the Son of God, touches the leper, Jesus is not made unclean. Instead the leper is made clean. Jesus' holiness overshadows the leper's uncleanness! The contagious power of Jesus' holiness prevails over the contagious power of the leper's disease! The very fact that the leper's disease is healed demonstrates that Jesus could not have been defiled by such contact!

Jesus' Instruction

But there is more to this encounter. For Mark's account does not end there. After making him clean, Jesus "sternly charged him and sent him away at once, and said to him, 'See that you say nothing to anyone, but go, show yourself to the priest and offer for your cleansing what Moses commanded, for a proof to them" (verses 43-44). His instruction consisted of two things—not to say anything to anyone about this miraculous healing (particularly, who did it); and, instead, to show himself to the priest and offer sacrifices for his cleansing. We know the reason for the second command. He had to be declared clean by the priest to be reinstated back into the covenant community. But why the first?

This has been Jesus' consistent practice since He began His ministry. Earlier in Mark 1, He told the unclean spirit to be silent when it addressed Jesus as the Holy One of God. Now He tells the healed leper not to tell anyone. Why this secrecy? One reason seems to be for the right timing. Jesus knew that His growing popularity would trigger the jealousy of the religious leaders and lead to their conspiracy to kill Him. His death was inevitable but it had to happen at the divinely appointed time. For there were still things to be done before the designated time of His inevitable death, one of them being the training of His disciples. So, on many occasions, Jesus forbade people (and demons) from speaking out on His true identity. And Jesus orchestrated everything perfectly—through the obedience as well as the disobedience of people and demons—to perfectly time His death as the true Passover Lamb. Jesus does everything well. He never fails.

The Final Exchange—The Great Exchange

But I would like us to see the final exchange, which takes place at the end of the story. Despite Jesus' instruction, the leper "went out and began to talk freely about it, and to spread the news, so that Jesus could no longer openly enter a town, but was out in desolate places, and people were coming to him from every quarter" (verse 45). We see the transformation of the leper. He came to Jesus a leper. He leaves as a clean man. He was a social outcast, having to move around in desolate places out of people's sight and way. Now he freely moves among people, talking and sharing. He was an object of scorn and disgust. Now, as he shares about what Jesus has done for him, he speaks to people's admiration and amazement.

But do you see what happens to Jesus as a result of this encounter? He can no longer openly enter a town. He has to move around in desolate places. Do you see? That was exactly what the leper's life was like!

Where the leper used to be, Jesus is now. And where Jesus used to be, the leper is now. They traded places. This encounter is not just about Jesus exercising His omnipotent power to heal the leper, from which Jesus comes out unscathed. No! This encounter foreshadowed what would take place on the cross. Jesus would take our place before the judgment seat of God and endure the punishment of our sin so that we could stand in His place of honor and glory before His heavenly Father.

What is your life's story? Has your life intersected with Christ? If so, do you appreciate how radically your life has been changed? Can anything be of greater significance than meeting Christ and entering into relationship with Him? You are no longer a slave of your past! If you are in Christ, you are a new creation (2 Cor. 5:17)! His righteousness is your righteousness. His victory is your victory. His life is your life!

I grew up in a Buddhist-atheistic home. And God brought me to the States and to Himself. Now I am a minister of the gospel! What an amazing change! All that I am and do now are reverberations of my encounter with Christ. And my encounter with Christ will affect my children, and hopefully, their children and many more generations to come! And I pray that God would be pleased to use my ministry to affect many. Oh, what praise and thanksgiving our wonderful Savior deserves from us! And we don't have to hold back from declaring the excellencies of Him who has called us out of darkness into His marvelous light (1 Peter 2:9), out of our sickness into His health (W.T. Sleeper, "Out of My Bondage, Sorrow, and Night")! Now we don't have to keep it a secret! For Jesus died at the time appointed by God and He rose again. There is no longer any need for secrecy until the time of His death. Now we are called to boast of Him as much as we want! And if we do not, the stones will cry out! Let us, then, make this the chief aim of our life—to boast of Christ and His wonderful salvation for sinners! We only have this lifetime to suffer for Him as He so willingly suffered for us. For one day, we will boast of Christ through all eternity without any hindrance and persecution!

Jesus' Cursing Of A Fig Tree

[12] On the following day, when they came from Bethany, he was hungry.
[13] And seeing in the distance a fig tree in leaf, he went to see if he could
find anything on it. When he came to it, he found nothing but leaves, for it
was not the season for figs. [14] And he said to it, "May no one ever eat fruit
from you again." And his disciples heard it.
[15] And they came to Jerusalem. And he entered the temple and began
to drive out those who sold and those who bought in the temple, and he
overturned the tables of the money-changers and the seats of those who sold
pigeons. [16] And he would not allow anyone to carry anything through the
temple. [17] And he was teaching them and saying to them, "Is it not written,
'My house shall be called a house of prayer for all the nations'? But you
have made it a den of robbers." [18] And the chief priests and the scribes
heard it and were seeking a way to destroy him, for they feared him, because
all the crowd was astonished at his teaching. [19] And when evening came
they went out of the city.
[20] As they passed by in the morning, they saw the fig tree withered away
to its roots. [21] And Peter remembered and said to him, "Rabbi, look!
The fig tree that you cursed has withered." [22] And Jesus answered them,
"Have faith in God. [23] Truly, I say to you, whoever says to this mountain,
'Be taken up and thrown into the sea,' and does not doubt in his heart,
but believes that what he says will come to pass, it will be done for him.
[24] Therefore I tell you, whatever you ask in prayer, believe that you have
received it, and it will be yours. [25] And whenever you stand praying,
forgive, if you have anything against anyone, so that your Father also who is
in heaven may forgive you your trespasses."
Mark 11:12-25

If you thought that Jesus was just a Mr. Nice Guy, a consummate guru of political-correctness, think again! This passage should shatter that perception to pieces. See what Jesus did in our passage.

Jesus cursed a fig tree (verse 14) and it withered away to its roots by the next day (verse 20). Not only that, Jesus entered the temple and wreaked havoc there. He overturned the tables and drove out the merchants from it. Are these the actions of a Mr. Nice Guy? No! Then was He Mr. Crazy, Mr. Temperamental? That is not true, either. We must be careful not to apply our modern, American sensibilities to what Jesus does in our passage. This passage is eminently relevant and applicable to our situation and life, I assure you. But in order to see that, we must consider this incident in light of its own context. And the context of what Jesus does here is, as in other passages, the Old Testament.

A God To Reckon With

Before we deal with the difficulties related to this incident, let us affirm certain things first. This incident shows that Jesus actually has the authority to curse and the power to bring it about. The Bible does not allow us to view Him as a spineless Santa Clause, whose uniform response to whatever we do is always "Ho! Ho! Ho!"—"Ho! Ho! Ho!" when we lean on Him in times of need and "Ho! Ho! Ho!" when we trample on Him with unbelief and rebellion. Jesus showed much compassion to the weak and needy who sought His help and mercy. But Jesus did not countenance evil and wickedness, especially of an arrogant, impenitent kind. Can a person be "good" if he does not oppose and despise evil?

Why do we marvel at His grace as "amazing" grace? If grace is all God's got, what is so amazing about that? We sing of His amazing grace because it comes from the One, who is holy, holy, holy, three times holy. Righteousness and truth are the foundation of His throne; therefore, sin cannot dwell in Him; He cannot let any sin go unpunished. God has prepared a day of reckoning when all things will be exposed, when all sins and sinners will receive their due punishment. This is why the grace God shows us is so amazing! It comes from the One who has all the right to condemn sin and punish sinners. In fact, He is obligated to execute justice as the good and righteous Judge of all. The more we understand God's holiness and righteousness, the greater will be our appreciation for His grace and mercy.

But where is justice in Jesus' cursing the fig tree? A tree doesn't have any soul, any moral capacity to do right or wrong. And why did He curse the tree? Because He couldn't find any fruit! Was He just lashing out His anger at this innocent, helpless tree?

The Bible does not allow us to view [Christ] as a spineless Santa Clause, whose uniform response to whatever we do is always "Ho! Ho! Ho!"—"Ho! Ho! Ho!" when we lean on Him in times of need and "Ho! Ho! Ho!" when we trample on Him with unbelief and rebellion. Jesus showed much compassion to the weak and needy who sought His help and mercy. But Jesus did not countenance evil and wickedness, especially of an arrogant, impenitent kind.

Cursing The Fig Tree: A Symbolic Act

That Jesus condemned a tree, which cannot sin, shows that it was a symbolic act. Here, Jesus was enacting a famous biblical song in Isaiah 5. There God lamented the fact that the choice vine He had planted in His fertile hill was producing only wild grapes. The choice vine, of course, was Israel, transplanted by God from Egypt to the promised land. Jesus in this symbolic action showed that the situation had not changed at all. In fact, the situation had gotten even worse. He showed this by cursing the tree on the spot. By the next day, the tree withered to the roots. The time of God's patience was over. The Son of God came to demand fruit from Israel. But Israel would persecute and execute the Son of God. Here, Jesus acted as the final Prophet, delivering God's judgment against Israel for its unfaithfulness and fruitlessness.

But what about that nagging clause in verse 13—"for it was not the season for figs"? Isn't this a most unreasonable thing to do—to demand fruit from a tree when it is not the season? And it was God who established the laws of nature—for the trees to bear fruit in their seasons.

But that is exactly the point. What Jesus is doing here does not fit the laws of nature. His action is meant to show that He brings in the power and principle of another world! His action points to a different world, a better world, where trees bear fruit all the time, in season and out of season. The force of life in that world is so vigorous and so prolific that there is no barrenness of winter. There is no need for spring and summer for growth and maturation. In that land of vigorous life and plenty, all kinds of fruits are always in season. Jesus' words burst forth out of that world. They are an indictment against this world. They expose the imperfections and limitations of this world by the light of the glory of the other world. The first creation, as good and beautiful as it was, was not meant to be our eternal abode. It was meant to be replaced by a new, better creation. That is why the first creation was liable to Satan's attack. That is why Adam and Eve were made naked, yet to be clothed with the robe of impeccable, everlasting righteousness.

So keep in mind the *symbolic* nature of Jesus' act, that the fig tree was a *symbol* of Israel. People do not have designated seasons to bear fruit for God. For the fruit God demands from His people is that of faith and obedience. Whether we are engaged in our Lord's Day worship or in our daily work, we are always to render the fruit of faith and obedience to God. Therefore, God has the right to demand fruit from His people in season and out of season.

This is true also because God provides for us always, in season and out of season. He gives us the sun as well as the rain, and we need both. He who made the day for our work and activity also made the night for our sleep and rest, and we need both. The view from the mountain peaks of success is great. But also good for the soul are the occasional valleys of humiliation.

Cleansing The Temple: Another Symbolic Act

As a chosen nation, delivered from the Egyptian bondage and endowed with the oracles of God, Israel owed God fruitfulness, in season and out of season. But Israel failed, miserably, fully incurring God's curse. This is reinforced by what Jesus did next (verses 15-19). He went into the temple to cast out the merchants and money-changers. This was how bad things had gotten. The temple, the most sacred place in Israel, was overrun with merchants and corrupt priests.

He chased them out, delivering the divine indictment: "Is it not written, 'My house shall be called a house of prayer for all the nations'? But you have made it a den of robbers" (verse 17). This, too, was in the prophetic tradition. God told Jeremiah to stand at the gate of the temple and proclaim God's word of warning against the people of Judah, who were coming to the temple, supposedly to worship God (Jeremiah 7:2ff). Can you see Jeremiah blocking the gate of the temple and pushing people back like a mad man? And it was in this passage that we find the words that Jesus quoted: "Will you steal, murder, commit adultery, swear falsely, make offerings to Baal, and go after other gods that you have not known, and then come and stand before Me in this house, which is called by My name, and say, 'We are delivered!'—only to go on doing all these abominations? Has this house, which is called by My name, become a den of robbers in your eyes" (Jeremiah 7:9-11)?

And now someone far greater than Jeremiah the prophet was here. Jeremiah was but one of God's servants, the prophets. But Jesus was the Son of God, the Messiah. Jesus had all the right, therefore, to be angry with a righteous anger and to cleanse His Father's house.

Of course, the temple Jesus cleansed (which was being built by Herod) was only a type, a shadow. Even Solomon, who built the original temple a millennium earlier, wondered, "But will God indeed dwell on the earth? Behold, heaven and the highest heaven cannot contain you; how much less this house that I have built" (1 Kings 8:27)? If Solomon's temple was but a shadow of the true, heavenly temple, how much less was this temple being built by Herod? Even so, insofar as it was a picture of the heavenly temple, violating its sanctity was violating the sanctity of the true temple.

Still, a picture of a thing is not the thing itself. The earthly temple was just a picture of the true temple. It was temporary and destructible (as it was eventually destroyed in 70 A.D.). And Jesus' cleansing of the temple was a symbolic act. It did not cleanse the temple permanently. I'm sure, after a time, the merchants came back and it was business as usual again. So, then, what would it take for Jesus to cleanse the temple completely and permanently? The answer is hinted at in the following section.

From Fruitlessness To The Fruitfulness Of All Peoples

As we move to the next section (verses 20-25), we are back at the fig tree that was cursed by Jesus. This is one of the typical "Markan sandwiches." James R. Edwards describes them in this way: "Mark begins story A, introduces story B, then returns to and completes story A."[9] This arrangement shows that these two events are very closely related to each other. So the day after cleansing the temple, we find Jesus and the disciples passing by the fig tree again. The disciples notice that the tree is withered completely to its roots. They marvel and alert Jesus to what has happened.

But Jesus' response surprises us. He does not speak of the cursed tree at all! Instead, Jesus goes on to talk about faith and what amazing things are possible when we pray in faith. Wait a minute! Have we misread Jesus' cursing of the fig tree? It had nothing to do with Israel's judgment? Was it simply about the power of prayer? Not necessarily. Jesus was no longer explicitly addressing the unfruitfulness of Israel and its religious leaders. However, He was still dealing with essentially the same issue, focusing on the other side. Instead of dealing with Israel's unfruitfulness, Jesus was now speaking of what fruitfulness looked like—demonstrated through faith in God (verse 22), especially as it expresses itself in faith-filled prayer (verses 23-24).

This was already in Jesus' mind when He "cleansed" the temple. As He cleansed the temple, He referred to it as "a house of prayer for all the nations" (verse 17). This is interesting because the temple was preeminently a place of sacrifice. Only in Isaiah 56:7 is the temple called a house of prayer. But Isaiah 56 is an important and fascinating passage. There God spoke of a time when Gentiles and even eunuchs would be included in the covenant community, when God would bring Gentiles and eunuchs to His holy mountain, to His holy temple, which would be called a house of prayer for all peoples. And now, Jesus was highlighting this aspect of the temple—God's house of prayer for all peoples! While the nation of Israel was being condemned for its unfruitfulness, a hope for all peoples was being offered by Jesus!

---

9 James R. Edwards, *Markan Sandwiches*, Novum Testamentum XXXI, 3 (1989), p. 193.

And isn't it fascinating that, in Isaiah 56, the eunuchs were commanded not to say, "Behold, I am a dry tree" (verse 3)? Though they were like a dry tree, they would be made fruitful in the kingdom of God. They would be included in a new Israel, which would be made up of both Gentiles and Jews. This new Israel would become fruitful, not by their own strength, but by the strength of God. Thus Jesus' emphasis on faith. Thus Jesus' emphasis on prayer. Should we be surprised? We read in Psalm 127: 1, "Unless the LORD builds the house, those who build it labor in vain." If our physical accomplishments are impossible without God, how much more impossible are our spiritual tasks, the works that have eternal significance?

From Dry Withered Tree To Fruit-Bearing Tree Of Life

But how would God bring this about? How would God make dry, withered trees to be fruitful again? How would He restore the sanctity of His temple as a house of prayer for all peoples? How would He bring Jews and Gentiles together into this house of prayer?

The solution certainly could not come through the merchants and money-changers who defiled the temple and the priests who allowed it and benefited from it! Nor could it come through anyone who needed to be cleansed by the temple sacrifice, which included the high priests. The solution could not, and cannot, come from this world of change and decay, of futility and death! Then how? You know the solution God provided for the fallen world, don't you?

The answer is found in the One whose presence brings the life and power of the other world—the kingdom of God, a world of perpetual and bountiful fruitfulness! The answer is found in the One whose zeal for the house of the Lord drove Him to drive out the merchants and money-changers from the temple!

But we know that the temple could not be cleansed simply by driving the merchants and money-changers out of it. It must be cleansed of our sin, which was why the temple sacrifices had to be instituted in the first place! Chasing out the merchants and money-changers of the temple does not cleanse our sin. As David realized a long time ago, even offering thousands and tens of thousands bulls and goats cannot take away our sin (Psalm 51:16). What Jesus did at the temple was only a preview of what He would do out of His zeal for His Father's house. This zeal compelled Him to abandon the glories of His heavenly throne and come into this world. And this zeal would compel Him to go all the way down into the depths of hell itself in order that He might fully pay the penalty of our sin! To that end, only a few days later, Jesus would go to the cross to bear the wrath of God in our place.

And do you see the irony? Jesus would die on the cross, on a dry, withered tree. As He hung upon the dry, withered tree, He took upon Himself our fruitlessness, our lifelessness, becoming the dry tree that we all were. And when He died, He buried it in the ground, in death. But Jesus rose again from the dead! When He rose again from the dead, He rose again as the Tree of Life, who bears twelve different kinds of fruit all throughout the year, in season and out of season (Revelation 22:2). If we can have life, it is only because, by grace through faith, we are united with Him who is the Resurrection and the Life! And if we can bear any fruit, it is only because we are grafted into Him who is the true Vine, the everlasting Tree of Life!

Because we are grafted into the Tree of Life, we can bear fruit in season and out of season. Not just when we bask in the warmth of His favor but also when we stay awake in the cold night of His fatherly discipline. Not just when we stand on top of the world, on the mountain peaks of success, but also when we walk through the valley of humiliation and affliction. Not just with our confident profession of faith in the Lord but also with our heartfelt confession of sin and decisive repentance from it.

Prayer, Indispensible To Fruitfulness

That is why prayer is so indispensable to a fruitful Christian life and ministry. For prayer is the clearest expression of our humble and complete dependence on Christ, the true fruit-bearing Tree. And in Jesus Christ, we will all be fruit trees, which always bear fruit for God—succulent, delicious fruit to God's great delight. And this fruit we can begin to bear if we are in Christ, as we pray by faith in the One who raised Jesus from the dead! We can be bold and daring in our prayers because we are grafted into the One who is not only able to do all things but also possesses all things in heaven and earth!

Because we are grafted into the Tree of Life, we can bear fruit in season and out of season. Not just when we bask in the warmth of His favor but also when we stay awake in the cold night of His fatherly discipline. Not just when we stand on top of the world, on the mountain peaks of success, but also when we walk through the valley of humiliation and affliction. Not just with our confident profession of faith in the Lord but also with our heartfelt confession of sin and decisive repentance from it.

As one classic hymn that we sing puts it:

Thou art coming to a King,
Large petitions with thee bring;
For His grace and power are such,
None can ever ask too much;
None can ever ask too much.[10]

---

10 John Newton, "Come, My Soul, Thy Suit Prepare," *Trinity Hymnal* (Phila-delphia: Great Commission Publications 1994), 628.

.

"When You Go Out To War"

[20:1] "When you go out to war against your enemies, and see horses and chariots and an army larger than your own, you shall not be afraid of them, for the LORD your God is with you, who brought you up out of the land of Egypt. [2] And when you draw near to the battle, the priest shall come forward and speak to the people [3] and shall say to them, 'Hear, O Israel, today you are drawing near for battle against your enemies: let not your heart faint. Do not fear or panic or be in dread of them, [4] for the LORD your God is he who goes with you to fight for you against your enemies, to give you the victory.' [5] Then the officers shall speak to the people, saying, 'Is there any man who has built a new house and has not dedicated it? Let him go back to his house, lest he die in the battle and another man dedicate it. [6] And is there any man who has planted a vineyard and has not enjoyed its fruit? Let him go back to his house, lest he die in the battle and another man enjoy its fruit. [7] And is there any man who has betrothed a wife and has not taken her? Let him go back to his house, lest he die in the battle and another man take her.' [8] And the officers shall speak further to the people, and say, 'Is there any man who is fearful and fainthearted? Let him go back to his house, lest he make the heart of his fellows melt like his own.' [9] And when the officers have finished speaking to the people, then commanders shall be appointed at the head of the people.
[10] "When you draw near to a city to fight against it, offer terms of peace to it. [11] And if it responds to you peaceably and it opens to you, then all the people who are found in it shall do forced labor for you and shall serve you. [12] But if it makes no peace with you, but makes war against you, then you shall besiege it. [13] And when the LORD your God gives it into your hand, you shall put all its males to the sword, [14] but the women and the little ones, the livestock, and everything else in the city, all its spoil, you shall take as plunder for yourselves. And you shall enjoy the spoil of your enemies, which the LORD your God has given you. [15] Thus you shall do to all the cities that are very far from you, which are not cities of the nations here. [16] But in the cities of these peoples that the LORD your God is giving you for an inheritance, you shall save alive nothing that breathes, [17] but you

shall devote them to complete destruction, the Hittites and the Amorites, the
Canaanites and the Perizzites, the Hivites and the Jebusites, as the LORD
your God has commanded, [18] that they may not teach you to do according
to all their abominable practices that they have done for their gods, and so
you sin against the LORD your God.
[19] "When you besiege a city for a long time, making war against it in order
to take it, you shall not destroy its trees by wielding an axe against them. You
may eat from them, but you shall not cut them down. Are the trees in the field
human, that they should be besieged by you? [20] Only the trees that you
know are not trees for food you may destroy and cut down, that you may build
siegeworks against the city that makes war with you, until it falls."
Deuteronomy 20:1-20

One of the major complaints we get about Christianity is, "Why does Christianity have to be so bloody bloody? Why can't you just have a loving, gracious forgiveness and be done with sin? Why do you have to insist on the bloody cross for the forgiveness of sin? And why does your God have to be so cruel? How can He command nations to be wiped out, including women and children?"

Of course, we want peace. So people say, "Make love, not war!" "War is not the answer!" "Give peace a chance!" We realize how blood calls for blood and more blood. Just take a look at what is going on in the Middle East—what havoc centuries-old politics of hatred and vengeance have wrought in that region. War is ugly and repulsive. There is nothing pleasant about it—all the senseless casualties of human lives—the precious lives of someone's beloved husband or son or brother—all the senseless destruction of people's homes and businesses and farms and arts and histories and memories, etc.

When Peace Is Not An Option

But are all wars bad? Could there be such a thing as a just war? In the realm of international politics, a just war may be a hard thing to justify, of course. However, we also know that not all peace is good. There may be so-called peace in North Korea and Myanmar and some other countries under a tyrannical regime. But can we call that true peace? How good and desirable is peace when evil exists? Can a society or an individual be called good when evil is tolerated and allowed to run rampant?

If God is indeed good, He cannot be the quintessence of political correctness, a cosmic Santa Clause figure, who laughs "Ho! Ho! Ho!" to anything and everything. If God is good, He must hate evil with the most intense, absolute, and infinite hatred. And in all of us, there is a yearning for all evil to be wiped away and uprooted from this world. What we see in today's passage is a picture of that side of God's goodness which is not so pleasant but is absolutely necessary.

Two Kinds Of War

As you can see, this passage speaks of two different kinds of war Israel would be engaging against other nations: 1) wars against the nations outside the promised land; 2) wars against the nations within the promised land.

If God is indeed good, He cannot be the quintessence of political correctness, a cosmic Santa Clause figure, who laughs "Ho! Ho! Ho!" to anything and everything. If God is good, He must hate evil with the most intense, absolute, and infinite hatred. And in all of us, there is a yearning for all evil to be wiped away and uprooted in this world.

It is interesting to note that the Lord prescribed different tactics and goals for each of the two. With regard to the nations outside the promised land—"all the cities that are very far from you" (verse 15)—Israel was to offer terms of peace before attacking them (verse 10). If the enemy nations surrendered in peace, they were not executed. They were simply subjugated to forced labor. But if they refused to surrender, only then would Israel attack them. And even after the battle was won, they were not "devoted to complete destruction." The males were put to death but the women and children and everything else were spared.

It was a completely different story for the seven nations within the boundaries of the promised land. No terms of peace were to be offered.

No negotiation or truce was allowed. Those nations were to be "devoted to complete destruction." This meant that every living thing had to be slaughtered—not just the male soldiers but also the women and the children and the livestock and everything else that had breath. This is what is known as *herem* warfare.

Why The Differences?

It is quite clear that it had to do mainly with the promised land. But it was not simply that God arbitrarily decided to give the land to the Israelites and, since the Canaanite nations happened to be there, they had to be wiped out. It is more complicated than that.

We must keep in mind that the promised land was not just a land chosen for Israel's dwelling. It was to function also as a holy land, set aside from the rest of the world. It was a place where God would make His dwelling in the midst of His people. A temple would be built there at God's designated place. His people would worship Him there.

As a holy land, the promised land had to be kept pure from defilement in a special way. So, should the land be defiled in any way, it had to be cleansed by blood: "For the life of the flesh is in the blood, and I have given it for you on the altar to make atonement for your souls, for it is the blood that makes atonement by the life" (Leviticus 17:11).

This is one reason that *herem* warfare was used in the conquest of the promised land. It was not a "normal" war, with nations vying for political dominance or territorial expansion, etc. In a sense, it was more than just a religious war, with nations going at each other on account of the differences of their religions. It was ultimately a cultic war. By "cultic," I do not mean things associated with cults and occults. "Cultic" here refers to that which is related to worship, particularly to its rituals. Completely devoting something to destruction by *herem* warfare was like offering a sacrifice to the Lord. The land that had been defiled by the sins of its inhabitants had to be cleansed by the shedding of their blood.

In the case of the Canaanite nations, there was a sense of finality to it. When God promised to give the land of Canaan to Abraham, He told him that he and his descendants would have to wait. Before his descendants could take possession of the land, they would be taken away from the promised land and enslaved to another nation for four generations—that is, 400 years. Why such a long wait? "[F]or the iniquity of the Amorites [a general title referring to the Canaanites] is not yet complete" (Genesis 15:16). These words seem to imply that God does not always deal with individuals and nations with immediate retribution for every sin. He has appointed to each his/its own measure of wickedness. When an individual or a society fills up that measure, then comes the divine judgment (cf. 1 Thessalonians 2:16). That was what happened to the generation of Noah, to Sodom and Gomorrah, and to the Canaanites.

What is important to keep in mind here is that these were previews and pictures of the Final Judgment. When the measure of wickedness which God has assigned to the whole world is filled up, then will come God's Final Judgment. When that Day shall come, there will be a complete, full eradication of evil and sin from the world. Israel's conquest of Canaan was to coincide with the time of God's judgment on its nations, which was a picture of the Final Judgment. Israel was God's instrument of judgment on them.

God's Assurance, God's Soldiers

And since it was *God's* judgment upon the Canaanite nations, He would not leave it up merely to Israel to carry it out. In our passage we find God's assurance to be with them to bring them victory: "When you go out to war against your enemies, and see horses and chariots and an army larger than your own, you shall not be afraid of them, for *the LORD your God is with you*, who brought you up out of the land of Egypt…. [T]he LORD your God is he who goes with you *to fight for you against your enemies, to give you the victory*" (verses 1, 4). What greater assurance could the Israelites have, what better assurance did they need, than this—that the almighty God would go before them and fight for them! So David, just a young shepherd boy, was able to face Goliath the giant without fear and knock him out with a slingshot: "You come to me with a sword and with a spear and with a javelin, but I come to you in the name of the LORD of hosts, the God of the armies of Israel, whom you have defied" (1 Samuel 17:45)! If God be with us, surely one can chase a thousand, and two can put ten thousand to flight (Deuteronomy 32:30; cf. Leviticus 26:8)!

Since God was Israel's strength and victory, their victory did not depend on the number of their soldiers. So here we see God's gracious provision for some men to be excused from war in order that they might enjoy the blessings of the promised land—those who built new houses, those who planted new vineyards, and those who were engaged to be married (verses 5-7).

But those who would fight in the army of God must be men of faith. Not that God cannot use even faithless men to accomplish His purpose. He used Nebuchadnezzar to punish His rebellious people. He even used donkeys and roosters! But the glory He seeks in dealing with His people is not that of a perfect chess player. The glory He seeks is the glory that comes when His people love Him and obey Him against all odds because they trust Him and treasure Him. So the officers of Israel were to charge the men, "Is there any man who is fearful and fainthearted? Let him go back to his house, lest he make the heart of his fellows melt like his own" (verse 8).

To fight in the army of God, one did not need to be strong or skilled—the battle is the Lord's and the Lord is the One who gives victory. But he could not be a coward—the kind of coward who could not muster up courage even at God's assurance because of unbelief. (And it is possible that this was another reason that other men were excused from the battle. Having things that were yet to be enjoyed in the promised land—a new house, a new vineyard, or a new wife—might make them more fearful of dying in the battle.) This didn't mean that the fearful ones were cut off from the covenant community. They might have even been allowed to share in the spoils (cf. Numbers 31:12). But to be excluded from the battle on account of one's fear was obviously a shameful thing. And it could even be a dangerous thing, a sign of complete unbelief. (We all have those areas in our life, in which we find it difficult to completely trust the Lord. But if we do not cultivate faith even in these areas, it can foster the kind of unbelief which can lead to the denial of faith altogether, and thus prove that we were never part of the elect, 1 John 2:19.)

So What?

So what does all this talk of wars and battles have to do with us Christians?

Of course, even in our Christian walk, there are wars to be fought. Unlike the wars of Israel, however, the Christian warfare does not take on the military dimension. Christians can participate in military wars, of course, as part of their civic duty to the nations of their citizenship, insofar as they are for a just cause—to defend their respective nations against enemy invasion, for example. But "the weapons of our warfare are not of the flesh but have divine power to destroy strongholds" (2 Corinthians 10:4). "For we do not wrestle against flesh and blood, but against the rulers, against the authorities, against the cosmic powers over this present darkness, against the spiritual forces of evil in the heavenly places" (Ephesians 6:12).

As you can see, the differences (between the wars of Israel and the Church) are due to the different ways in which the kingdom of God manifests itself. Israel was a theocracy. Although God was its ultimate king, it had the forms and characters of a national, geopolitical entity. The Church, on the other hand, is not a geopolitical, civic entity. It is not confined to one nation or an ethnic group. It transcends ethnic, national boundaries and political ideologies. And there is no holy land. There is only God's holy people.

Although there are these differences, our spiritual wars correspond to the wars of Israel in many ways. Just like the wars of Israel, our battles are divided into two categories: 1) wars within ourselves and within our covenant community; 2) wars outside of ourselves and our covenant community.

Wars Within

What do I mean by wars within ourselves and within our covenant community? These wars are against the flesh, against the deeds of the body (Romans 8:13), against the desires of the flesh (Galatians 5:15), against the works of the flesh—"sexual immorality, impurity, sensuality, idolatry, sorcery, enmity, strife, jealousy, fits of anger, rivalries, dissensions, divisions, envy, drunkenness, orgies, and things like these" (Galatians 5:19-21). What are we to do with these things? We are to show no mercy to them. We are to put them to death. We are to use the *herem* warfare against these things.

How about in our covenant community? As long as we live in this world, the visible church will never be pure. By God's own design, wheat and weed will grow together even in the church (Matthew 13:29-30). Not knowing the heart of man, we will not know for sure who the elect are and who are not. However, we are warned, "A little leaven leavens the whole lump" (1 Corinthians 5:6; Galatians 5:9). Though we do not know what is in the heart of man, we can, and must, deal with what surfaces in the words and actions of the members. Though not perfectly, "each tree is known by its own fruit" (Luke 6:44). When a sin becomes known, we must deal with it. Paul severely rebuked the Corinthian church for their failure or unwillingness to discipline a member of their church, who was living with his stepmother (1 Corinthians 5). But the goal of church discipline is not to punish the sinners; it is to reclaim and restore wayward sheep. Elders should not be trigger-happy.

It should be very encouraging for you to know how our denomination's Book of Church Order defines church discipline. When we hear the phrase, "church discipline," we think of the formal, judicial process which can lead to excommunication if the offender refuses to repent. But that is only a part of church discipline. In a broader sense, church discipline includes everything that the church does for the spiritual well-being and growth of its members—worship, Bible studies, prayer meetings, fellowship, counseling, providing opportunities to serve, etc.—"that every one of [the members] may be presented faultless on the day of the Lord Jesus."[11] The goals of church discipline, even when it "involves

---

11 *Book of Church Order* (Lawrenceville: The Office of the Stated Clerk of the General Assembly of the Presbyterian Church in America 2014), 27-4.

judicial action, are the rebuke of offenses, the removal of scandal, the vindication of the honor of Christ, the promotion of the purity and general edification of the Church, and *the spiritual good of offenders themselves.*"[12]

The church of Jesus Christ is a holy community, purchased by the blood of Jesus Christ, set apart from the world unto the worship and service of God. But it is made up of imperfect sinners who are brought into this holy community by the grace of God, not by their own merit. No one in this community should pretend that he is perfect and has it all together. We should not be surprised and shocked when any of us sins. As sinners, forgiven by the grace of God ourselves, we should not *condemn* those whose sins are exposed. But while we should not condemn sinners, we must not *condone* their sins, either. We must *confront* their sins and help those that are in sin to repent of their sins and overcome them. As a community, we must devote to complete destruction all sins that are public and gross so that the offenders might be delivered from them and the peace and purity of the church of Jesus Christ might be maintained.

No one in this community should pretend that he is perfect and has it all together. We should not be surprised and shocked when any of us sins. As sinners, forgiven by the grace of God ourselves, we should not *condemn* those whose sins are exposed. But while we should not condemn sinners, we must not *condone* their sins, either. We must *confront* their sins and help those that are in sin to repent of their sins and overcome them. As a community, we must devote to complete destruction all sins that are public and gross so that the offenders might be delivered from them and the peace and purity of the church of Jesus Christ might be maintained.

Wars Without

But what about our dealings with those who are outside the church? As Israel was supposed to do, we offer them terms of peace. We do that not by bringing our armies and weapons. We do that by sharing the gospel of Jesus Christ. And the terms of peace we offer are so much

---

12 *Book of Church Order*, 27-3.

greater than those offered by Israel, aren't they? It is not just to spare their lives only to subjugate them to forced labor for us. We offer them God's forgiveness and acceptance; we offer them equal citizenship in the kingdom of God; we offer them the privilege to be co-heirs with Jesus Christ to all the riches of our heavenly inheritance. We offer them our loving service. What a wonderful and delightful task it is to extend such an invitation!

But of course, if they reject it, and continue to do so, they are heaping up on themselves the burning coals of God's wrath. We must keep in mind that we are no longer the agents of bringing temporal, physical punishments to those who reject the gospel. Our mission is to continue to bring the gospel to others (though we must not forget to issue the warning against the danger of rejecting the gospel). And when people reject the gospel, we do not give up but continue to pray for them and love them and share with them (as long as God allows it), leaving judgment to God.

A Call To Arms

Who should be engaged in this battle? Its spiritual nature does not exclude anyone—not women, not even children. For in spiritual warfare, there is no safe place to retreat away from the battlefield. We are at war in every aspect and every moment of our life. We cannot afford to be cowards. For our battle is unavoidable.

But if we must not be cowardly, it is because Jesus Christ has already won the victory. Our great King, the great Captain of our soul, has gone to the battlefield and fought our enemies singlehandedly. He defeated our sin and the world and death and the devil and his demonic hosts. He did not fight this battle with swords and spears. These deadliest of our enemies are not the kind that can be defeated with weapons and armies. He fought this battle with His perfect righteousness and His perfect obedience to God's will even to the point of laying down His life on the cross. And having paid for the penalty of our sin, He rose again from death, shattering the chains of death forever. Thus He conquered our sin and this world and death and Satan.

If we have placed our faith in Jesus Christ, the Word of God assures us that His victory is ours. And He who desires to share His victory with us desires to share His glory with us as well. In Shakespeare's *Henry V*, King Henry promises this to all those who would fight with him against the French despite being greatly outnumbered:

> This day is call'd the feast of Crispian.
> He that outlives this day, and comes safe home,
> Will stand a tip-toe when this day is nam'd,
> And rouse him at the name of Crispian.
> He that shall live this day, and see old age,
> Will yearly on the vigil feast his neighbours,
> And say "To-morrow is Saint Crispian."
> Then will he strip his sleeve and show his scars,
> And say "These wounds I had on Crispian's day."
> Old men forget; yet all shall be forgot,
> But he'll remember, with advantages,
> What feats he did that day. Then shall our names,
> Familiar in his mouth as household words—
> Harry the King, Bedford and Exeter,
> Warwick and Talbot, Salisbury and Gloucester—
> Be in their flowing cups freshly rememb'red.
> This story shall the good man teach his son;
> And Crispin Crispian shall ne'er go by,
> From this day to the ending of the world,
> But we in it shall be remembered—
> We few, we happy few, we band of brothers;
> For he to-day that sheds his blood with me
> Shall be my brother; be he ne'er so vile,
> This day shall gentle his condition;
> And gentlemen in England now-a-bed
> Shall think themselves accurs'd they were not here,
> And hold their manhoods cheap whiles any speaks
> That fought with us upon Saint Crispin's day.

And yet a far more glorious honor awaits all those who engage in this battle by faith in their victorious King Jesus! Let us be bold and courageous and dare to suffer and even die for our glorious King! For if we suffer with Him, we will be glorified with Him also (Romans 8:17)!

Acquit The Innocent, Condemn The Guilty

[1] "If there is a dispute between men and they come into court and the judges decide between them, acquitting the innocent and condemning the guilty, [2] then if the guilty man deserves to be beaten, the judge shall cause him to lie down and be beaten in his presence with a number of stripes in proportion to his offense. [3] Forty stripes may be given him, but not more, lest, if one should go on to beat him with more stripes than these, your brother be degraded in your sight."
Deuteronomy 25:1-3

When I delivered this sermon, I intentionally wore my tie crooked because I heard of a pastor who did this on one occasion. Children in the congregation were especially quick to notice this. I did it intentionally, to make a point about our sense of right and wrong, and how important it is. Again, children are very sensitive to this. Not too long after they begin to talk and reason, we hear them say, "That's not fair! That's not right!" We must admit that few things bother us like unfairness and injustice, even when it comes to the distribution of candies and chocolates among children!)

Imagine living under a crooked and evil regime, which has no respect for justice! Imagine the police station being the last place you would want to go to when crimes are committed against you because they would not budge without you bribing them—worse yet, because they would have been already bought off by the criminals!

We have this innate sense of justice because we are made in the image of God. But it is not always easy to administer justice with equity and wisdom. To see how difficult it is, all you need—again—is to raise children. This business of upholding justice can be quite daunting when communities are formed, resulting in a web of complex interpersonal and business relationships. So God has entrusted the government with

131

the responsibility to administer and maintain justice in society. Even in today's short passage, we can see God's concern for justice.

A Case Law, Based On Justice

Our passage for today, like last week's, is a case law. It, too, is a long, "if-then" statement. This law is mainly about how to administer proper punishment to the guilty party when there is a dispute between individuals. The crimes in view are not capital crimes deserving capital punishment. In such cases, scourging was inflicted. But the scourging was not to be more than 40 lashes. The Jewish practice was to inflict 39 lashes for the maximum. "They abated one for fear of having miscounted (though one of the judges was appointed to number the stripes), or because they would never go to the utmost rigor, or because the execution was usually done with a whip of three lashes, so that 13 stripes (each one being counted for three) made up 39, but one more by that reckoning would have been 42" (Matthew Henry).

We see that the main concern of this case law is the equitable administration of justice, even in the punishment of criminals. But what is not lost sight of is the dignity of man, especially the dignity of a member of the covenant community of Israel, even though he may be a criminal. Note the reason for the limit set on scourging: "Forty stripes may be given him, but not more, lest, if one should go on to beat him with more stripes than these, your brother be degraded in your sight" (verse 3). He is still called "your brother."

Justice And The Justification Of Believers

The foundation of the case law is obviously justice. And this concept of justice is summarized in the phrase delineating the responsibility of the judges: "acquitting the innocent and condemning the guilty" (verse 1). This phrase is important not only for the social administration of justice but also for our redemption. Let us see how.

As Christians, when we hear the word "justification," how do we understand the term? When unbelievers hear the term, they hear something negative—such as giving excuses and rationalizing one's mistakes or wrongdoings. But that is not what the Bible means by it.

When Christians hear the term in sermon or Bible study, they probably think of something along the lines of what the Apostle Paul says in Romans 4:5: "And to the one who does not work but believes in him who justifies the ungodly, his faith is counted as righteousness...." We think of justification as an act of God's grace toward sinners. The Westminster Shorter Catechism gives a wonderful, precise definition of justification: "Justification is an act of God's free grace, wherein he pardons all our sins, and accepts us as righteous in his sight, only for the righteousness of Christ imputed to us, and received by faith alone" (Answer #33).

But we must appreciate how radical and scandalous this statement is from a judicial point of view! In fact, it is the very opposite of the judicial justice the court of law must uphold, "acquitting the innocent [literally, the just or righteous] and condemning the guilty" (verse 1). Keep in mind that the word translated as "acquitting" can also be translated as "justifying." The New American Standard Version even translates it, "they justify the righteous and condemn the guilty."

What does it mean to justify in the court of law? It is for the judge to declare the defendant to be innocent because he *is* innocent! It is the opposite of condemnation. To condemn is for the judge to declare the defendant to be guilty because he *is* guilty!

What is presupposed in today's passage is the responsibility of Israel's judges to maintain justice in society. What is the judge supposed to do as an agent of justice? He is to justify the innocent and condemn the guilty. Imagine what would happen if the judge did the opposite—justifying the guilty and condemning the innocent. A reign of terror and evil would prevail. In fact, the very foundation of society would be destroyed and the fabric of social order would be unraveled. Few things are more angering than watching the guilty walk away scot-free, aren't they? Especially when you are the victim! So we read in Proverbs 17:15, "He who justifies the wicked and he who condemns the righteous are both alike an abomination to the LORD."

Of course, there are wicked judges. What is more, even the best judges are all too fallible, limited as they are in knowledge and wisdom and insight into human character and heart as well as having to deal with insufficient evidence. So even Solomon, that wisest of human kings, felt compelled to pray at the dedication of the temple, "If a man sins against his neighbor and is made to take an oath and comes and swears his oath before your altar in this house, then hear in heaven and act and judge your servants, condemning the guilty by bringing his conduct on his own head, and vindicating the righteous by rewarding him according to his righteousness" (1 Kings 8:31-32). Solomon's unwavering confidence was that, even when all human judges failed, people could look to God to execute His perfect justice, condemning the guilty and vindicating (or, justifying) the righteous.

But what does Paul say? "And to the one who does not work but believes in him who justifies the ungodly, his faith is counted as righteousness"! How does Paul present God? As the One "who justifies the ungodly"! How scandalous! How blasphemous it sounds! He is presenting God as doing exactly what He warned (with threats!) the human judges not to do, doing what a wicked judge does!

Thanks To Someone Else's Righteousness

But why are we not shocked by this scandalous claim? Because of what Christ has done on our behalf, of course! Paul did not make that scandalous claim out of a vacuum, did he? He said in the previous chapter, "For by works of the law no human being will be justified in his sight, since through the law comes knowledge of sin. But now the righteousness of God has been manifested apart from the law, although the Law and the Prophets bear witness to it—the righteousness of God through faith in Jesus Christ for all who believe" (Romans 3:20-22).

Paul points out that no human being can be justified before God by works of the law. God cannot justify us if He is to judge us according to *our* merit. We are not innocent; we are not righteous; we are literally "guilty as hell." As a just and righteous Judge, He must condemn each and every one of us as guilty and cast us one and all into eternal punishment.

But Paul also declares to us that "now the righteousness of God has been manifested apart from the law…the righteousness of God through faith in Jesus Christ for all who believe" (Rom. 3:21, 22). This was no emergency measure put together at the last moment because things did not work out as God originally intended. Paul declares that the righteousness of God that has been manifested in Jesus Christ is what the Law and the Prophets testified to, though it was apart from the law.

What is this righteousness of God apart from the law? It doesn't mean that this righteousness had nothing to do with the law of God. Righteousness cannot be without the law. For the biblical notion of righteousness is inseparably connected with keeping the law—both its stipulations and its spirit. A righteous person is the one who keeps the law. When Paul speaks of this righteousness of God, which is apart from the law, he is not saying that it is without keeping the law. Rather, he is distinguishing it from *our* own righteousness obtained by *our* own efforts of keeping the law. "For by works of the law no human being will be justified in his sight" (Romans 3:20). His focus is who it is that keeps the law—we ourselves or Someone else.

This righteousness of God is through faith in Jesus Christ (Romans 3:22). It is "apart from the law" because it is through *faith*, not by *our* works of obedience to the law. But it is not without the law because it is through faith *in Jesus Christ*, who has fulfilled the law and obtained perfect righteousness on our behalf. You see, God's grace does not just come from His love. It flows from a dual fount—of His love *and* of the righteousness of God in Christ. Why is this important?

Justice Not Set Aside

Because God's grace cannot be just gracious. If God's grace were simply gracious, it would be evil. It would be like a judge justifying the wicked. Then God would be violating His law, denying His essential divine character. If He denied His righteousness in being gracious to us, He would no longer be God. He cannot deny Himself and still be God (2 Timothy 2:13). That is why God's grace must be a *righteous* grace, flowing from the dual fount of His love and Christ's righteousness.

Consider what would be the result if we were saved merely by God's *gracious* grace. Without the righteousness of Christ, ours would be no more than a *shameful* redemption, if that. We know what people think of those who get away scot-free from their rightful punishment only because they were rich enough to hire the best lawyers money could buy, or because they were close enough to the president to obtain a presidential pardon. Would we be any different if we were saved by God's gracious grace alone? We might be able to escape from the punishment but not from the stain of guilt and shame. What kind of redemption would that be if we still have to live with guilt and shame?

Paul declares that Jesus "was delivered up for our trespasses and raised for our justification" (Romans 4:25). Why Jesus had to be delivered up and be crucified for our trespasses is clear. He had to take our place before the judgment seat of God and pay the punishment of our sin. But why did Jesus have to be raised for our justification? Isn't it sufficient that Jesus died for our sins?

Yes, the death of our Lord was absolutely necessary: "without the shedding of blood there is no forgiveness of sins" (Hebrews 9:22). And it was absolutely sufficient *for the forgiveness of our trespasses* (Romans 4:25). But it was *not* sufficient *for our justification*! Jesus had to be raised—not just die—for our justification (Romans 4:25). It is in this sense that Paul says in 1 Corinthians 15:17, "And if Christ has not been raised, your faith is futile and you are still in your sins." How so?

Jesus Raised For Our Justification

You see, all that we say about the death of Jesus Christ would be an empty claim unless Jesus rose again from the dead. For it is one thing to claim that Jesus died for our sins. But what would be the proof that He actually did? If He did not rise again from the dead, how do we know that He did not die as we all die—in sin? For the wages of sin is death. And even if He did die for our sins, we can never have the full assurance that all our sins are fully paid for. For as long as He remains dead, we must assume that He is paying for our sins. He cannot rise from the dead until all our sins are paid for. (This is not to say that it took Jesus three days to pay for our sins. Jesus remained in the grave for a time to demonstrate that He was fully dead, not just fainted!) But by

His resurrection from the dead Jesus demonstrated that: 1) He did not die for His own sin but for our sins; 2) He paid for all our sins fully and completely; 3) there is, therefore, no condemnation for those who place their faith in Him—not now, not ever; 4) death has been conquered and it is no longer a punishment for our sin!

That is why Paul also claims that Jesus Himself was justified: "Great indeed, we confess, is the mystery of godliness: He was manifested in the flesh, *vindicated* [or, justified] *by the Spirit*, seen by angels, proclaimed among the nations, believed on in the world, taken up in glory" (1 Timothy 3:16). How can we say that Jesus was justified if we use the definition given in Rom. 4:5—that God justifies the ungodly? No, Jesus was justified in the sense of Deuteronomy 25:1. God justified Jesus because He *was* innocent of sin, because He *was* righteous. He kept all the demands of the law, loving God with all of His heart and soul and mind and strength and loving His neighbors to the point of laying down His life even while we were yet sinners! And as we saw, His resurrection was *His* justification by God, God declaring, "My Son, You are not guilty! You are righteous!" What is more, God declared, "I have accepted Your sacrifice for the sins of Your people once for all! By Your death, you have paid for all their sins, fully and completely, even to the least and smallest of their sins! Break the shackles of death and rise again from the dead! For You cannot remain in the grave under the reign of death any more!"

Jesus was justified in the sense of Deuteronomy 25:1. God justified Jesus because He *was* innocent of sin, because He *was* righteous. He kept all the demands of the law, loving God with all of His heart and soul and mind and strength and loving His neighbors to the point of laying down His life even while we were yet sinners! And as we saw, His resurrection was *His* justification by God, God declaring, "My Son, You are not guilty! You are righteous! ....I have accepted Your sacrifice for the sins of Your people once for all! By Your death, you have paid for all their sins, fully and completely...! Break the shackles of death and rise again from the dead! For You cannot remain in the grave under the reign of death any more!"

An Unshakeable Foundation

Do you see? The basis of our justification is the justification of Jesus Christ! For Jesus was justified as our Representative and Redeemer by His resurrection. Through faith in Him, therefore, we can be justified before God even though we are guilty and ungodly! The foundation of our justification is firm and unshakable because it is none other than the life and death and resurrection of Jesus Christ—His righteous justification before God! God sees us as if we had never sinned because Jesus paid for all our sins by His death. God sees us as if we had loved Him with all of our heart and soul and mind and strength, as if we had loved our neighbors as ourselves perfectly, because Jesus lived that way on our behalf! That is why our justification is by faith in Christ!

Oh, how glorious is our justification in Jesus Christ! His grace for unworthy sinners triumphed without surrendering His righteousness! So much so that the Apostle Paul was able to glory in our justification as the manifestation of God's righteousness (Romans 3:21-22)!

This is why the Apostle John can proclaim, "If we confess our sins, he is faithful and just to forgive us our sins and to cleanse us from all unrighteousness" (1 John 1:9). Did you notice that he doesn't say, "If we confess our sins, he is *loving and gracious…*"? He actually says, "If we confess our sins, he is *faithful and just* to forgive us our sins"! *Now* we know how God can be faithful and just to forgive the ungodly. If Jesus did pay for all our sins once for all, God cannot punish us *again* for our sins. God's justice forbids it! So it is out of His justice that He forgives us when we plead guilty to our sins with our confession! Because of Jesus Christ, God *cannot* condemn us! He is no longer our Judge. He is our Father.

What should be our response to this gospel truth—that the grace, by which we are saved, is not just gracious but also righteous? We realize that our justification, being *declared* pardoned and righteous—cannot be separated from our sanctification, being *made* righteous in our character and life! For it is unto righteousness and holiness we are saved! We are not just saved from the punishment of sin; we are also saved from the power of sin and eventually from the presence of sin itself! Yes, God accepts us the way we are, with all of our guilt and shame and brokenness. He calls us to come as we are, not *after* we make ourselves more presentable to Him! But God loves us too much to leave us in guilt and shame and brokenness! The righteousness of Christ, which covers us in our justification, is infused into us for our sanctification, enabling us to be like Him more and more! Let us grow ever more secure in our understanding of the glory of our justification in the justification of Jesus Christ! And as we do so, let us grow ever more in righteousness and holiness in the likeness of our Lord!

Worship in Spirit and Truth

[19] The woman said to him, "Sir, I perceive that you are a prophet.
[20] Our fathers worshiped on this mountain, but you say that in Jerusalem
is the place where people ought to worship." [21] Jesus said to her, "Woman,
believe me, the hour is coming when neither on this mountain nor in
Jerusalem will you worship the Father. [22] You worship what you do not
know; we worship what we know, for salvation is from the Jews. [23] But the
hour is coming, and is now here, when the true worshipers will worship the
Father in spirit and truth, for the Father is seeking such people to worship
him. [24] God is spirit, and those who worship him must worship in spirit
and truth." [25] The woman said to him, "I know that Messiah is coming (he
who is called Christ). When he comes, he will tell us all things."
[26] Jesus said to her, "I who speak to you am he."
John 4:19-26

Now we have an ongoing debate between the proponents of "contemporary" worship and "traditional" worship. Actually, that may not be an accurate description of the current state of affairs. The wave of contemporary worship has so swiftly and decisively washed over the American evangelical world that there's really no debate over it any more, it seems. Many who visit our church may be shocked to find out that there are still people who worship without praise bands and Power Point. But there are still some people who hold on to the traditional form of worship, however small and rapidly declining their number may be. And they do so for different reasons. Some do so because they simply don't like changes. But others do so because of certain theological reasons. In the same way, some of those who advocate contemporary form of worship do so because of theological reasons while others simply accept it as an inevitable result of changing times.

I'm sure we all recognize *how* we worship is important—whether you are a lay person trying to choose which church to attend or a part of the leadership in the church who are entrusted with the responsibility of designing and leading the worship service. And I'm sure we prefer a certain way of worshipping God to other ways. But how we worship shouldn't be just a question of *our* preference, right? After all, our worship is not just a social event we plan for ourselves. It involves God first and foremost. Even when we organize a birthday party for someone, we must take into account what he or she likes and wants. To worship God is to pay tribute to God, to acknowledge God's supreme worth to us as the one and only true God, our Redeemer and our Provider. So it is important for us to think through our preferences and reasons biblically and theologically. I hope this message will help us do precisely that and, in doing so, explain our philosophy of worship.

"In Spirit And Truth"

In today's passage, Jesus prescribes for us the character of our worship with the phrase, "in spirit and truth." Let us examine this passage together and discover the principles that should dictate our worship.

In His conversation with this Samaritan woman, our Lord speaks of a new age of worship. "Woman, believe me, the hour is coming when neither on this mountain nor in Jerusalem will you worship the Father" (verse 21). In fact, our Lord goes on to announce that a new age has arrived. "But the hour is coming, and is now here, when the true worshipers will worship the Father in spirit and truth" (verse 23). Our Lord characterized the worship of this new age in four words: "in spirit and truth."

What does it mean to worship God "in spirit and truth"? Does it mean having some kind of ecstatic, mystical, spiritual experience while privately meditating for a long time? Or does it mean worshipping God in a sincere, heartfelt way? Or does it mean maintaining a well-balanced worship characterized by passion (in spirit) and doctrinal accuracy (in truth)?

No one would dispute that true worship requires sincerity and earnestness. Simply going through the motions, mindlessly performing external ceremonies, cannot be true worship. And it should also be based on the truth about God. What's the point of getting all excited and emotional about something when it is not true? Finally, worship should be a moving experience—something that stimulates our mind and touches our heart and directs our will. Ravi Zacharias often quotes Archbishop William Temple on worship: "Worship is the submission of all of our nature to God. It is the quickening of the conscience by his holiness; the nourishment of mind with his truth; the purifying of imagination by his beauty; the opening of the heart to his love; the surrender of will to his purpose—all this gathered up in adoration, the most selfless emotion of which our nature is capable."

A Change In Location

But is that all our Lord is talking about in today's passage? Most likely not. Jesus uses the phrase "in spirit and truth" in contrast to something else. In contrast to what? To hypocrisy, formalism, or insincerity? No. "In spirit and truth" is placed in opposition to "neither on this mountain nor in Jerusalem" in verse 21. This pairing of contrast is made clear by the repetition of the same idea of the coming hour in both verses: "Woman, believe me, *the hour is coming* when neither on this mountain nor in Jerusalem will you worship the Father" (verse 21). "*The hour is coming*, and is now here, when the true worshipers will worship the Father in spirit and truth" (verse 23). The worship of the previous era was in Jerusalem (and in the era before that, in other locations). The worship of this new era is instead "in spirit and truth"!

Does this make sense? Isn't this like comparing apples with oranges? How can worshipping in Jerusalem (location) be compared with worshipping in spirit and truth (if this phrase refers to our attitude of sincerity)?

However, most commentators agree that the word "spirit" in verse 23 does not refer to our own spirit but to the Holy Spirit. Raymond Brown says, "In fact, one could almost regard 'Spirit and truth' as a hendiadys… equivalent to 'Spirit of truth' [in John 16:13]."[13] This

13 Raymond Brown, *The Gospel According to John*. AB, vol. 29 (New York: Doubleday 1966), p. 180.

helps us make sense of the comparison our Lord is making, doesn't it? In a way, Jesus *is* talking about a change in our worship location—from worshipping in Jerusalem (or in any other specific geographical location) to worshipping in the Holy Spirit.

The question of the day is, then, what does it mean to worship in the Holy Spirit?

Worshiping in the Holy Spirit

Worshipping in the Holy Spirit means, at the most basic level, true worship is not confined to a specific geographical location. For the Jews at that time, true worship was inextricably bound up with the temple in Jerusalem. It was certainly not at Mount Gerizim (which is what "this mountain" in Samaria probably refers to)! Jesus mentioned Mount Gerizim only because He was speaking with a Samaritan woman. Mount Gerizim was one of the two mountains, along with Mount Ebal, upon which the twelve tribes of Israel, six on each mountain, responded to the words of blessings and curses—blessings by the six tribes on Mount Gerizim and curses by the six tribes on Mount Ebal (Deuteronomy 11:29; Joshua 8:33-35). Other than this specific occasion, Mount Gerizim had no significance in terms of Israel's worship. It was an important place of worship for the Samaritans. It was not the place God designated for Israel's worship in the Promised Land. Jerusalem alone was. That is why Solomon built the temple there.

But Jesus does something shocking here, doesn't He? By listing Mount Gerizim and Jerusalem together, side by side, He gives the impression that both places are of the same category—especially when you consider the fact that both Mount Gerizim and Jerusalem are together contrasted with the Holy Spirit. Our Lord is suggesting that, in this new age of worship in the Holy Spirit, Jerusalem is really no different from Gerizim! Do you realize how radical this is? At that time, Jerusalem being the only legitimate location of worship, to worship in Gerizim was to sin against God and His command! When you read the biblical history of Israel's kings, many kings were criticized for not removing "the high places" where the people of Israel offered their sacrifices throughout the land.

So then, in this new age of worship in the Holy Spirit, there is no longer any one official location where all the people of God must come for true worship! God's people can gather at any place and offer to God true worship—even at Mount Gerizim, even in San Diego, even in Hollywood or Las Vegas!

But how can this be if God designed Jerusalem to be the only legitimate place of worship? Is Jesus contradicting God's law in the Old Testament? No. What did Solomon say at the very moment he dedicated the temple to the Lord? "But will God indeed dwell on the earth? Behold, heaven and the highest heaven cannot contain you; how much less this house that I have built" (1 Kings 8:27)! As magnificent as it was, the temple was too small for God to dwell in. It was too small even for all the Jews to worship in all together! Besides, God is not just the God of Israel, is He? God is the God of all the nations, of heaven and earth! Abraham was chosen so that all the families of the earth might be blessed in him (Genesis 12:3)! So we should not be surprised to find passages like Malachi 1:11 in the Old Testament, in which God declares, "From the rising of the sun to its setting my name will be great among the nations, and *in every place* incense will be offered to my name, and a pure offering. For *my name will be great among the nations*, says the LORD of hosts." Worship will be offered to God all throughout the world, not just in Jerusalem.

What is it about worshipping in the Holy Spirit that makes this kind of radical transition possible?

A geographical location cannot make our worship true and acceptable to God. This whole world is fallen in sin. No location is sacred in and of itself. It can be made holy and sacred only by the special presence of a holy God. So Mount Sinai was transformed into a holy mountain when the Lord descended upon it in fire (Exodus 19:18). The tabernacle, too, was no more than a man-made tent until the glory-cloud covered it and the glory of the LORD filled it (Exodus 40:34). The same was true of Solomon's temple (2 Chronicles 5:13). The glory-cloud was, of course, the theophanic manifestation of the Holy Spirit. And what we must not miss here is how no one could enter these sanctuaries when the glory-cloud (the Holy Spirit) descended on them! The people of Israel had to watch from a distance!

Now we can understand the significance of worshipping God in spirit and truth, in the Holy Spirit! A new era of worship has arrived in Jesus Christ, in which the people of God are worshipping in the Holy Spirit rather than watching from a distance. The people of the Old Testament had to stay away from the Holy Spirit for fear of death and destruction. For God is a consuming fire! Sinners coming into direct contact with God cannot withstand the heat of His holy wrath against sin. But now the people of God can worship in the Holy Spirit! In fact, they are being built up into a holy temple where God dwells forever! So Paul says in Ephesians 2:19-22, "So then you are no longer strangers and aliens, but you are fellow citizens with the saints and are members of the household of God, built on the foundation of the apostles and prophets, Christ Jesus Himself being the cornerstone, in whom the whole structure, being joined together, grows into *a holy temple in the Lord.* In him you also are being built together into *a dwelling place for God by the Spirit.*"

The New Temple In Christ: People Who Worship By The Spirit

This could not happen unless the problem of our sin was completely taken care of! In the age of animal sacrifices at the temple, God's people had to stay away from the sanctuaries that were filled with the Holy Spirit. But on the Day of Pentecost, the Holy Spirit descended upon the 120 disciples of Jesus in the form of fire and rested on each of them. That indicated that all their sins had been paid for. How? By the once-for-all sacrifice of Jesus Christ, by the blood of the Lamb of God, which alone can wash away our sin! As a result, the people of God themselves have been made into a dwelling of God, God's holy, living temple!

Obviously, then, we no longer need to worship at a temple. By temple, I mean a physical structure that is built according to divine specifications. We are blessed to gather and worship at this church building. But a church building is not a temple. And it doesn't even have to be a church building, does it? Many congregations worship at schools and hotels and even movie theaters. Our church began at Richard Kim's townhome in La Jolla, CA and even met at the choir room at nearby All Hallows. Some places may be less conducive to worship than others. But in this new era of worship, it's the people who worship in the Spirit that sanctifies a space, not the other way around.

Does the fact that we no longer worship at the temple affect how we worship? Obviously, we no longer offer animal sacrifices and burn incense. We no longer have a priestly tribe who serve at the temple, assisting in offering sacrifices and singing in choirs. Is that all? No. We must keep in mind the general character of the nation of Israel and its temple. Israel was a temporary, provisional, and earthly representation of the kingdom of heaven. As such, the kingdom of Israel had to represent the invisible, spiritual realities of

In the age of animal sacrifices at the temple, God's people had to stay away from the sanctuaries that were filled with the Holy Spirit. But on the Day of Pentecost, the Holy Spirit descended upon the 120 disciples of Jesus in the form of fire and rested on each of them. That indicated that all their sins had been paid for. How? By the once-for-all sacrifice of Jesus Christ, by the blood of the Lamb of God, which alone can wash away our sin! As a result, the people of God themselves have been made into a dwelling of God, God's holy, living temple!

the kingdom of heaven in physical, tangible forms. The power of God showed itself through Israel's military victories. Obedience to the law was rewarded with material blessings and prosperity in the Promised Land. Although heaven and the highest heaven could not contain God (I Kings 8:27), a magnificent physical temple was built as a tangible sign of God's presence in the midst of Israel. No precious materials were spared to build the temple in order to reflect God's majestic splendor. Even the high priest, who served the Lord in His temple, was given holy garments, made for glory and for beauty (Exodus 28:2).

Taking place in this kind of environment, the worship in the old covenant had to be elaborate and impressive in a physical manner to show forth the glory of God in tangible ways. The temple choirs were organized to sing the Psalms with the accompaniment of many musical instruments. The worship at the temple was designed to stimulate and overwhelm the physical senses of man in order to communicate the glories of the invisible, spiritual realities.

With the coming of Jesus Christ, things have changed radically. Jerusalem and Mount Gerizim are contrasted with the Holy Spirit. Jerusalem and Mount Gerizim represent the earthly manner of worship. The Holy Spirit represents the heavenly manner of worship. What is the difference? It is like teaching children. When we try to teach something new to young children, we must work with their limited vocabulary and knowledge. When a child asks what a pear is, you may start by telling him that a pear is like an apple, emphasizing the similarities (like how it is round like an apple) between the two so he can have some bearing. Then, as he grows, he begins to appreciate pears for what they are, for their unique qualities that are quite different from apples (although they are both round fruits).

The same was true of God's dealing with His people. In prescribing Israel's worship, God was speaking as to a child, emphasizing the similarities between heaven and earth. But in the new covenant, God is speaking to us as to a mature person, focusing more on the distinctive features of heaven.

Another way to put it is this. In Israel, God showed the invisible glory of heaven by the visual aid of earthly glory, emphasizing the similarities. In this new age of worship, God directs our eyes away from the perishable glories of this world toward heaven by the simplicity and plainness of worship, emphasizing the differences. We can say that the Israelites worshipped by sight whereas we are called to worship by faith. Isn't that clear? Take a look at the Table of the Lord, for example. How humble is its appearance! Doesn't it force us to look beyond it to the realities it points to—the glorious feast in heaven? Doesn't that speak volumes about what should characterize our worship—not the pomp and glitz of earthly glories but the simplicity and plainness that point toward the heavenly reality? If not, we should all try to build the most impressive, magnificent church buildings and have the biggest orchestras and choirs. And we should flock to such churches because that's where true worship can take place! But is that true?

Are You Worshipping In Spirit And Truth?

The question is, Are you worshipping in spirit and truth? How can we know? We don't see the fire of the Holy Spirit resting upon us. That doesn't happen even in a most charismatic church. How can we know?

You are worshipping in spirit and truth if you sincerely believe in Jesus Christ. For "no one speaking in the Spirit of God ever says 'Jesus is accursed!' and no one can say 'Jesus is Lord' except in the Holy Spirit" (1 Corinthians 12:3). Anyone who sincerely confesses Jesus as Lord has been baptized by the Holy Spirit and therefore has the Holy Spirit dwelling in him. And when the Call to Worship is issued at the beginning of our Lord's Day services and believers gather in the name of Jesus Christ, we know we are worshipping in spirit and truth.

But of course, true worship is more than just being here. If we are the holy temple of God, if the Holy Spirit dwells in each of us and among us as a corporate body, how should we conduct ourselves in our worship? Think of the temple that was filled with the glory of the Lord and how the people of Israel were filled with fear. They dared not enter the temple. But we are there. We *are* the temple of the Lord, filled with the glory of the Lord! Can we be lax? Can we be distracted? And if temptations should arise, should we not resist them quickly and decisively rather than yielding to them?

Worshipping By Faith, Not Sight

At the outset, I talked about the debate between contemporary and traditional forms of worship. But it may not be the most helpful way to frame the issue. Rather, it should be between earthly versus heavenly, whether it caters to sight or to faith. Let us remember that we no longer need the visual, auditory extravagance of the old covenant temple worship to arouse our religious sentiments, to get us prepared for worship. Nothing in this world, nothing made with human hands, can do justice to the surpassing glory of God revealed through Jesus Christ God's Son. The simplicity and plainness of the new covenant worship is designed to stimulate our eyes of faith, not our physical eyes, to see the invisible, heavenly glory of God. Knowing our weakness, our Lord graciously provided the Sacraments, the visible signs to aid us in our pilgrim journey toward heaven. However, the Sacraments are the only and sufficient visual aids for our worship. And even these Sacraments of the new covenant take the form of plainness and simplicity without any trace of extravagance.

It is said, "When man ceases to worship God, he does not worship nothing but worships everything." What a blessing it is, then, to believe in the one and only true God, who created us and planted that longing for our Maker in our soul! Nothing can truly satisfy us until our souls find satisfaction in God.

Brothers and sisters, we have been invited to participate in glorious new covenant worship! In this worship, we are not to depend on anything other than the simple elements of the new covenant worship to see the glory of God. We don't need an impressive church building, a hundred-voice choir accompanied by an orchestra, and other visual and audio aids to feel the presence of God. For we have been given the Spirit of Christ, who dwells in us. Without His work of illuminating the word of God, no oratory of man, no matter how eloquent and powerful, can give us a saving knowledge of God's Word. And if we have that Spirit of God working in our hearts, we can hear God speaking to us through the least gifted of God's servants. Without the Spirit of adoption, no warmth of human words can enable us to cry out to the almighty God, "Abba! Father!" And we have that Spirit of God working in our hearts, praying for us with groanings too deep for words! By that Spirit, we have the privilege to enter into the heavenly temple itself. Here in this temple, we are not to look at the mere copies and shadows of the glory of God but to look directly to Jesus Christ and marvel at the glory of our God and Savior! And to think that we are being built up into that heavenly temple, full of God's glory!

Praise: "They Sang a New Song!"

[4:8] And the four living creatures, each of them with six wings, are full of eyes all around and within, and day and night they never cease to say,
"Holy, holy, holy, is the Lord God Almighty,
who was and is and is to come!"
[9] And whenever the living creatures give glory and honor and thanks to him who is seated on the throne, who lives forever and ever, [10] the twenty-four elders fall down before him who is seated on the throne and worship him who lives forever and ever. They cast their crowns before the throne, saying,
[11] "Worthy are you, our Lord and God,
to receive glory and honor and power,
for you created all things,
and by your will they existed and were created."
[5:9] And they sang a new song, saying,
"Worthy are you to take the scroll
and to open its seals,
for you were slain, and by your blood you ransomed people for God
from every tribe and language and people and nation,
[10] and you have made them a kingdom and priests to our God,
and they shall reign on the earth."
[11] Then I looked, and I heard around the throne and the living creatures and the elders the voice of many angels, numbering myriads of myriads and thousands of thousands, [12] saying with a loud voice,
"Worthy is the Lamb who was slain,
to receive power and wealth and wisdom and might
and honor and glory and blessing!"
[13] And I heard every creature in heaven and on earth and under the earth and in the sea, and all that is in them, saying,
"To him who sits on the throne and to the Lamb
be blessing and honor and glory and might forever and ever!"
[14] And the four living creatures said, "Amen!" and the elders fell down and worshiped.
Revelation 4:8-11; 5:9-14

151

The worship of God demands our whole being to be engaged—our intellect, our emotion, and our will. For it is God who calls us to worship Him. His honor demands it. His glory deserves it. His beauty inspires it. Even when we deal with another human being, it is considered rude to keep looking at our watch or have wandering eyes. How much worse it is when we are dealing with the one and only true, all-glorious God! In worship, our whole being should be engaged from beginning to end, in every element of worship.

Let's turn our attention to the singing of praise to God. Singing of praise, as someone has suggested, is prayer set to music. We readily associate music with emotions. Music evokes our emotions in the profoundest and most wonderful ways. In the singing of praise, then, the emotionality of prayer is amplified further by the emotionality of music. The presence of praise in worship validates the importance of our emotions in the worship of God. Thus it calls us in a powerful way to engage our whole being in the worship of God—our emotions along with our intellect and will.

But does it matter what we sing in worship? Different occasions call for different types of songs. We wouldn't sing "Happy Birthday" at someone's funeral. And we certainly wouldn't sing dirges at someone's wedding. Then what songs are appropriate for worship? Whatever makes us feel spiritual and emotional? Or any song, as long as it has some kind of Christian message or theme? Would it be okay to sing "Veggie Tales" songs?

According to Ephesians 5:19, we are to sing "psalms and hymns and spiritual songs." They are most likely synonyms, all referring to the same thing. What's interesting, though, is that categories other than the Psalms are included in the list of sacred songs ("hymns" and "spiritual songs"). What makes a song "sacred"?

Songs Centered Upon God, His Goodness To His People

It has got to be its subject matter—the glory of God *and* His covenant relationship with His people. This is what is so wonderful about biblical religion. In our biblical religion, we don't come to know God merely as an abstract being conjured up by some philosophical speculations. Nor do we come to know God as He is in and of Himself without any relation to us, as "a god who doesn't care, who lives away, out there." We come to know God as He has revealed Himself to us, in covenant relationship with us—through His words and deeds in history as our covenant Lord. Though He is high above the heavens, though His glory extends far beyond all measure, He has graciously bound Himself to us through an eternal covenant. As our covenant Lord, He has created us, cares for us, and redeems us. So we sing psalms, hymns, and spiritual songs in grateful response, in awe of His glory and His goodness.

Psalms and hymns and spiritual songs are therefore directed to God. They ascribe to God glory and strength, majesty and honor. They acknowledge all the wonderful things that God has done for us, the great and mighty acts of God in history. They express our faith and confidence in the Lord, our joy and gratitude for His wonderful mercy. These sacred songs can address us as well. When they do, they exhort us to worship the Lord and praise Him, to hold fast to our faith and hope in Him and to walk in obedience to His will.

But is it okay to sing any song as long as it sings about the right subject matter—of God and His glory and our gratitude for His grace? There are thousands and thousands of "Christian" songs and I'm sure new "Christian" songs are added every day. Are they all appropriate for worship? (Notice, here we are speaking of "appropriateness"—not of right and wrong, necessarily.) There are certain things we must take into account.

Appropriate For Worship

The worship song, insofar as it is a congregational song, shouldn't be so individualized and personal. Not everything we write about has a universal appeal and significance. In God's providence, not even everything Jesus said and did was recorded in the Bible for all Christians to know and believe. Not every "Christian" song is appropriate for worship.

We must remember that worship is a corporate event. Worship songs are sung when God's people (of various singing abilities) are gathered together. So the songs we sing at worship shouldn't be too complicated and difficult to sing—something only professional singers can sing because the notes are too high or too low or the tune is too complex.

The tune should also have a reverential quality to it. We know that different tunes affect us differently, both physically and emotionally. Even the worship songs we sing are not all celebratory in terms of emotion. There are songs that sing of the gravity of our sin and our desperate need of a Savior. There are songs that call for repentance. There are songs we sing in times of loss, etc. But no matter what, the worship song should have a spirit of reverence, which recognizes God's presence among His people and draws us away from total self-indulgence and self-absorption.

We also have to keep in mind that the music is there to support the words we sing, not to draw attention to itself. That is why hymns do not usually have a long interlude between the verses, if at all, in which the musicians can do all kinds of fancy things to wow the people. What is important is God's people singing to God, not how well the band can play the music. (Of course, they should play well enough so they don't distract people with all their mistakes!) It is somewhat like the relationship between natural revelation and special revelation. Natural revelation is wonderful and it is able to communicate God's invisible attributes even without words (Romans 1:20). But it cannot show us the way of God's salvation in Jesus Christ. We can also say that natural revelation is there to show the specialness of special revelation. The same can be said of music. It can reflect the beauty of God and His creation in powerful ways. But it is insufficient to clearly communicate the greatest work of God—our redemption—without words.

New Works Of God, New Songs Of Praise

But this doesn't settle everything. There are those, though small in number, who believe that only the 150 Psalms of the Bible should be sung in worship. After all, these are divinely inspired songs! What's more appropriate to sing in worship than these songs that are inspired by God Himself! I'm sure they have many more reasons.

We should not dismiss what they say. Their desire to uphold the sanctity of worship should be respected. And they challenge us not to neglect these sacred, inspired songs in the Bible in our insatiable quest for new and fresh songs. However, their restriction doesn't do justice to the message of the Psalter itself. In several Psalms (33, 40, 96, 98, 144, 149) the people of God are exhorted to sing a new song to the Lord. What does this new song refer to? At the most basic level, the Psalmists are reminding God's people that God's infinite glory and honor, grace and mercy deserve a continual supply of new songs, for the theme of God and His glory can never be exhausted.

However, this phrase, "a new song," carries with it a very important redemptive-historical significance. In Isaiah 42:10 a divine command is issued: "Sing to the LORD a new song, his praise from the end of the earth...." This divine command is preceded by a divine promise: "Behold, the former things have come to pass, and new things I now declare; before they spring forth I tell you of them" (Isaiah 42:9). Thus the Lord establishes a direct link between His command to sing a new song and His declaration that He would do something new.

Seen in this light, the exhortation in the Psalms to sing a new song to the Lord flowed out of the redemptive-historical anticipation of a new work that God would do for His people—something much greater than what He had done, much greater than the exodus and the conquest of the Promised Land. Indeed, we see a definite link between God's great and mighty acts in history and the songs God's people sing of them in response. When God created the heavens and the earth, we are told that the angels sang praises to God (Job 38:7). And when God delivered the people of Israel out of Egypt and brought them safely through the Red Sea, the Israelites sang a song of deliverance to God and danced (Exodus 15). And when David consolidated the nation of Israel and subjugated all the surrounding nations and brought the Ark of the Covenant to Jerusalem, the priests led the whole nation in singing praises to God (1 Chronicles 16).

God's new work would naturally require new songs to acknowledge it. The Psalter itself leaves room for new songs. In fact, the Psalter demands that new songs be sung when God does something new. The sacred songs we sing in worship therefore cannot be restricted to the 150 Psalms of the Old Testament. Indeed, those psalms must be recast in the light of the wonderful new thing that God would do!

A Prime Example

In Revelation 4-5, we have a demonstration of this redemptive-historical link between God's work and our sacred songs, as well as what the new song is about. John the Seer is taken up into heaven in the Spirit and sees a form of God sitting on the throne. He sees surrounding God's throne 24 thrones, with the 24 elders sitting on them, clothed in white garments and golden crowns on their heads. He also sees four living creatures in the center around the throne. John sees them, along with the angels, singing praises to the Lord. He records for us five praises.

The first is found in 4:8: "Holy, holy, holy, is the Lord God Almighty, who was and is and is to come!" In this song, we are taken back to the beginning, before time, as God is praised for His holiness and eternal being.

The second one is in 4:11: "Worthy are you, our Lord and God, to receive glory and honor and power, for you created all things, and by your will they existed and were created." In this song, God is praised for His creation.

We find the third in 5:9-10: "Worthy are you to take the scroll and to open its seals, for you were slain, and by your blood you ransomed people for God from every tribe and language and people and nation, and you have made them a kingdom and priests to our God, and they shall reign on the earth." Here, in the third praise, the recipient is changed from the One sitting on the throne to the One who was slain. He is the Lamb who purchased His people with His blood and made them a kingdom and priests to God. This Lamb-figure is praised for having been found worthy to open the scroll and break its seals by being slain as a sacrifice. What happened?

Chapter 5 opens with John noticing the scroll with seven seals placed in the right hand of God. He also hears the angels proclaiming, "Who is worthy to open the book and to break its seals?" When no one is found, John weeps bitterly because the seals must be broken for the accomplishment of God's salvation. Then appears the One called "the Lion of the tribe of Judah, the Root of David," and "a Lamb standing," as if "slain," having "seven horns and seven eyes." He approaches the One on the throne and takes the book (verses 2-8). It is this event that prompts the third praise to spring forth. Let us note here that this third praise is introduced as "a new song" (verse 9).

The fourth one (5:12) follows the third praise: "Worthy is the Lamb who was slain, to receive power and wealth and wisdom and might and honor and glory and blessing!" The Lamb is praised for being worthy to receive "power and wealth and wisdom and might and honor and glory and blessing."

And we have the final praise in 5:13: "To him who sits on the throne and to the Lamb be blessing and honor and glory and might forever and ever!" This hymn is directed both to the One who sits on the throne and to the Lamb. To both are ascribed eternal blessing and honor and glory and dominion. The Lamb thus receives equal honor with the One who sits on the throne. The exaltation of the Lamb is thus made complete.

All Of History In 25 Verses

What did John witness in these two chapters? What duration of time do you think is covered by the events of these two chapters? There are only 25 verses and not much action takes place in those verses. We see the hosts of heaven singing praises to the One sitting on the throne and the Lamb appearing and taking the scroll from Him. Could it have taken 30 minutes? An hour?

However, when we pay attention to the lyrics of the five praises and their arrangement, we realize that what John witnessed was the entire history of the world up to the death, resurrection, ascension, and exaltation of

Jesus Christ. Notice the progression of redemptive history indicated by the praises:

- God's eternal attributes (4:8)
- His creation (4:9)
- Redemption accomplished as represented by the Lamb being slain (5:9, 10)
- The exaltation of the Lamb (5:12)
- The enthronement of the Lamb as the culmination of His exaltation (5:13)

As you can see, the themes of these praises are none other than the greatness of God and His mighty acts in history. In the light of God's matchless splendor in heaven nothing will be worth singing about except the glory of God and His wonderful works in history. What are the masterpieces of music? What are the songs that climb to the top of the charts? All of them will be drowned out by the praises of the saints singing of the matchless glory of the Lord of hosts.

But let us not fail to notice a very important point—a definite and significant transition occurs in the progression of the praises. "A new song" is introduced with the third song (5:9): "They sang a new song...." This new song is associated specifically with the saving work of Jesus Christ. Thus identified is the "new song" that the Psalmists and the prophet Isaiah invoked God's people to sing. The call to sing a new song came with God's declaration that He would do something new, something so radically and marvelously new that everything He had done in the past would be a thing to be forgotten: "Remember not the former things, nor consider the things of old. Behold, I am doing a new thing..." (Isaiah 43:18-19)! This new work of God was new in a most radical way—it was done "in the frailty of His Son," as sung by Michael Card in "El-Shaddai." So we are told in Revelation that the heavenly beings "sang" this new song. Compare this with the call to sing a new song in the Old Testament. There the new song is presented as something yet to be done. Now we are called to sing a new song that sings of the wonderful redemption of God, now completed in Jesus Christ! Jesus is the theme of the new song!

New In Quality: Forever, Lasting, Cannot Be Changed Or Improved

But there is another aspect to the "new" songs we are to sing. There is a very significant use of the word "new" in the Bible, which goes beyond just referring to something that comes after something that is old. It is used in contrast to the old, particularly to the meaning of the old as something that passes away and is no more. So "new" in this sense refers to something that does not pass away, something that does not have anything newer coming after it. It is new in the sense that it lasts forever and cannot be changed or improved.

> What John witnessed was the entire history of the world up to the death, resurrection, ascension, and exaltation of Jesus Christ....
> The themes of these praises are none other than the great and mighty acts of God in history. Before the presence of God in heaven nothing will be worth singing about except the glory of God and His wonderful works in history. What are the masterpieces of music? What are the songs that climb to the top of the charts? All of them will be drowned out by the praises of the saints singing of the matchless glory of the Lord of hosts.

This word is used in that sense in Jeremiah 31:31-32: "Behold, the days are coming, declares the LORD, when I will make a *new* covenant with the house of Israel and the house of Judah, not like the covenant that…they broke…." This new covenant God will make is not just something that simply replaces the old (with the possibility of itself being replaced yet with a newer covenant). This new covenant is the last and everlasting covenant because, unlike the old covenant that was broken, it will never be broken.

The word is used in a similar way in Revelation 21:1: "Then I saw a *new* heaven and a *new* earth, for the first heaven and the first earth had passed away, and the sea was no more." This new heaven and new earth is eternal because in it "death shall be no more, neither shall there be mourning, nor crying, nor pain anymore, for the former things have passed away" (Revelation 21:4).

We must view the "new" song that the Bible calls us to sing in the same sense. This new song is inextricably bound up with the new covenant, the new heaven and new earth, etc.! There isn't another covenant to replace the new covenant in Jesus Christ. There isn't anything new that will come after it to surpass its glory. There is no newer revelation necessary. There is no newer prophet to give the newer revelation, as some cults claim!

The New Never Growing Old Or Tiresome

So, then, this call to sing a new song means more than coming up with newer songs to add to the repertoire of worship songs. It doesn't preclude that since the theme of God's amazing grace in Jesus Christ cannot be exhausted, even through all eternity! But it does make us pause and check our insatiable appetite for something new all the time. In this age of "newer is better," we get bored of things so easily and are constantly on the lookout for newer and more exciting things. We jump from one fad to another and it seems like the same is unfortunately true with church music, too. We go after the latest and the newest, not necessarily because the new is better but simply because the new is new. But we need to treasure the old hymns, not to mention the Psalms. They testify to God's faithfulness to His people throughout the ages. These "old" songs are an important part of church history and the language of God's people. It is said, "Those that fail to learn from history are doomed to repeat it." And how we squander away our treasures if we neglect these sacred songs that have withstood the test of time! This is not to say we don't need new songs. These new songs testify to the timelessness of the biblical truths that are "eternally contemporary."

But, more importantly, let us not be bored with the gospel of Jesus Christ, the new work God promised and fulfilled, the new work that cannot be outdone, even by God Himself! If we cannot be satisfied with the love of God in Jesus Christ, what can satisfy us? If we cannot derive comfort from the gospel of Jesus Christ, what can comfort us? If we say we have to have this and have that, or I cannot be happy until this happens, what are we saying about Christ and about ourselves? May we never grow tired of the gospel! And may the Lord renew His steadfast love every morning so that we may sing the new song to Him! Because of His ever-renewing love for us, because of His infinite love that knows no end, even when we sing the old, familiar hymns and psalms and spiritual songs, we can sing them as if they were new—with an ever-deepening joy of salvation in Jesus Christ.

Let Us Sing To Him A New Song!

What are the songs you sing in your life? Do you just go from one hit song after another? A life that has something to sing about is a meaningful life. A life that has something worthwhile to sing about is a truly blessed life. A truly blessed life is what we have in Jesus Christ. Let us sing to Him a new song!

Let us sing of the wonder of Jesus' birth, the mystery of the incarnation of God:

> *All praise to thee, eternal Lord,*
> *Clothed in a garb of flesh and blood;*
> *Choosing a manger for thy throne,*
> *While worlds on worlds are thine alone.*
> *Once did the skies before thee bow;*
> *A virgin's arms contain thee now:*
> *Angels who did in thee rejoice*
> *Now listen for thine infant voice.*[14]

Let us sing of His life, His sacrificial love for us:

> *Thou who wast rich beyond all splendor,*
> *All for love's sake becamest poor;*
> *Thrones for a manger didst surrender,*
> *Sapphire-paved courts for stable floor.*
> *Thou who wast rich beyond all splendor,*
> *All for love's sake becamest poor.*[15]

---

14 Martin Luther, Tr. In *Sabbath Hymn Book, 1858,* "All Praise to Thee, Eternal Lord," *Trinity Hymnal* (Philadelphia: Great Commission Publications 1994), 219.

15 Frank Houghton, "Thou Who Wast Rich beyond All Splendor," *Trinity Hymnal,* 230.

Let us sing of His sacrificial death for our atonement:

> *What thou, my Lord, hast suffered was all for sinners' gain:*
> *Mine, mine was the transgression, but thine the deadly pain.*
> *Lo, here I fall, my Savior! 'Tis I deserve thy place;*
> *Look on me with thy favor, vouchsafe to me thy grace.*[16]

Let us sing of His glorious resurrection:

> *Thine be the glory, risen, conqu'ring Son;*
> *Endless is the vict'ry thou o'er death hast won;*
> *Angels in bright raiment rolled the stone away,*
> *Kept the folded grave-clothes where thy body lay.*
> *Thine be the glory, risen, conqu'ring Son,*
> *Endless is the vict'ry thou o'er death has won.*[17]

And with great expectation, let us sing of His promised return:

> *O Lord, haste the day when the faith shall be sight,*
> *The clouds be rolled back as a scroll,*
> *The trump shall resound and the Lord shall descend,*
> *'Even so'—it is well with my soul!*[18]

---

16 Bernard of Clairvaux, Tr. by James W. Alexander, "O Sacred Head Now Wounded," *Trinity Hymnal*, 247.
17 Edmond Budry, Tr. by Richard B. Hoyle, "Thine Be the Glory," *Trinity Hymnal*, 274.
18 Horatio G. Spafford, "It is Well with My Soul," *Trinity Hymnal*, 691.

By Faith We Please God

[5] By faith Enoch was taken up so that he should not see death, and he was not found, because God had taken him. Now before he was taken he was commended as having pleased God. [6] And without faith it is impossible to please him, for whoever would draw near to God must believe that he exists and that he rewards those who seek him.
Hebrews 11:5-6

It is said, "If it's worth doing, it's worth doing well." Similarly: "If it's worth believing, it's worth giving our all." Of course, not everything we believe is worth risking all. But there are some things, though mighty few, that are worth it. Why do we believe what we believe and do all that we do in the name of faith? In the case of Abel, whose faith is highlighted in the verses leading up to our passage, his life was cut short on account of the jealousy of his brother. His life was characterized by his worship, which was accepted by God. But was it worth it—his sacrifice and his short-lived life?

And this was not limited to Abel, was it? So many people suffer in this world. Even Christians suffer tremendously. Sometimes the intensity of it is so great we get overwhelmed just listening to their list of troubles. Is it worth holding on to our faith in Jesus Christ? The author of this letter to the Hebrews answers that question by putting Abel's and Enoch's lives side-by-side. "By faith Enoch was taken up so that he should not see death" (verse 5). This is a strange sentence. "By faith Enoch…" should be followed by what he did—like, "By faith Abel offered" a better sacrifice. Instead, we have the passive voice: "By faith Enoch was taken up…." It sounds like faith took Enoch up to heaven.

The True Role Of Faith

But we know that cannot be the meaning of the sentence. Faith has no ability to take us up to heaven, no matter how strong or sincere.

It may be a powerful motivator. Prompted by it, we may be driven to accomplish quite a few things. But willing ourselves up to heaven is not one of them. We know that faith was not what took Enoch up to heaven because we are clearly told only a few words later, "and he was not found, because *God had taken him*" (verse 5).

Then what was the role of faith? We are given the answer, starting at the end of verse 5: "Now before he was taken he was *commended as having pleased God. And without faith it is impossible to please Him....*" Faith is that by which Enoch was commended as having pleased God who took him up to heaven. So the Hebrews writer concludes his commentary on Enoch's life, "And without faith it is impossible to please [God]..." (verse 6). Assumed in those words are at least four things: 1) it is a very *difficult* thing to please the Lord; 2) it is *imperative* and even *necessary* to do so; 3) it is a most *desirable* thing; and finally, 4) it is nevertheless still *possible* to please the Lord.

It Is A Very Difficult Thing To Please The Lord

When the Hebrews writer says, "Without faith it is impossible to please Him," he is assuming that pleasing the Lord is a very *difficult* thing to do. It is indeed impossible, no matter how hard we try or what means we employ. There is only one possible way of doing it and that is by faith!

This should not be difficult to see. How difficult is it for an employee to "please" the employer? We may not see how difficult this is until we become employers ourselves. Some of our members who have their own businesses can tell us how difficult it is to come by a good and trustworthy employee, much less an employee after their own heart, who truly cares about the company, loves his job, is grateful for it, and shows his gratitude by working really hard. But we don't have to be a business owner to get this point. All one has to do is organize an event or lead a project—how difficult it is to get willing cooperation from others!

It is a sobering thing to ask. Do we know what our employers and superiors actually think of us? Are they really pleased with us and our work? And what about those that are closest to us—our wives and our husbands and our children and our parents? We know how difficult it is to please—really, really please—another person. It may seem impossible at times.

But should we be surprised by this? Are *we* pleased with *ourselves*? Is any of us half the man (or woman) we would like to be? So when someone complains about us, we should say, as Spurgeon did, "That's much too kind. Only if you knew what I was really like...." And if we cannot even please ourselves—and we love ourselves more than we deserve, I think—how can we think that we can please God? Is it ever possible for a sinner to please a holy God? If we are honest with ourselves, we would have to say it is indeed impossible to please a holy God.

It Is Imperative And Necessary

Some may say, "Who cares? Why should we try to please God anyway?" Well, what is also assumed in today's passage is that it is *imperative* and even *necessary* to please the Lord. To see this point all we have to do is to ask a simple question. What is the alternative of not pleasing the Lord? Jesus said, "If anyone does not abide in me he is thrown away like a branch and withers; and the branches are gathered, thrown into the fire, and burned. If you abide in me, and my words abide in you, ask whatever you wish, and it will be done for you" (John 15:6-7). There are only two possibilities: to abide in Christ and bear much fruit, or to be thrown away like a branch to be burned. It is either heaven or hell. Either we are for Christ or against Him. There is nothing in between. If we do not please the Lord, we are under God's wrath. So much is at stake! It is important—it is absolutely necessary to please God.

It Is Desirable

It is also assumed, then, that pleasing the Lord is a very much *desirable* thing. The most obvious reasons are given in the verse itself: "for whoever would draw near to God must believe that he exists and that he rewards those who seek him." If the God of the Bible exists, who created the heavens and the earth and is the Lord over all, and if He delights in rewarding those who draw near to Him, what can be more

165

desirable than to please Him? Some of us who are parents know what it is like to be delighted with our children—how it opens up our hearts with such generosity and warmth! We can only imagine what can flow out of God's infinite bounteousness when He is delighted with us! And that is exactly what Jesus told us: "If you abide in me, and my words abide in you, ask whatever you wish, and it will be done for you" (John 15:7). Pleasing God is most desirable because it does not just get us out of God's wrath but also places us in God's magnanimous favor.

It Is Nevertheless Possible

And finally and most importantly it is assumed that it is nevertheless *possible* to please the Lord. This is indeed good news, isn't it? But how can we please the Lord? We have established that this most desirable thing, this most urgent and important thing, is also a most impossible thing. Surely, for a sinner to please a holy God is more difficult than for a camel to go through the eye of a needle! The Word of God affirms that it is impossible by any other means—except by faith.

What is it about faith that even a sinner can please God?

What Does It Mean To Exercise Christian Faith?

Faith is more than an act of intellectual assent. The element of intellectual assent must be there in faith. For we cannot just believe without knowing what it is that we believe. But faith does not stop at knowing. It is an act of personal trust.

Here is an illustration that you may have heard of. An acrobat once tied a rope across Niagara Falls and, in front of a huge crowd, performed the amazing feat of walking on the rope across the falls and back. And he did not just walk on the rope. He did front flips and back flips and dazzled the crowd gathered there. When he got off the rope, the crowd cheered and roared with admiration. After bowing in acknowledgment he tied a chair on his back and asked the crowd, "Do you think I can carry a person on my back and walk across?" The crowd cheered with resounding affirmation. Then he asked for a volunteer from the crowd. The crowd suddenly became silent. No one dared to volunteer.

This shows what it means to have faith. It is not just to admire the acrobat's skills. It is to *trust* him enough to get into that chair on his back and stake one's life on it. What honors a person more than that kind of trust? Faith is a personal trust of that nature and magnitude.

But there is still more to the Christian faith. Trusting in the Lord is not for an idle, acrobatic entertainment, is it? Going across Niagara Falls is not a matter of mere intellectual curiosity or adventure. The cliff we are standing on is the Cliff of Human Mortality. It is about to crumble down into the falls of divine wrath and judgment. In order to live, we must cross the falls on the tight rope of perfect obedience. There is absolutely no other way. We see in front of us those who dare to cross the falls. They are falling off the rope left and right, swallowed whole by the thundering torrent of God's righteous wrath. And we realize that we can do no better. Drunk with sin, our vision is blurry, our hands shaky, and our legs hopelessly wobbly. To venture out would be an act of utter foolishness, quixotic beyond measure.

Christ extends His nail-pierced hands toward us and offers His scourged back. He promises to carry us safely across to the other side. Can we take that offer without fully accepting two facts—our utter inability to do it ourselves and Christ's complete ability to do so? This should be no-brainer. But many find it most difficult. Why? For the same reason that we consider driving ourselves safer than taking a flight, only because *we* are in control!

But with what can we impress God? Our intelligence? Our degrees and accomplishments? Our wealth? Our fame? What do we have that we have not received from Him? We can see why nothing other than our humble faith can please God and how, without it, we cannot please Him. We should also see why our lack of faith would offend God so much. It is not that God delights in humiliating us unjustly and unduly. It is that our faith acknowledges and conforms to the dual *truth*: our utter inability to save ourselves and God's total competence to do so. Our faith rightly, justly, and duly honors God.

Enoch's Faith

We can see the foundational importance of such faith. Whatever we do without it will lead to pride and arrogance, denying the full, dual truth. That is why it is so fascinating to see what the Hebrews writer, under divine inspiration, does here. In Genesis 5 we read, "Enoch *walked* with God after he fathered Methuselah 300 years and had other sons and daughters. Thus all the days of Enoch were 365 years. Enoch *walked* with God, and he was not, for God took him" (Genesis 5:22-24). Twice (verses 22, 24) we are told that Enoch walked with God. "The Hebrew phrase 'to walk with God' is expressive of a close intimacy and fellowship with God (Genesis 6:9)."[19] To walk is also a metaphor for the way one conducts himself (e.g., "Blessed is the man who walks not in the counsel of the wicked…" [Psalm 1:1]).

> Christ extends His nail-pierced hands toward us and offers His scourged back. He promises to carry us safely across to the other side. Can we take that offer without fully accepting two facts—our utter inability to do it ourselves and Christ's complete ability to do so? This should be no-brainer. But many find it most difficult. Why? For the same reason that we consider driving ourselves safer than taking a flight, only because *we* are in control!

So, reading the Genesis account, one may think that Enoch was a righteous person in his own right. The Hebrews writer shatters such thinking when he says, "*By faith* Enoch was taken up…, having pleased God." It was not by his works but by faith. Not that he did nothing but believe. His faith motivated him to walk with God, to order his life in such a way that it would be a continual fellowship with God. But his faith was not in *himself* as a good and moral person. His faith was *in God* who exists and rewards those who seek Him. (The language of God "rewarding" may cause some to think that Enoch somehow deserved it. Not so. To whom does the Lord give the reward? To those who fulfill the Law on their own? No! To those who seek *Him* as their reward! This language highlights just how great God's generosity really is to reward

---

19 Peter T. O'Brien, *The Letter to the Hebrews*. PNTC (Grand Rapids: Eerdmans 2010), pp. 404-405.

us for what we ought to have done anyway [Luke 17:10], for our acts of faith in Him regardless of how feeble and imperfect they are.)

What We Must Believe—According To Abel And Enoch

This leads to *what* we must believe. The answer is given clearly. "Whoever would draw near to God must believe that He exists and that He rewards those who seek Him"(verse 6). Does this seem too generic? According to v. 6, many could qualify—they don't even have to be Christians! Even those of other religions seek their gods because they believe that their gods exist and that they reward those that seek them!

But we must remember that this verse is not to be taken in isolation. It comes after 10 chapters (214 verses) that precede it! And the author has affirmed again and again in no uncertain terms that Jesus Christ is the only Mediator between sinners and a holy God, the only Great High Priest who alone can usher us into the presence of God! And it is only because of Jesus that we can draw near to God and expect His reward instead of His punishment. Only by being washed by His precious blood and dressed in His righteousness alone can we ever hope to please God! And it is by faith we receive all such blessings in Jesus Christ.

And what God did for Enoch testifies to us that our eternal life in heaven is the ultimate reward for those who by faith please God. This becomes all the more poignant when we look at Abel's life and Enoch's in juxtaposition, as presented in Hebrews.

We observe that they both pleased God because they both were commended by God—Abel as righteous (verse 4) and Enoch as having pleased God (verse 5). And if it was by faith that they were commended by God, then they were commended as righteous on the same ground— the perfect righteousness of Jesus Christ, the promised Seed of the woman, who was the ultimate object of their faith.

But the way their earthly lives ended could not be more different! Abel was murdered by his own brother. Enoch did not even taste death because God took him up to heaven before he died (verse 5)! How could

God consign Abel to such a tragic end? Some may ask, "What is the point of pleasing God? What if God has ordained my life to be like Abel's instead of Enoch's?"

Interestingly, Enoch's life answers that question, doesn't it? It is because this world is not all there is! Enoch was taken up from this world to heaven. Heaven is our final, eternal abode, not this world! So John Owen exhorts us, "They must walk with God here who design to live with him hereafter, or they must please God in this world who would be blessed with him in another." And Owen goes on to encourage us in our faith when he adds:

> That faith which can translate a man out of this world, can carry him through the difficulties which he may meet withal in the profession of faith and obedience in this world—herein lies the apostle's argument. And this latter, the Lord Jesus Christ hath determined to be the lot and portion of his disciples. So he testifies, John 17:15: 'I pray not that thou shouldest take them out of the world; but that thou shouldest keep them from the evil.' [20]

Following Jesus, The Resurrection And The Life

Only two in the entire history of man were translated from this world to heaven without dying—Enoch and Elijah. Even Jesus Himself died before He was raised up to heaven in His resurrected body. Whatever question we may have about God's dealings with Abel, it is ultimately answered in Jesus' death and resurrection. For no one pleased God more than Jesus, God's only begotten Son. Yet God allowed Jesus to die on the cross for the redemption of sinners. How can we complain that we, being sinners, should suffer in any way, even unjustly at times for the sake of the gospel? After being released from prison, Peter and John rejoiced that "they were counted worthy to suffer dishonor for the name" (Acts 5:41). We suffer for the sake of Christ when we endure our trials with patience and by faith show the surpassing value of possessing God as our inheritance.

20 John Owen, *An Exposition of the Epistle to the Hebrews with Preliminary Exercitations* (Edinburgh: Johnstone and Hunters, 1854, Amazon Kindle Edition), vol. 7, location 793.

Jesus said, "I am the resurrection and the life. Whoever believes in me, though he die, yet shall he live, and everyone who lives and believes in me shall never die. Do you believe this" (John 11:25-26)? Enoch and Elijah were the forerunners of those who will be alive when Christ shall return and enter into heaven without seeing death. Some may see the return of Christ before they die. But most of us will die before then. What then? May we confess with the Apostle Paul, "[I]t is my eager expectation and hope that I will not be at all ashamed, but that with full courage now as always Christ will be honored in my body, whether by life or by death. For to me to live is Christ, and to die is gain" (Philippians 1:20-21).

The Rich Privilege Of Pleasing God

Is this all about sacrifice on our part? Of course not! We know what it is like to be able to please someone we love and care for, don't we? At times we realize that it is more pleasurable to please someone else than to be pleased—as it is more blessed to give than to receive. So, when we find a perfect gift for someone we love, we can't wait till we give it to that person, till we see that face of surprise and delight!

What a privilege it is, then, that we are able to please the almighty and holy God! It cannot be a burden and it must not be considered as such! This is so, all the more, when we consider that this almighty and holy God is the One who took the first initiative to please us—not in a way that gratifies the sinful desires of our flesh but satisfies the deepest and noblest longings of our hearts that are restless until they find their rest in Him! To do that, God did not spare any expense, not even the ultimate cost of sacrificing His only begotten Son! And what did our Lord Jesus do, who translated Enoch out of this world into heaven so that he should not see death? By incarnation He translated Himself out of heaven into this world so that He might taste death on our behalf! What wondrous love is this! And our God is ever ready to be pleased with our faith, however small and weak, and with our humble service that flows from it.

If something is worth believing, it is worth giving our all. Is Christ worth living for and dying for? Is Christ worth doing what is good and true and beautiful no matter what the cost? Is Christ worth putting away our sins that give us ever diminishing returns? Surely, Christ is worth our all in a most deserving way! So then, let us place our faith in Him and live by faith to please our wonderful God! Let us not just praise Him and admire Him from afar with our lips! Let us get into the chair on His scourged back and trust Him to carry us safely across the falls of divine judgment! Let us not grow weary but be courageous in doing good, no matter how difficult, since our goal in life is not to live as long and comfortably as it is possible in this world but to walk with God in this world so that we may rest in Him forever in heaven! And let us be daring in our faith as we seek His kingdom and His righteousness by prayer and by good deeds, knowing that our God exists and He rewards those who seek Him!

Mount Sinai And Mount Zion

[12] Therefore lift your drooping hands and strengthen your weak knees, [13] and make straight paths for your feet, so that what is lame may not be put out of joint but rather be healed. [14] Strive for peace with everyone, and for the holiness without which no one will see the Lord. [15] See to it that no one fails to obtain the grace of God; that no "root of bitterness" springs up and causes trouble, and by it many become defiled; [16] that no one is sexually immoral or unholy like Esau, who sold his birthright for a single meal. [17] For you know that afterward, when he desired to inherit the blessing, he was rejected, for he found no chance to repent, though he sought it with tears.

[18] For you have not come to what may be touched, a blazing fire and darkness and gloom and a tempest [19] and the sound of a trumpet and a voice whose words made the hearers beg that no further messages be spoken to them. [20] For they could not endure the order that was given, "If even a beast touches the mountain, it shall be stoned." [21] Indeed, so terrifying was the sight that Moses said, "I tremble with fear." [22] But you have come to Mount Zion and to the city of the living God, the heavenly Jerusalem, and to innumerable angels in festal gathering, [23] and to the assembly of the firstborn who are enrolled in heaven, and to God, the judge of all, and to the spirits of the righteous made perfect, [24] and to Jesus, the mediator of a new covenant, and to the sprinkled blood that speaks a better word than the blood of Abel.

[25] See that you do not refuse him who is speaking. For if they did not escape when they refused him who warned them on earth, much less will we escape if we reject him who warns from heaven. [26] At that time his voice shook the earth, but now he has promised, "Yet once more I will shake not only the earth but also the heavens." [27] This phrase, "Yet once more," indicates the removal of things that are shaken—that is, things that have been made—in order that the things that cannot be shaken may remain. [28] Therefore let us be

grateful for receiving a kingdom that cannot be shaken, and thus let us offer to God acceptable worship, with reverence and awe, [29] for our God is a consuming fire.
Hebrews 12:12-29

The Hebrews author puts before you two mountains—Mount Sinai and Mount Zion.

Of course, Mount Sinai is not explicitly mentioned in this passage. However, it is obvious that the mountain described in verses 18-21 is Mount Sinai. When the people of Israel came out of Egypt and arrived at Mount Sinai, God descended upon that mountain to enter into covenant with them. The manner in which God came down upon Mount Sinai is described in Exodus 19:16: "On the morning of the third day there were thunders and lightnings and a thick cloud on the mountain and a very loud trumpet blast, so that all the people in the camp trembled." As you can see, this is what is described in verses 18-21.

Mount Zion, on the other hand, is identified with Jerusalem, "the city of David (2 Samuel 5:9; 1 Chronicles 11:7; 2 Chronicles 5); even the temple."[21]

Mount Sinai and Mount Zion are arguably the two most important mountains in the history of redemption. Interestingly, the two came to be important for contrasting reasons. Mount Sinai was in the wilderness while Mount Zion was in the promised land; Mount Sinai was temporarily transformed into a holy mountain when God came down upon it in His glory cloud while Mount Zion was chosen as a place of God's (more or less) permanent dwelling among His people; no one could approach Mount Sinai, except Moses, while the people of Israel lived on Mount Zion, upon which the city of Jerusalem was situated.

---

21 A.R. Fausset, *Fausset's Bible Dictionary*, "Zion." (http://www.bible-history.com/faussets/Z/Zion/).

Two Mountains, Two Choices

Why does the author of the Hebrews mention these two mountains? He is not interested in simply giving history lessons on the importance of these two mountains. He argues that one must be abandoned for the sake of the other, that only one is the proper destination of the people of God and not the other. "For you have not come to what may be touched [i.e., Mount Sinai].... But you have come to Mount Zion..." (verses 18, 22).

But we quickly realize that what is in view here is not the physical mountains. Notice how Mount Zion is identified as "the city of the living God, the *heavenly* Jerusalem" (verse 22).

This makes sense, doesn't it? Think about the occasion of this book. The author was writing to Christians, whether Jews or Gentiles or both, who were contemplating going back to Judaism. That is why he has been demonstrating Jesus' superiority over all things, particularly over the elements of Old Testament Judaism. If the author were talking about the physical mountains only, nothing would be wrong with them going back to Judaism. For in going back to Judaism, they would be going to (the physical) Mount Zion, where the (physical) temple was located, with its Old Testament priesthood and animal sacrifices. But that is precisely what the author is telling them not to do!

But you may ask, "What does all this have to do with me? I am certainly not thinking of going back to Old Testament Judaism!" Very true, and I am glad! However, what the author says is eminently applicable even for us. We can see this when we see the true nature of the comparison and contrast he is giving.

What is the essence of the contrast between the two? According to the Hebrews writer, Mount Sinai represents what is earthly ("what may be touched," verse 18). Mount Zion, on the other hand, represents what is heavenly ("the city of the living God, the *heavenly* Jerusalem," "innumerable *angels* in festal gathering," "the assembly of the firstborn who are enrolled *in heaven*," verses 22-23). This earthly-heavenly contrast is made explicit in verse 25: "For if they did not escape when they refused him who warned them on earth [i.e., Mount Sinai], much less will we escape if we reject him who warns from heaven [i.e., Mount Zion]."

Seen in this light, we see how applicable this contrast is to us. After all, what is the fundamenal struggle in our Christian life? Wouldn't you agree that it is the choice between heaven and earth, between the blessings and glories and joys of heaven and those of earth? That is why the Hebrews author has been emphasizing our Christian life as a life of faith and faith as "the substance of things hoped for and the evidence of things not seen" (Hebrews 11:1, KJV).

What our choice should be between the heavenly and the earthly is obvious. What is earthly is temporary, fleeting, transient, short-lived as well as fallen, defiled, marred, and broken. In our passage, the author presents the transiency of the earthly as "shakable" (verses 26-27). At Mount Sinai, God only shook the earth. But there is yet to come another day of shaking. When that day comes, the whole universe will be shaken ("not only the earth but also the heavens," verse 26). And once this shaking is done, those things that are shakable will be removed while the things that cannot be shaken will remain.

The Empty Allure Of What Can Be Touched And Seen

Then why are we drawn to what is temporary and shakable?

Because these things of Mount Sinai may be touched (verse 18). These are the things we can see with our eyes and touch with our hands. They are immediately accessible to our senses. So we associate what is real with what is tangible. The things that may be touched have the lure of immediate gratification.

Yet a moment's reflection can show that there is more to what is real than just what is tangible. Much of our conduct and thought is actually determined by things that are invisible and immaterial—such as our sense of right and wrong, good and evil, just and unjust, etc. There are many things we will not allow ourselves to do simply because we believe them to be wrong, even though we may have the freedom and ability to do them. It may be visiting certain websites, buying certain magazines, trying certain illegal drugs, or trying a hand at shoplifting, etc. Though fallen, we still have an inner moral compass, however imperfect it may be. They say that, even in prison, certain criminals must be separated from other inmates. Why? Because their crimes are considered so heinous and repulsive that other inmates may take justice into their own (criminal) hands!

And how about our inner need to "keep up with the Joneses"? Do we want what others have because it is good or simply because others have it and we don't (because the grass looks greener on the other side)? If so, can we say that that invisible thing that drives us to keep up with the Joneses—whether it is simply our greed or insecurity or inferiority complex—is less real than the thing itself?

But here is the problem with Mount Sinai, with the things that may be touched. Though they seem to be immediately available to us, we cannot attain the full possession of them. This is powerfully demonstrated in the description of Israel's Mount Sinai experience. Though they came to what may be *touched* (verse 18), they were given a dire warning: "If even a beast *touches* the mountain, it shall be stoned" (verse 20).

Look back on your life and think of the things you once wanted more than anything at that time. Were you able to buy them or get them? What did it feel like to finally get them? But how long did that sense of bliss last? And where are those things now? Do you still have them? If so, do they still possess the glow of allure for you? The moment we attain something of this world, a greater void is created. We realize that what we really wanted was more than what we are holding in our hands. So we pursue even better and greater things. But it doesn't take long to discover that these things yield ever-diminishing returns.

The Limitations Of The Law

But, of course, what is ultimately in view here is not the treasures of this earth. Mount Sinai represents the utter impossibility of the fallen man to have access to God by the works of the Law. After all, Mount Sinai is where the Law was given. This is definitely in view, although our passage does not explicitly mention the Law in association with Mount Sinai. After all, what were the "*words* [of God that] made the hearers beg that no further messages be spoken to them" (verse 19)? According to Exodus 20, those were the words of the Ten Commandments, which God spoke to them from Mount Sinai in the midst of "a blazing fire and darkness and gloom and a tempest and the sound of a trumpet." In fact, the Ten Commandments are referred to in Hebrew as "the Ten *Words*" (Exodus 34:28).

This is the very tension that characterized what happened at Mount Sinai. Mount Sinai was the place of covenant ratification. There God and Israel entered into covenant relationship—for God to be *their* God and Israel to be *His* people. And yet the people were forbidden from approaching the mountain upon which God descended. They were not allowed to enter into the presence of God!

This was to show the limitations of the Law. The Law is good and righteous and holy. But it cannot make us good and righteous and holy—even with all of its clear stipulations of what to do and what not to do, with all of its promises of blessings for obedience and its threats of curses for disobedience. Instead, the heart that is defiled by sin "uses God's good commandment for its own evil purposes" (Romans 7:13, NLT). If this is true of the Law of God, how much worse are the systems of morality and ethics devised by men in various other religions and civic societies?

No wonder that what dominates the description of the Mount Sinai incident is gloom and fear and trembling and separation! How horrible it would have been if that were all there was to true religion?

But that was not the case, praise God! The Apostle Paul says in Galatians 3:19 that the Law was *added* to the gracious promise of God. Why? So that the Law could expose how truly sinful we are and highlight our desperate need for a Savior. It was designed to tear us away from all the illusions about our own righteousness and goodness. It was designed to thrust us to the throne of God's grace and induce us to beg for His mercy. It was designed to drive us to Christ our only Redeemer. Indeed, it was designed to move us on to Mount Zion, "the city of the living God, the heavenly Jerusalem" (verse 22)! If so, how foolish it was for the Christians at that time to go back to Mount Sinai, to Old Testament Judaism, to the administration of law and works-righteousness!

The True Mount Zion

Now consider the description of Mount Zion. What characterizes it is not separation but union. At Mount Sinai, the people were forbidden from entering the mountain of God's presence. Not so with Mount Zion, the city of the living God. There in the heavenly Jerusalem are found innumerable angels in their festal gathering along with the redeemed people of God ("the assembly of the firstborn who are enrolled in heaven"). The union of these two groups provides a shocking contrast to what happened at Mount Sinai. The angels took part in what happened at Mount Sinai (Deuteronomy 33:2). Both Stephen and Paul speak of the Law as delivered by angels (Acts 7:38, 53; Galatians 3:19). That means, at Mount Sinai, the people of Israel were separated not only from God but also from the holy angels. But on Mount Zion, the two are joined together in a great assembly! What is more, they dwell together in the presence of God, the judge of all (verse 23) and Jesus, the Mediator of a new covenant (verse 24).

together in a great assembly! What is more, they dwell together in the presence of God, the judge of all (verse 23) and Jesus, the Mediator of a new covenant (verse 24).

Mount Zion is also a place of great joy. The angels' gathering is described as "festal," a gathering of joyful celebration. This is true in greater measure of human beings. They are referred to as "the assembly of the firstborn who are enrolled in heaven" (verse 23). "The reference [to them as 'the assembly'] sustains the note of joy and fellowship in worship introduced with verse 22b ['innumerable angels in festal gathering'] and indicates that the redeemed take their place in the festive assembly at Zion."[22] They take part in this great celebration as "the firstborn"— referring to their adoption as sons of God! In fact, we who are redeemed by the blood of Jesus Christ are brought nearer to God in kinship than the holy angels of God, as God's true sons (Hebrews 12:7)! And we are "enrolled in heaven"—that is, our names are recorded in the Book of Life—yes, in the genealogical record of the family of God as His sons and daughters! So, then, how much greater should be our celebration as the redeemed of the Lord!

Interestingly, however, God is described as "the judge of all" (verse 23). This title is not so festive, is it? For it reminds us of the punishment we deserve as sinners. But we can see why this title of God is highlighted in this passage. It is to show the surpassing greatness of our redemption. For this fearful title is followed by "and to the spirits of the righteous made perfect"! Do you see it? So perfect and so secure is our union with God that we don't have to squirm at the mention of God as the Judge of all! Why? Because we are made righteous and perfected in righteousness. How so? By Jesus Christ, the Mediator of a new covenant and His efficacious blood (verse 24)!

A Two-Fold Application

There is a two-fold application of the message that we find here.

---

22 William L. Lane, *Hebrews 9-13* WBC (Dallas: Word Books 1991), vol. 47b, p. 468.

1. <u>The Gospel Is Not To Be Taken Lightly</u>: "See that you do not refuse him who is speaking. For if they did not escape when they refused him who warned them on earth, much less will we escape if we reject him who warns from heaven" (verse 25). The logic here is very simple, isn't it? If the sin of rejecting the Law of God was bad, how much worse is the sin of rejecting the grace of God? If the sin of dismissing the *promise* of God was bad, how much worse is the sin of dismissing the glorious *fulfillment* of His promise in Jesus Christ? If God gave us His only begotten Son in the new covenant (verse 24), what more or better things can God give us? Even for the omnipotent God, that would be impossible! So utterly and detrimentally foolish it would be, therefore, to leave Christ because God did not give us this or that in this world!

2. <u>The Things That Truly Matter Are Secure</u>: Do not be discouraged by the adversities and trials you face in this world. Rather, rejoice that your name is inscribed indelibly in the Book of Life, in the palm of His hand! Your hope is not anchored in what may be touched, Mount Sinai. Your hope is grounded in Mount Zion, the city of the living God, the heavenly Jerusalem! "Therefore lift your drooping hands and strengthen your weak knees, and make straight paths for your feet, so that what is lame may not be put out of joint but rather be healed" (Hebrews 12:12-13)! Let us not act like our life is over because our wish has not come true and what we cherish in this world has been lost. All those things that are of this world will be shaken on that final day. They will not remain anyway! We belong to Mount Zion. What we possess in Jesus Christ—our eternal life in Jesus Christ, God's eternal love for us in Jesus Christ, every spiritual blessing in the heavenly places in Christ Jesus, and God Himself as our eternal inheritance—can never be lost. They will remain forever, grace upon grace, from glory to glory!

Looking Away From Self, To Christ

I would like to conclude today's message with an excerpt from Spurgeon:

The Christian views his evidences from the top of Sinai, and grows alarmed concerning his salvation; it were better far if he read his title by the light of Calvary [i.e., Mount Zion]. "Why," saith he, "my faith has unbelief in it, it is not able to save me." Suppose he had considered *the object* of his faith instead of his faith, then he would have said, "There is no failure in *him*, and therefore I am safe." He sighs over his hope: "Ah! my hope is marred and dimmed by an anxious carefulness about present things; how can I be accepted?" Had he regarded *the ground* of his hope, he would have seen that the promise of God standeth sure, and that whatever our doubts may be, the oath and promise never fail. Ah! believer, it is safer always for you to be led of the Spirit into gospel liberty than to wear legal fetters. Judge yourself at what *Christ* is rather than at what *you* are.[23]

This is not to say that what we do doesn't matter, whether we believe or not believe. What is Spurgeon urging us to do? To look to Christ as the unfailing object of our faith, as the ground of our hope! To look to Christ like that—isn't that what a saving faith does, however weak it may be? And we must look to Christ and not turn away in despair and disbelief!

We may say that Mount Sinai represents us—our (vain) attempt at self-righteousness, at earning God's approval; our desire for the things of this world as the ground of our self-worth and happiness. Mount Zion represents Christ in all His sufficiency for us in this life and in the age to come. Why would we go back to ourselves? Have we not seen enough of our failures and brokenness? Let us run to Christ, to Mount Zion! And if we have come to Mount Zion, let us abide there, where there will be unceasing festivity forever, where we will rejoice with a joy inexpressible without ending, where God and angels and the redeemed people of God will be joined together in a celebration of eternal gladness!

---

23 Charles H. Spurgeon, Morning and Evening: Daily Readings by C.H. Spurgeon. (Edinburgh: Christian Focus Publications 2014), p. 525.

"I Rejoice In My Sufferings For Your Sake"

[1:24] Now I rejoice in my sufferings for your sake, and in my flesh I am filling up what is lacking in Christ's afflictions for the sake of his body, that is, the church, [25] of which I became a minister according to the stewardship from God that was given to me for you, to make the word of God fully known, [26] the mystery hidden for ages and generations but now revealed to his saints. [27] To them God chose to make known how great among the Gentiles are the riches of the glory of this mystery, which is Christ in you, the hope of glory. [28] Him we proclaim, warning everyone and teaching everyone with all wisdom, that we may present everyone mature in Christ. [29] For this I toil, struggling with all his energy that he powerfully works within me.

[2:1] For I want you to know how great a struggle I have for you and for those at Laodicea and for all who have not seen me face to face, [2] that their hearts may be encouraged, being knit together in love, to reach all the riches of full assurance of understanding and the knowledge of God's mystery, which is Christ, [3] in whom are hidden all the treasures of wisdom and knowledge.

Colossians 1:24-2:3

"I rejoice in my sufferings for your sake...." Do you have anyone who loves you enough to *suffer* for you? Do you have anyone who loves you enough to *rejoice* in his/her suffering*s* for your sake—not just in a one-time suffering but in *many* sufferings? How blessed are those who have someone like that in their lives, someone to say to them with all sincerity, "I rejoice in my sufferings for your sake!" Someone who will stand by you no matter what. Not just in times of your success and victory. But also in times of your failure, even in times of your sufferings for wrongdoing. How cold and bleak is life when we don't have anyone like that!

Let's also turn it around and ask ourselves, "Do I have anyone whom I love enough to suffer for him? Do I love anyone enough to consider it my joy to suffer for her sake?" Maybe it is more tragic to have no one of whom to say what the Apostle Paul said to the Colossians—no one to love deeply, no one to say with all of our heart, "I rejoice in my sufferings for your sake…." Paraphrasing what our Lord said (Acts 20:35), we can say, "It is more blessed to love than to be loved." Think about this. We don't get happy because just *anybody* loves us. We get happy when someone *we* love and value loves us back. Even in being loved, our love matters much.

If we have no one to love deeply, maybe it is not because we lack the people to love. Maybe it is because our hearts are cold—like the bare, frozen garden of the selfish giant in a children's story, which was always winter because the selfish giant didn't want to share it with anyone else. That's the tragedy of it—a heart that cannot love. Who is truly rich? Someone with a lot of money or someone with a few true friends to love? I pray that God would make us rich with many true friends. Even more so, I pray that God would make each of us a true friend to many and make us truly rich among men. In fact, I pray that God would make us realize how rich we are already because we belong to Christ our truest Friend and to His church!

Paul's Joy To Suffer For His Beloved

Listen to Paul's words to the Colossians: "*I rejoice* in my sufferings for your sake…." There was no doubt that the Colossians were blessed to have someone like Paul to love them and to love them as he did. What did Paul say? He declared that *his* was the joy because *he* suffered for their sake! The joy was *his* because *he* had someone to suffer gladly for! No doubt he lived the words of Christ that it is more blessed to give than to receive (Acts 20:35)!

It is easy to see throughout the whole passage how intense Paul's love *for the Colossians* was. In this short passage of nine verses he says his sufferings were for them four times: "for your sake" (1:24); "for the sake of his body, that is, the church" (1:24); "the stewardship from God that was given to me *for you*" (1:25); "I want you to know how great a struggle I have *for you* and *for those* at Laodicea and *for all…*" (2:1).

What is even more amazing is the fact that Paul had not even seen them in person (2:1)! We say, "Out of sight, out of mind." This is true even of our friends and families. "A close neighbor is better than a distant relative." There is a world of difference between praying for the missionaries we have met and known and for those we have not. How impressive, then, was Paul's love for the Colossians whom he had never met! The Colossian church was not founded by Paul. It was most likely founded by Epaphras (1:7), an associate of Paul's. But as an Apostle appointed for Gentile missions (1:25), his concern extended beyond the churches he himself planted. He was deeply concerned with *all* the Gentile converts and cared for them greatly.

We can also easily observe how *costly* Paul's love for the Colossians was: "my *sufferings*" (1:24); "I am filling up what is lacking in Christ's *afflictions*" (1:24); "for this I *toil, struggling* [that is, laboring intensely] with all his energy that he powerfully works within me" (1:29); "for I want you to know how great a *struggle* I have…" (2:1). But *how* did he suffer specifically *for them*?

We know that he suffered for the Colossians through his prayers. He was extremely glad to hear of their conversion. Since then, he had not ceased to give thanks to God for them and pray for their welfare and growth (1:4, 9). We know how "labor-intensive" prayer can be—to pray for others consistently and persistently when there are so many people to pray for and so many other things that demand our attention. Yet Paul gladly labored for them in his prayers.

We don't know how else Paul "suffered" specifically for the Colossians. Other than his prayers, Paul doesn't specify. But this much is clear from what we can glean from this letter. Just like a soldier on the front line of the battle who bravely faces suffering and death on account of his beloved family and country, so did Paul face the afflictions that came his way. Paul did what he did, first and foremost, for the glory of his Savior and Lord. But he knew glorifying Christ could not be separated from serving Christ's people. He worked tirelessly to preach the gospel throughout the world. He was met with all kinds of obstacles and threats in doing so. He was mocked and ridiculed. He was flogged and thrown into prison. He was even stoned by the enemies of the gospel. There were people who vowed never to eat or drink again until they killed him (Acts 23:12). But he did not give up his gospel ministry, especially to the Gentiles. He kept his faith and did not stop fighting the good fight for the gospel because he was not ignorant of the impact of his life and ministry, or the failure thereof—how damaging it would be for the Christian community if he should bring shame to the gospel by cowardice and unfaithfulness.

Amazing Love For Gentiles

Paul's love for the Colossians was all the more amazing when we consider that they were Gentiles in the flesh (1:28). We know how intense and deep and long-lasting ethnic-racial conflicts can be. There are many areas in the world in which ethnic hostilities have existed for hundreds and thousands of years. And they don't show any sign of stopping any time soon. From the biblical perspective, however, the greatest of them all was the Jew-Gentile conflict in the Old Testament. We all know about the antagonistic relationship between the Jews and the Gentiles at that time. Paul characterized it as enmity, being separated by "the dividing wall of hostility" (Ephesians 2:14).

The Jew-Gentile conflict was the greatest because it was ordained by God Himself, sanctioned by His law. It was designed to represent the conflict between the city of God and the city of man, between the kingdom of heaven and the kingdom of this world. Whatever conflict may exist among the nations and races, they are no more than in-house squabbles. Despite their conflicts, Gentiles were ultimately united together in rebellion against God and His kingdom (cf. Psalm 2:1-3). These national, racial conflicts were nothing in comparison to the depth of the Jew-Gentile conflict.

What would it take for Paul, a Jew and a Pharisee, to love these Gentiles this way? The Bible answers, nothing short of a new creation to end the present order of things and bring about a new one! So deeply did the Jew-Gentile conflict run that nothing less than a new creation could bring about its resolution! And that's exactly what happened in Jesus' death and resurrection—His resurrection being the beginning of a new heaven and a new earth in which there is neither Jew nor Greek (Galatians 3:28)!

Christ's Resurrection: The New Creation Set In Motion

This resurrection of Christ was not just a curious, rare oddity in history. It was truly a watershed, an event that changed the world forever. It was indeed the initiation of a new heaven and a new earth—not just in a metaphorical sense but in a true, historical sense. You may ask, How is that true? Even secular scholars will acknowledge the enormous religious, social, and even political impact that Christianity has had on world history. But that is hardly a new creation in the literal sense of the word, is it? The universe doesn't look that much different now than what it used to look like before the resurrection—the mountains and the rivers and the oceans look pretty much the same and the same laws of nature govern our physical universe as they have done since the creation. Where is this cosmic new creation?

What we have in the resurrection of Jesus Christ is the *inauguration* of the new creation, the intrusion of the power and life of heaven into this world order. There have been many invasions of heaven into this world throughout redemptive history. All the miracles were such invasions. All of God's supernatural revelation, such as His theophanic appearances and His words to the prophets, were such heavenly invasions as well. However, we can say that they were but preliminary forays that were launched in advance of the main invasion—namely, the resurrection of Jesus Christ. How so? The miracles accomplished only temporary results. Take healing for instance. We have no guarantee that those who were healed were never subject to other illnesses after their healing. We know for certain that all of them eventually succumbed to death and died, even those who were raised from the dead. These miracles were but fireworks of the supernatural in the darkness of the natural—*brilliant* in their glow but *short-lived* in their duration.

The resurrection of Jesus Christ was the decisive, main invasion from heaven, for which all other incursions were but previews. His resurrection was not just a spark which was quickly swallowed up again by the darkness of death. He was raised in His body unto eternal life, never to die again—"an empty grave is there [still] to prove [our] Savior lives" (as the song *Because He Lives* reminds us). Do you see? In this world of atrophy and death, a resurrection unto eternal life took place! Something that is completely foreign to this world is introduced and implanted.

The resurrection of Christ is like an irreparable puncture that is made to the massive dam of the natural realm—death. It may not be noticeable at the beginning. But the moment the puncture is made, the dam is so critically damaged that it is only a matter of time before the dam crumbles down! The dam of death has been irreparably punctured by the resurrection of Christ. It can no longer keep us within the confines of this world and this present age. An opening is made to the other side— to the kingdom of heaven, to the age to come, to eternal life. For now, the rippling effects of His resurrection are manifested in the inner new creation of individual believers, in our being born again from above. But a day is coming for the redemption of our bodies in the resurrection, as well as the cosmic renewal of the whole universe into a new heaven and a new earth!

A New Humanity

How is all this related to Paul's love for the Colossians? This new creation, inaugurated by Jesus' death and resurrection, has resulted in the creation of a new humanity, in which Jews and Gentiles are brought together in unity (Ephesians 2:15)!

This is what is referred to by "the mystery hidden for ages and generations but now revealed to his saints" (1:26). What is this mystery? Paul describes it this way in verse 27: "how great among the Gentiles are the riches of the glory of this mystery, which is Christ in you, the hope of glory." To put it simply, the mystery is the salvation of the Gentiles along with the Jews, the union between Jews and Gentiles.

This is not to say, of course, that the *idea* of Gentile salvation is brand new. It was clearly present in the Old Testament. Take a look at God's dealings with Abraham, the Father of the nation of Israel. God's blessings to him culminated with the promise to bless *all the families of the earth* in him (Genesis 12:2-3) and his Seed (22:18). And God changed his name from Abram ("exalted father") to Abraham ("father of a multitude of nations," Genesis 17:5) in order to signify this.

This aspect was buried under the Jew-Gentile conflict for ages and generations, under the rules and regulations concerning Israel's religious, ethnic purity. Israel had to be set apart from other nations in order to preserve the line of promise and ensure the coming of God's anointed One. The idea of Gentile salvation had to lie dormant until the Messiah came. The hidden mystery of God was *not* the *idea* of Gentile salvation; it was rather the *realization* of the promise in Christ Jesus. This is the background for Paul's affection for the Gentile Christians who were once his enemies.

But Jesus is not just a means through which this mystery is revealed. See how Paul further elaborates on the true essence of this mystery, what constitutes the "riches of the glory of this mystery": "Christ in you [i.e., Gentile Christians like the Colossians]" (1:27); "all the riches of full assurance of understanding and the knowledge of God's mystery, which is Christ, in whom are hidden all the treasures of wisdom and knowledge" (2:2-3). What is the mystery of God, which had been hidden for ages and was only lately revealed? Christ in us, who were once Gentiles in the flesh!

How marvelous is this mystery lately revealed—Christ in us! When we behold Christ's beauty and excellencies, we don't admire Him from a distance as spectators do at museums. Rather, we admire Him as *our* Redeemer and Lord! His beauty is the beauty of *our* Savior and Friend! His excellencies are the excellencies of *our* Redeemer and Lord! All of His beauty and excellencies are all the more beautiful and excellent because they are the glories of the One, who is in us as *our* Savior, *our* Lord, *our* strength, *our* life, *our* beauty, *our* excellencies! Oh, to think that He is all of that to us, who were once Gentiles in the flesh, having no hope and without God in the world!

189

From Deepest Hatred To Deepest Love

Paul was gripped by that reality, by that mystery of God in Christ Jesus! He knew that Christ's resurrection, the new creation commenced by it, brought about a radical change in the Jew-Gentile relationship, a new creation. This gospel grabbed a hold of him and made him an example of its awesome power. So you see Paul's profound affection for the Colossians. So you see the communion of deep affection between Paul and the Colossians. The dividing wall of hostility was broken down and completely leveled. The age-old enmity was removed.

The resurrection of Christ did not just neutralize the antagonistic relations, however. The dividing wall of hostility is replaced with the strong, firm bond of brotherly love. The age-long enmity is replaced with the kind of love we see in Paul for the Colossians. In Christ's death and resurrection, in this new creation, a deepest hatred is put to death and raised anew as a deepest love. Both Jews and Gentiles are born again as fellow citizens of the kingdom of heaven. Mortal enemies are made loyal friends, who would gladly suffer and die for one another. Discrimination is transformed into warm reception and self-sacrifice. Thus Paul, a Jew, rejoiced in his sufferings for the Colossians, who were once Gentiles—because He saw Christ in them!

But if we speak of the magnitude of Paul's love for the Colossians, it is only to highlight and magnify the surpassing love of Jesus Christ for sinners. Do not forget that Paul's affection for the Colossians was but a ripple, an echo, of Christ's love. Oh, how much greater must be the love of Christ for us, which drove Him to the cross to die in our place!

Paul's Ministry, In Union With Christ

So then, what does Paul mean when he says in verse 24, "in my flesh I am filling up what is lacking in Christ's afflictions for the sake of his body, that is, the church"? It doesn't mean that there is anything qualitatively deficient in Christ's affliction for our redemption. He declared on the cross, "It is *finished*!" (John 19:30) All of His affliction for the sins of His people was finished when He breathed His last and died on the cross. Nothing can add to His affliction for the forgiveness of our sins—not the labors of our hands, nor our zeal that knows no respite, nor our tears that flow forever without ceasing. All of Paul's suffering for the gospel could not add to the perfect efficacy of Christ's suffering for our sin.

But there is a kind of affliction we suffer *because* we are redeemed, because we are united with Christ. This kind of affliction is not punitive in nature—we do not suffer it as God's punishment for our sins. But we do suffer it as members of the body of Christ to build it up to its intended maturity and completeness. So Paul says in 1:28-2:3:

> Him we proclaim, warning everyone and teaching everyone with all wisdom, that we may present everyone mature in Christ. For this I toil, struggling with all his energy that he powerfully works within me. For I want you to know how great a struggle I have for you and for those at Laodicea and for all who have not seen me face to face, that their hearts may be encouraged, being knit together in love, to reach all the riches of full assurance of understanding and the knowledge of God's mystery, which is Christ, in whom are hidden all the treasures of wisdom and knowledge.

Paul's afflictions were not to bring about our forgiveness of sins; his afflictions were about building up the body of Christ to a fuller maturity, both in number and faith. Again, we must not forget that Paul's suffering and labor were a part of Christ's own work of building up the body of Christ. We are told in 1:22 that Christ is working to present us holy and blameless and above reproach before God. In fact, Paul said, "For this I toil, struggling with *all his energy that he powerfully works within me*" (1:29). We can see it reflected in Paul as he proclaims Christ, warning everyone and teaching everyone with all wisdom, that we may present everyone mature in Christ (1:28). We see here Paul's ministry in union with Christ's.

So then, if Paul was able to rejoice in his sufferings for the Colossians, it was because Christ rejoiced in His sufferings for us. Michael Card sang, "And why did they nail His feet and hands? His love would have held Him there!" Surely, it was not the nails that kept the almighty Son of God up on the cross, was it? Even if the Roman soldiers and the Jews repented and "unnailed" Him, He would not have come down until He shed every drop of His blood and water. For He went up there voluntarily, knowing that without His sacrificial love there would be no salvation for us. And He did it with joy. "For the *joy* that was set before him [he] endured the cross, despising the shame..." (Hebrews 12:2). We have seen how such rejoicing in suffering is impossible without a great love. And oh, how great His love was that the holy and righteous One should lay down His life for such worms as we!

Christ was able to rejoice in His sufferings also because He knew His sufferings for us would not be in vain. His death would procure our full reconciliation with God and He would be raised from the dead to usher in the kingdom of eternal life. Oh, how He must have rejoiced to see us fully pardoned, fully made holy, blameless and above reproach through His work of redemption! Paul was given the privilege of participating in that work, which cannot fail. No matter how great his afflictions were, Paul was able to rejoice because he knew that his labor was not in vain (1 Corinthians 15:58), because he possessed Christ's joy in his union with Christ.

Don't you want to know this joy of Christ? Christ rejoiced in all of His sufferings for us. He suffered all that He did so we can rejoice as He did—rejoice even in our sufferings! We may feel sad because no one seems to rejoice in his sufferings for us, let alone care for us. But can we be so dejected when we have Christ as our true Friend, who rejoiced in His sufferings for us? It's so wonderful to have such a Friend who loves us so. But I dare say there is a deeper joy—the joy He experienced as He suffered for us. Oh, how deep Christ's joy must have been if it enabled Him to endure the infinite wrath of God on the cross! This joy of Christ we will not know unless we are willing to suffer for others as Christ did for us.

Suffering For One Another's Sake

Let us not forget that all of us who are members of the body of Christ are given the privilege of taking part in the work of Christ, which cannot fail. Regardless of success or failure we can rejoice in our struggle and labor for our Lord and His church. For our labor is not in vain in Christ. God, who sees in secret, will greatly reward us for our deeds of service unto Him. How wonderful this is when being able to do something for another is a reward in itself! So then, look around to see who might need your work of service, your sacrifice, your forgiveness, your humility, your encouragement! Let us start with those that are near and dear to us (while certainly not stopping with them, for even Gentiles and tax collectors know how to love their own)! As we do things for them, let us not do it in a grumbling spirit! Isn't it so easy to do things just because they have to be done, all the while letting everyone around us know just how much we hate doing them? How all that can change if we can commit to live for the good of others, to make it our joy even to suffer for them, as Christ did for us! Our most unsavory drudgeries will turn into the noblest of tasks!

> We may feel sad because no one seems to rejoice in his sufferings for us, let alone care for us. But can we be so dejected when we have Christ as our true Friend, who rejoiced in His sufferings for us? It's so wonderful to have such a Friend who loves us so. But I dare say there is a deeper joy—the joy He experienced as He suffered for us. Oh, how deep Christ's joy must have been if it enabled Him to endure the infinite wrath of God on the cross! This joy of Christ we will not know unless we are willing to suffer for others as Christ did for us.

Even when we are apart from one another, working at home or at our office, let us be mindful of one another so we can say to one another when we meet again, "I worked hard, I suffered, I did not shrink away from the hardships of keeping my faith and fighting the good fight, for you and your encouragement! And I rejoiced in my sufferings for your sake!"

May the Lord bless us all with the very heart of Christ to rejoice even in our sufferings for others! For the day will come when we shall live forever in the kingdom of heaven, where there is no suffering or pain or death. We won't be able to suffer for Christ any longer! And we shall rejoice forever in the sufferings we suffered for the sake of Christ, seeing that none of our sufferings was in vain but richly rewarded far beyond what we deserve!

Final Greetings

*[7] Tychicus will tell you all about my activities. He is a beloved brother and
faithful minister and fellow servant in the Lord. [8] I have sent him to you for
this very purpose, that you may know how we are and that he may encourage
your hearts, [9] and with him Onesimus, our faithful and beloved brother,
who is one of you. They will tell you of everything that has taken place here.
[10] Aristarchus my fellow prisoner greets you, and Mark the cousin of
Barnabas (concerning whom you have received instructions—if he comes to
you, welcome him), [11] and Jesus who is called Justus. These are the only
men of the circumcision among my fellow workers for the kingdom of God,
and they have been a comfort to me. [12] Epaphras, who is one of you, a
servant of Christ Jesus, greets you, always struggling on your behalf in his
prayers, that you may stand mature and fully assured in all the will of God.
[13] For I bear him witness that he has worked hard for you and for those
in Laodicea and in Hierapolis. [14] Luke the beloved physician greets you,
as does Demas. [15] Give my greetings to the brothers at Laodicea, and to
Nympha and the church in her house. [16] And when this letter has been read
among you, have it also read in the church of the Laodiceans; and see that
you also read the letter from Laodicea. [17] And say to Archippus, "See that
you fulfill the ministry that you have received in the Lord."
[18] I, Paul, write this greeting with my own hand. Remember my chains.
Grace be with you.*
Colossians 4:7-18

What should we do with these greetings? We can see why they are
here. Such greetings were part of the letter-writing convention
of ancient times. But they seem so personal. How can something this
personal belong in the Bible? As the Canon of Christianity, the Bible
is the final, absolute authority for our faith and living. Commands and
doctrines, we expect to find in the Bible. Psalms and wisdom literature,
too. We can also see the reason for historical narratives in the Bible. But

these personal greetings? How can such personal greetings belong to the Canon, which all Christians are called to believe and accept?

What is more, we have no idea who many of these people were that are mentioned in these greetings. What possible practical, spiritual benefits can these personal greetings yield to us? Yet we have them in the Bible as part of our Canon.

> Paul...surrounded himself with many co-laborers....He called them "brothers," "fellow workers," "fellow bond-servants." Some of them he called his "fellow prisoner(s)" because they suffered together with him in prison. As they say, "If you want to travel fast, go alone. If you want to travel far, go together." Do you want to travel fast or do you want to travel far? Our Christian life is not an individual sport; it is a team sport. It is not a solo; it is a chorus.

Written under the inspiration of the Holy Spirit, this epistle has a legitimate place in the Word of God—yes, including these personal greetings. We must recognize that these greetings were personal because they involved specific individuals, not because they were trivial in any way. We must not forget that these greetings were the greetings of the *Apostle* Paul. As such, they still retained an official character. But as *personal* greetings, they give us brief yet intimate snapshots of Paul's ministry as well as the life of the Early Church. These personal greetings show in a different format what the Book of Acts does through its historical narratives. Indeed, I'd like to put forth before you that these final greetings provide us with a wonderful picture of what our church communities can, and ought to, be. We will begin by surveying the list of Paul's various associates. Then we will draw from it the characteristics of the Christian community.

Paul's Various Associates

In the first section, we have the people designated as the couriers of the letter, Tychicus and Onesimus (verses 7-9). Tychicus is described as "a beloved brother and faithful minister and fellow servant in the Lord" (verse 7). Onesimus is described as "our faithful and beloved brother, who is one of you [i.e., a member of the Colossian church]" (verse 9).

196

In the next section (verses 10-14), we have a collection of what is called "third-person greetings." Here we see Paul greeting the Colossians on behalf of his fellow workers. Mentioned are Aristarchus, who is described as Paul's "fellow prisoner," Mark the cousin of Barnabas, and Jesus who is called Justus (verses 10-11). Paul adds that they are the only Jewish men among his fellow workers for the kingdom of God and how they are a comfort to him (verse 11). Then Paul mentions Epaphras, who is one of the Colossians (verse 12), as well as Luke the beloved physician and Demas (verse 14).

In the next section (verses 15-17), we have Paul giving his instructions to the Colossians to greet others on his behalf. He is asking them to be his messenger. This is where we learn about other churches, such as the Laodicean as well as the house church in Nympha's house (verse 15). Paul asks that his letter be read among the Colossians as well as in the church of Laodicea. Then he asks them to convey his message to Archippus to fulfill the ministry that he had received in the Lord (verse 17).

In the final verse (verse 18), Paul "autographs" the letter, asks them to remember his chains and gives his benediction, "Grace be with you."

What do we learn about Paul's ministry and the life of the Early Church from the list of these names?

No Lone Rangers

First, we learn that Paul was no lone ranger; he did not carry out his ministry alone. It was a community effort. As you may know, the apostolic office was quite exclusive. Our Lord handpicked them as the official eyewitnesses of His ministry, death, and resurrection. As such, the apostolic office was not something that was handed down from one generation to the next. The Apostles had a distinct role and place in the Early Church. Paul was added to this group later on when the resurrected Lord called him on the road to Damascus. Even so, Paul did not work by himself, or just with the other Apostles. After all, the Apostles were a proof that our Lord Himself did not work alone. He alone was our

Savior. He alone could save us. But He surrounded Himself with many disciples, particularly the Apostles so they could lay the foundation of gospel ministry for future generations (Ephesians 2:20) to carry the gospel to the ends of the earth after He was gone (Matthew 28:18-20).

As our Lord did, Paul too surrounded himself with many co-laborers. Although they were not Apostles like himself, he called them "brothers," "fellow workers," "fellow bond-servants." Some of them he called his "fellow prisoner(s)" because they suffered together with him in prison. As they say, "If you want to travel fast, go alone. If you want to travel far, go together." Do you want to travel fast or do you want to travel far? Our Christian life is not an individual sport; it is a team sport. It is not a solo; it is a chorus.

Do you have people you are traveling with on this life-long journey to your heavenly home? Have you found them? Do you wonder who they are? I hope you are not wasting your time looking far and wide for your traveling companions. You just need to look around you. God has already handpicked your traveling buddies and placed them all around you—your fellow members at New Life (or whatever local body of Christian believers you may belong to) There are many others for sure. But in His providence and wisdom, God has brought us together as a basic unit to work together, to walk this pilgrim journey to our heavenly home, together, side by side, shoulder to shoulder, hand in hand. We are God's gifts to one another. We are God's support and supply to one another as the Spirit of God dwells and works within each of us. And I hope we don't forget this and treat one another as mere acquaintances. Let us be faithful and diligent in upholding and encouraging and working with one another for the furtherance of the gospel!

New Covenant Diversity

Second, pay attention to the *diversity* of Paul's brothers and fellow workers. In this passage, we see both Jews and Gentiles (cf., verse 11). There is also a (former) runaway slave (i.e., Onesimus, verse 9; cf. Paul's letter to Philemon), as well as those who had enough resources to host a church in their homes (e.g., Nympha, verse 15).

As you can see, what we have here is a snapshot of the new covenant community formed under the lordship of Jesus Christ. As a *new covenant* community, it is contrasted with the old covenant community, which was almost exclusively made up of the physical descendants of Abraham, who were sealed with the physical sign of circumcision. But the new covenant community is formed by "a circumcision made without hands," "by the circumcision of Christ" (2:11). It is a community that transcends ethnic barriers, made up of both Jews and Gentiles. For Jesus Christ came not only as the Seed of Abraham but also as the Seed of the Woman. Before Abraham was called out to start the chosen nation, even before there was any ethnic, racial, or national division in the world, there in the Garden of Eden God promised the Seed of the Woman—this chosen One would come and vanquish the serpent of old and redeem *all* of God's people, both Jews and Gentiles, through His suffering victory. In fact, even in His promise to Abraham, God promised to bless *all* the families of the earth in this chosen Offspring (Genesis 12:3; 22:18).

Despite all their differences—from ethnic to socio-economic—these people were united as one under the sovereign lordship of Christ. For Christ broke down the dividing wall of hostility between Jews and Gentiles, between the haves and the have-nots, etc. The diversity of Paul's coworkers demonstrates how Christ is bigger than all of our differences, wider than any chasm that separates us. Isn't it a wonderful blessing to see right here in our congregation a picture of the rich diversity of God's kingdom? Simply by being here together as a church, diverse in our ethnicity but united as one in Christ Jesus, we are a witness to the world and to one another. Together we witness to the truth of God's word and the faithfulness of our Savior to accomplish all that He has promised about His church and history—and to the colorful, rich diversity of God's kingdom!

An Intense Unity

Third, consider the intensity of this unity. This can be seen in the fact that Paul did not hesitate to work with these people. We know that it is one thing to accept someone into our circle of friends but it is another to work with him. We may love our friends dearly. But we may dread the idea of actually working with some of them! And think about the context of Paul's labor and what his coworkers meant for him. Paul's ministry took him to the front lines of the war between the domain of darkness and the kingdom of God's beloved Son (1:13). His co-laborers, then, were not just casual acquaintances; they were his platoon—his band of brothers in spiritual battle. He looked to them to stand with him shoulder to shoulder in the defense of the gospel. He looked to them to cover his back, to protect his flanks, and to support him in various ways, as he did the same for them.

Don't you want that? And isn't that what we all need in our spiritual battle? And isn't that precisely what our Lord has provided for us when He established His church and enlisted each of us in His army?

Not Yet Perfected

But maybe some of us are feeling discouraged because this portrait of the early church seems too idealistic. I should hasten to point out that the community in which Paul labored was far from perfect. The new covenant community, as wonderful as it is, is a community that is not yet perfected. Notice how Demas is included in these greetings. We hear of Demas again in 2 Timothy 4:10. There Paul says to Timothy, "Demas, in love with this present world, has deserted me and gone to Thessalonica...." For Demas to be included in Paul's circle of coworkers, he must have demonstrated many godly characteristics and actions. But he went astray on account of his love for the world. We don't know what happened to Demas, whether he repented of his love for the world and returned to faith and service in the end. But he is a sober reminder of Peter's words in 2 Pet. 1:10: "Therefore, brothers, be all the more diligent to make your calling and election sure."

We know that such a defector was present even in the inner circle of Jesus' Twelve Disciples. This shows that, for now, the wheat grows together with the tares in the church. "Therefore let anyone who thinks that he stands take heed lest he fall" (1 Corinthians 10:12). And we must be all the more diligent in challenging and encouraging one another to make "every effort to supplement [our] faith with virtue, and virtue with knowledge, and knowledge with self-control, and self-control with steadfastness, and steadfastness with godliness, and godliness with brotherly affection, and brotherly affection with love" (2 Peter 1:5-7). We must care for one another so that no one "falls through the cracks."

A Community Of Reconciliation And Restoration

The new covenant community is not perfect. Not only do wheat and weeds grow together in it, but the wheat also is not fully grown. We are set apart as saints, God's holy ones. But we are not yet glorified. We all have a long way to go in our sanctification. If so, how can a community made up of saints not self-destruct? Because this new covenant community is also a community of reconciliation and restoration. Consider Onesimus mentioned in v. 9. Do you know his story? He was a slave of Philemon who had run away. But sometime after that, he was converted and came into contact with Paul. In his letter to Philemon, Paul asks Philemon to forgive him and receive him as his brother in the Lord! Can you believe that? What a thing to ask—not only to forgive this runaway slave but also to receive him and honor him *as his brother*! Yet I am certain that Philemon could not mock at Paul's plea. For he must have known from his association with Paul that the Apostle himself would have done what he was asked to do! All we have to do is to take another look at how this former Pharisee received both Jews and Gentiles as his brothers and coworkers—in fact, as his comrades in battle—trusting them enough to work with them!

Consider also what Paul says concerning Mark the cousin of Barnabas. He is the author of the Gospel according to Mark. Though not an Apostle himself, he was very closely associated with Peter as his son in faith (1 Peter 5:13). If you recall, there was a rift between Barnabas and Paul over Mark. Mark was with Barnabas and Paul at the beginning of their first missionary journey (Acts 13:5). But for some reason Mark soon left them and returned to Jerusalem (Acts 13:13)—for a reason that made Paul question his loyalty and reliability. So when Barnabas wanted to take Mark along on the second missionary journey, Paul opposed, "insisting that they should not take him along who had deserted them in Pamphylia and had not gone with them to the work" (Acts 15:38, NASB). "A sharp disagreement" arose between Paul and Barnabas and they separated from each other!

But now Paul and Mark are reconciled. And it seems like Paul before writing this letter gave special words of commendation to the Colossians concerning Mark. Even in this letter, Paul asks them to welcome him, if he should come to them (verse 10). What a touching picture! What we don't see in Paul's words is a begrudging, cold, unfeeling, superficial reconciliation. What we see is rather a heart-felt, complete reconciliation, which enabled him to trust him enough to work together with him!

Brothers and sisters, that is the power of the gospel, isn't it? We can't say, "You cross me once and that is it!" If there is genuine repentance, there ought to be genuine acceptance. And that is what the world needs to see in the church of Jesus Christ—that broken relationships can be mended, wounds can be healed, and trust can be restored to the point that former enemies can work together! Why? Because that is one of the most difficult things to do in life! I believe that a most telling measure of spiritual maturity is one's willingness to forgive and be reconciled with his brothers and sisters. The power of the gospel is most clearly demonstrated when two people are genuinely reconciled, when their broken relationship is restored!

It is inevitable in this world that our relationships get strained and in some cases ruptured, even among fellow members. We will disappoint one another. We may even sin against one another. But something greater than our pride and ego, something greater than our failures and sins, binds us together. We all have been forgiven much by our Savior. And someone who has been cleared of a trillion-dollar debt cannot refuse to forgive a million-dollar debt when asked. In fact, our Savior who has forgiven us much commands us to bear with one another, forgive one another and love one another (Colossians 3:12-13). When we have accepted Christ's forgiveness, we have surrendered the right to hold on to our grudge and harbor a vengeful spirit. Besides, how can we refuse to forgive those God Himself has forgiven on account of Christ's perfect sacrifice? Haven't you experienced your hardened heart just melt away and your deepest wounds healed when you come down from your judgment seat and kneel before the cross? We can't forgive on our own. But when we stand in the shadow of the cross, it becomes the most natural thing to do! That's the power of the gospel! The new covenant community is established and sustained by this power of the gospel and it will someday be perfected by it!

Seeing Jesus Christ,
The Foundation And Head And Lord Of His Church

If Paul did not minister alone, it was not because he was a needy guy, who was deathly afraid of being alone, I'm sure. Neither was it simply because he was a great strategist and tactician who knew how to work with people and bring the best out of them. Nor was it because he was just a practical guy, who knew that there was too much work to be done and he could not do it all alone. What are we to see in all this—the manner of Paul's ministry and the rich variety of the new covenant community? Jesus Christ, the Foundation, the Head and the Lord of His church. As Paul declared at the beginning of the letter, "He is the head of the body, the church. He is the beginning, the firstborn from the dead, that in everything he might be preeminent. For in him all the fullness of God was pleased to dwell, and through him to reconcile to himself all things, whether on earth or in heaven, making peace by the blood of his cross" (1:18-20).

As finite, limited creatures, we need one another. We are the individual voices that make up the heavenly choir. The heavenly song, the redemptive chorus, cannot be sung just with the sopranos. We need the altos. We need the tenors as well as the basses. This song of redemption, which God composed and Christ conducts and the Holy Spirit accompanies, is so rich, so intricate, so harmonious that it requires every member and the unique tone and color of each voice! We cannot sing this song alone. We cannot belch out whenever and however we feel like. We must listen for one another. We must keep in step with one another. There is the perfect music score to be followed by everyone according to God's direction. We've got to keep our eyes on Christ, the great Conductor. But we must also listen to one another and keep the beat.

If the church is rich in its diversity, it is because Jesus Christ is the Lord of all, the Lord of heaven and earth and all that they contain! If Paul did not minister alone, if Christians are not to live out their Christian life and do ministry alone, it is because Christ Himself has designed it that way! That design humbles us because none of us is capable of doing it all alone. As finite, limited creatures, we need one another. We are the individual voices that make up the heavenly choir. The heavenly song, the redemptive chorus, cannot be sung just with the sopranos. We need the altos. We need the tenors as well as the basses. This song of redemption, which God composed and Christ conducts and the Holy Spirit accompanies, is so rich, so intricate, so harmonious that it requires every member and the unique tone and color of each voice! We cannot sing this song alone. We cannot belch out whenever and however we feel like. We must listen for one another. We must keep in step with one another. There is the perfect music score to be followed by everyone according to God's direction. We've got to keep our eyes on Christ, the great Conductor. But we must also listen to one another and keep the beat.

Of course, for now, none of us sings our notes perfectly. Our pitches are off often and so is our timing. Someone is singing too loudly and another is not singing loud enough. It is easy to be discouraged and disappointed. There is no doubt that our song will be perfect when we sing before God in our heavenly glory. But, for now, we are faced with our imperfections and the imperfections of other saints. Yes, being together with others may be more depressing than encouraging at times. But we must not, and we cannot, retreat back into our individual foxholes. We still need one another, both in positive and negative ways. We need help from others because we are not self-sufficient. But we also need—yes, need!—to lend our helping hands to grow in our spiritual maturity. We cannot live simply by inhaling; we need to exhale as well. We do not grow just by taking in; we need to give and exercise our gifts. Christ has placed us together so that we can show the love of Christ to one another when we are all imperfect for now.

The "Extra Work" Is Worth It

But even more importantly, if we must accept one another as brethren and work together as co-workers, it is because Christ has accepted us as His brethren and works together with us as His co-workers. We must not forget. It is Christ and Christ alone who can build His church—a church that is completely free not only from sin but also from every tinge of blemish and imperfection. He alone is able to build such a church. Yet He builds His church through His imperfect people, people who are still sinful. So, then, it cannot be because He needs our help, can it? Left to ourselves, we would only hinder the work, not help! There is nothing we can contribute—after all, what do we have that we have not received from Him? He must work in and through and with us to accomplish His purpose. And He works in and through and with us because His goal is to build us up and conform us to His own image.

This is undoubtedly "more work" for Christ. We know that, sometimes, it is "more work" to work with others. Yet He is only glad to work with us so He can train us and build us up. If so, how can we *not* bear with one another and work together, especially when we do need one another and their gifts? And we are not strangers that we should feel awkward and uneasy to work together. We are "fellow-servants" of Christ. We are in fact "brothers" in the Lord! We are to treat one another with love and respect and all the cooperation we can give because Christ has received us as His servants, as His co-workers. So Paul did not think it beneath him to work with others because he was an Apostle.

The coastal redwood can grow to be 325 feet in height. But surprisingly their root system is quite shallow, not going deeper than several feet. How can they grow so tall? Because their root system extends over 100 feet from the base and intertwines with the roots of other redwood trees.[24] As imperfect Christians, our roots may not be deep. But take a look around you. God has already blessed this small congregation with the richness of His kingdom. The bond that we have is thicker than blood. The unity that we have is deeper than the superficial common ground of the world—our social status, our economic class, our educational background, our ethnicity. Let us work together. Let us accept one another as brothers and coworkers! In doing so, let the light of His glory shine in and through us. There is choice to be made. Is it about us or about Christ? Is it about our ease and the security of our comfort zone or

---

24 See http://www.parks.ca.gov/?page_id=22257.

is it about His glory? We belong to the marvelous kingdom of God's Son. The day shall come when we shall see its glory in its fullness. We may be frustrated now with all the imperfections of the church. But knowing that her perfection is inevitable, let us strive together to build up this community—the community of the new covenant, the community of Christ, the community of reconciliation and restoration, the community that is imperfect but predestined for perfection. May the Lord be pleased to bless us and build us up to what He has called us to be!

The High-Priestly Benediction

[22] The LORD spoke to Moses, saying, [23] "Speak to Aaron and his sons,
saying, Thus you shall bless the people of Israel: you shall say to them,
[24] The LORD bless you and keep you;
[25] the LORD make his face to shine upon you and be gracious to you;
[26] the LORD lift up his countenance upon you and give you peace."
Numbers 6:22-26

In many Protestant and Reformed circles, the ministry of the Word is given a central role and rightly so. We can say that the Word of God, publicly read and preached and taught, is the primary means of grace. But primacy (or, centrality) does not mean exclusivity. Maintaining the primacy of the ministry of the Word doesn't mean we can neglect the other parts of worship. Some, though very few (I hope), come to church late just in time for the sermon portion. And some leave right after the message, even before the pronouncement of the benediction. We have to keep in mind that from the time of the call to worship to the pronouncement of the benediction, we are taking part in a holy assembly before the presence of God. And we are not to view the benediction as merely the announcement that the worship service is officially over. We should be present and actively participate in the worship service from the beginning to the very end.

Today, we are going to deal with a scriptural benediction, a high-priestly benediction which God entrusted to Aaron and his descendants. You may have heard this benediction pronounced quite regularly from church pulpits. Now you know where it comes from. And today we have an opportunity to take a look at it in detail. It is so easy for us to think of the benediction merely as something that marks the end of our worship service and not have a full sense of its power and significance. Preparing this message has made me think more deeply about the significance of the words I utter. It has also deepened my sense of the privilege that is mine as a minister of the gospel to pronounce these words of blessing upon the people of God. And I hope that you too will come to a greater appreciation for the benediction you receive at the end of the worship services you share in.

A Priestly Pronouncement, On God's Behalf

The Lord gave Aaron and his sons, the priests, the privilege to pronounce His divine benediction upon the people of Israel. It was only appropriate that the priests should receive this privilege. For they were intermediaries between God and His people.

On the one hand, the priests represented the people to God. They did this by offering sacrifices on behalf of the people. They did it when they took the sacrificial animals that people brought and sacrificed them at the altar for various offerings. They did it also when they regularly offered sacrifices to God—every day, on behalf of all Israel, they offered two one-year old lambs as burnt offerings, one in the morning and one at twilight. Thus they ministered unto God continually on behalf of the people of God, as their representatives to God. After all, as we learn in Leviticus 3, the Levites, including the priestly family of Aaron, were consecrated unto God as the substitutes for all the first-born sons.

On the other hand, the priests were also *God's* representatives to the people. Even previously, in this legal section of the book of Numbers, we see the priests receiving restitution (Numbers 5:8) and all the holy gifts (Numbers 5:9) from Israel on God's behalf. They had the responsibility to administer trials by ordeal as representatives of the divine Judge (Numbers 5:11-28). And, as many of you know, the tithes, which the twelve tribes offered to God, were given to the Levites and priests. In addition, they received portions of sacrificial animals that were offered to God. It was most fitting, therefore, that the priests, as God's representatives, would pronounce God's benediction upon His people.

It is important to remember that it was God who took the initiative in blessing His people and provided the very words for this blessing. How thankful we ought to be! For if God did not take the initiative, what could Aaron and his sons do? What merit did they have to pronounce these blessings? What power did they possess to bless others? What right did they have? Did they have any reason to believe that the benediction would become a reality if they chanted these words often enough and sincerely enough? Or was there anything magical in the words themselves? No! This benediction was what it was because God commanded it, because God wished it, because it was an expression of God's sovereign and gracious will toward His people.

Couplets And Clauses Packed With Meaning

This benediction consists of three couplets—three groups of two: 1) "The LORD bless you *and* keep you"; 2) "The LORD make His face to shine upon you *and* be gracious to you"; 3) "The LORD lift up His countenance upon you *and* give you peace." Regarding this three-fold construction, Keil and Delitzsch have said,

> As the threefold repetition of a word or sentence serves to express the thought as strongly as possible (cf. Jeremiah 7:4; Jeremiah 22:29), the triple blessing expressed in the most unconditional manner the thought that God would bestow upon His congregation the whole fullness of the blessing enfolded in His Divine Being.[25]

This three-fold benediction communicates, then, the *fullness* of God's blessing upon His people as well as the full *intensity* of God's desire to bless His people. And the three couplets and the six clauses that make up these couplets show the manifold facets of God's blessing. I won't be able to allocate equal time and space for each of these but I'll try my best to address the main points.

"The LORD Bless You"

"The LORD bless you and keep you." The benediction naturally begins with the words, "The LORD bless you...." The vocabulary of blessing is pretty much absent in our culture. It is not a word that is commonly

25 C.F. Keil and F. Delitzsch, Commentary on the Old Testament (http://www.studylight.org/commentaries/kdo/view.cgi?bk=3&ch=6)

used anymore. Its prominent meaning has a religious overtone and our increasingly secular culture has not much taste for that. Now, if the word is used at all, it is usually in the sense of giving one's approval to a plan, etc., as in "The CEO gave the project his blessing." That shouldn't surprise us. In a real sense, that is the extent of man's ability to bless. What power does man have to bless another?

But this priestly benediction comes from God Himself. In this blessing, it is *the Lord* who blesses. This is made unmistakably clear by the three-fold repetition of the name of the Lord: "The LORD..., the LORD..., the LORD...!" Twice is for emphasis. But thrice, a triple repetition, in the Bible signifies a superlative, especially when used of a name or attribute of God.

God is no mere man that His blessing should be limited to mere approval and moral support. "The earth is the LORD's and the fullness thereof, the world and those who dwell therein, for he has founded it upon the seas and established it upon the rivers" (Psalm 24:1-2). He owns the cattle on a thousand hills (Psalm 50:10). He who created all things and has them at His disposal is alone capable and qualified to bless. In fact, God is the ever-blessed One, from whom all blessings flow.

When we refer to God as the blessed One, it does not mean that He receives His blessing from someone greater than Himself, of course. At the most basic level, it is the superior who blesses the inferior. However, we see in the Bible God's people blessing the Lord. In fact, the Bible commands them to bless the Lord. This, of course, does not mean that we impart blessing to God. What can we as finite creatures add to the infinite, all-sufficient God? But the inferior can bless the superior in this way—not in the sense of imparting blessing but in the sense of acknowledging His insuperable greatness. To bless the Lord is to praise Him, to adore Him, to glorify Him for His infinite being and to thank Him for the abundance of grace He bestows on His people. So we read in Psalm 103:1-2, "Bless the LORD, O my soul, and all that is within me, bless His holy name! Bless the LORD, O my soul, and forget not all His benefits...."

What we see in this benediction is that the ever-blessed God, who alone is capable and qualified to bless, is delighted to bless His people. His blessing is not just a wish but a promise to fulfill. And His blessing is eternal and irrevocable. For He does not change like men. He is eternal and immutable. There is no shadow of turning with Him (as the shadow of the sun-dial moves and shifts throughout the day). He is no weakling that He should rescind His pledge. He is no mortal that He should fail to fulfill His promise. The blessing of the almighty God is not just a wishful thought. Unlike men, who can bless only in the name of God, God is able to bless out of His sovereign, unstoppable will, out of His infinite riches. He is the Fountain of all blessings. He possesses in Himself all goodness, love, wisdom and power. And He promises to bless His people.

"And Keep You"

This general promise to bless is given more specific expressions in the words that follow. The Lord, who promises to bless, also promises to keep His people. The original Hebrew word used here is *shamar*, which is a very important word in the Old Testament. The basic meaning of its root is "to exercise great care over." The word is used much in conjunction with the idea of covenant, as in "to keep, or fulfill, the covenant." It can also mean to "take care of" or to "guard." Adam was placed in the Garden of Eden not only to cultivate it but also to keep it (that is, to guard it against the invasion of Satan). The word has some other related meanings but it is used in our passage in the sense of God guarding and protecting His people.[26]

> The blessing of the almighty God is not just a wishful thought. Unlike men, who can bless only in the name of God, God is able to bless out of His sovereign, unstoppable will, out of His infinite riches. He is the Fountain of all blessings. He possesses in Himself all goodness, love, wisdom and power. And He promises to bless His people.

This reminds us of the context in which God's blessings come to God's people—the fallen world, with the evil one and his minions trying to

---

26 R. Laird Harris, TWOT, "*shamar.*"

destroy the people of God. What does it profit us to be blessed with all the wonderful things of God and be robbed of them by the enemy? We are so fragile and so vulnerable in so many ways! We are only a blink away from a tragic accident, a phone call away from a terminal disease, a stroke away from death! There are hundreds and thousands of ways for our lives and endeavors to go down in a miserable, spectacular failure. How grateful we are that God's blessing includes this crucial aspect of guarding and protecting His people—in this life and more ultimately in the world to come!

"The LORD Make His Face Shine To Shine Upon You And Be Gracious To You"

The benediction moves on to the second couplet: "The LORD make His to face shine upon you and be gracious to you." This couplet brings us closer to the true essence of God's blessing, doesn't it? The core of God's blessing is not some gifts God gives out to His people, however precious and many they may be. The core of God's blessing is God Himself. He blesses us by making His face shine on us. We can say this because, in Hebrew terms, to be in the presence of God is to be in the face of God.

We know all too well the temptation of idolatry—to be enamored with the gifts more than with the Giver Himself. How foolish! What is better—to have a fish for a meal or to learn how to fish? If so, how can receiving a gift from God (or hundreds and thousands of them, for that matter) compare with having God Himself, having God's face shine upon us with love and delight? What does it profit a man to gain the whole world and lose his soul, which can find its true life only in God? In fact, what is heaven without God? Heaven without God would be nothing but eternal boredom (as many suspect and are turned off by). But if God should give Himself to us, what blessings, what gifts would He withhold?

God knows that the light of His face is what we truly need. For it is the light of His face that casts away all darkness and gloominess. It alone can chase away the darkness of sin, the darkness of despair, the darkness of evil. Even the deep darkness of death cannot stand the light of His countenance. He spoke into the primordial darkness, "Let there be light,' and there was light" (Genesis 1:3). If God can bring into existence all things out of nothing, can even death withstand His life-giving power? The light that shone at the dawn of creation was but a dim shadow of the light that shines eternally from His divine countenance. And the sunshine that brings warmth and vitality to the world is only a shadow of the light of His countenance upon the souls of men! And God promises to make His face shine on His people with the ineffable light of His eternal glory. So great is His love that He cannot withhold from us the greatest gift of all—the gift of Himself!

This couplet goes on to say, "[The LORD] be gracious to you." The Hebrew word used here, *chanan*," often has the sense of showing kindness to the poor and needy."[27] This blessing reminds us of an important truth about us—we are poor and needy in the sight of God. Yet God is gracious to the poor and needy. We may take this for granted because even we can feel sorry for the victims of tragic events. We may even feel compelled to help them. But generally people don't like needy, clingy people who constantly want their help. But God does not despise us or reject us because we are poor and needy. He welcomes us, no matter how often we come to Him with our needs, no matter how big or how many our needs may be. How gracious God is! He is ever willing and ready to bless us by meeting our true, real needs. When we feel poor and needy, we don't need to despair and grow bitter. We can look to our gracious God and know that He will bless us and not despise us!

"The LORD Lift Up His Countenance Upon You And Give You Peace"

Now we come to the final couplet: "The LORD lift up His countenance upon you and give you peace." To lift up one's face is a Hebrew idiom. Listen to how this idiom is used in Genesis 4:6-7: "Then the LORD said to Cain, 'Why are you angry? And why has your countenance fallen? If you do well, will not *your countenance* be lifted up?" (NASB) Here we see two opposite expressions—having one's face fallen is the opposite

---

27 R. Laird Harris, TWOT, *"chanan."*

of having one's face lifted up. And to have one's face fallen is equated with being angry: "Why are you angry? And why has your countenance fallen?" To have one's face lifted up is then the opposite of being angry. It is to look upon him with favor and delight (Job 22:26) rather than with anger and resentment. This benediction calls on God to take delight in His people!

So, then, we see how naturally the next blessing flows from this: "[The LORD] give you peace." In our individualistic culture, we think of peace mostly in terms of inner tranquility. And peace in political terms means absence of war or conflict. But the Hebrew understanding of peace (*shalom*) is much more comprehensive. "Peace,' ...means much more than mere absence of war.... Completeness, wholeness, harmony, fulfillment, are closer to the meaning. Implicit in [*shalom*] is the idea of unimpaired relationships with others and fulfillment in one's undertakings."[28]

The peace that is promised here definitely includes inner tranquility. However, the blessing of peace is much more than just that. If we can see the connection between the two blessings of this last couplet, the peace spoken of here is a relational one—the peace between God and His people. It is the kind of peace that knows of no animosity and enmity between God and His people. It is the kind of peace that exists because God looks upon His people with favor and delight and the people reciprocate that loving gaze with a gaze of gratitude and adoration. He who lifts up His countenance on us will lift up our head toward Him. Such is the peace He promises to give.

But How Can This Be?

But can this pledge be fulfilled? Can this benediction be fully realized? Remember where this benediction is placed. It comes at the end of a legal section (Numbers 5-6). This legal section has dealt with the laws concerning the holiness and purity of the covenant community. These laws speak clearly of uncleanness, sin, guilt, defilement and curse as well as God's demand for purity, atonement, innocence, and holiness.

---

28 TWOT, "shalom."

So, then, as we come to this benediction after the law section, we cannot forget about the holiness of God and the reality of our sinful condition. The question that cannot be avoided is, "Can a holy God truly bless such sinful people?"

And take a look at the extent of the blessings promised. We said that the three-fold expression of this benediction points to the fullness of the blessings promised. I wonder what things the Israelites thought of when they heard these words. God's protection through their long journey to the promised land? His provision for food and drink, clothes and shelter in the wilderness? And the victory over their enemies in Canaan? And the abundance of crops and cattle in the land flowing with milk and honey? How about you?

But even the vision of the Israelites surely reached beyond the horizon of their immediate needs and the material blessings of the promised land! They must have realized that the blessings promised in this benediction went far beyond their present experience of God's grace. Consider God's blessing of making His face shine on them. When Moses came down from Mount Sinai with the tablets of the law, the skin of his face shone and the people were afraid to come near him (Exodus 34:30). If they could not bear the reflected light of God in Moses' face, how could they withstand—let alone enjoy!—the light of God's countenance shining on them directly?

But a more important question is what *God* had in mind when He entrusted this benediction to Aaron and his priestly sons. This benediction showed that God desired to bless His people. But how much?

God must have known the true condition of His people—the depth and extent of their sinfulness, which deserved His wrath and not His blessings. As a holy God, He could not truly bless sinful men. If He were to make His face shine on them, it would be an all-consuming fire of judgment rather than a blessing. Do you see? God could not bless His people with these words unless He had in His mind the perfect atonement of His Son for their sins! The foundation of this benediction is not some generic benevolence of God. The foundation of this benediction is none other

215

than Jesus Christ and His work of salvation! You see, the benediction coming after a law section not only reminds us of the holiness of God and the sinful condition of man. It also points so marvelously to the triumph of God's blessing in Jesus Christ over man's sinfulness and the curse of the law. For this benediction is the final word of God in this law section! The benediction of God has the last word! And Jesus Christ is God's final Word (Hebrews 1:2)!

In order that the disposition of our holy God toward us might be that of blessing and not of curse, Jesus Christ became a curse for us. In order that God might keep us for eternity, Jesus was forsaken by the Father, crying, "My God, My God, why hast Thou forsaken Me?" In order that God might make His face shine on us, Christ endured God's abandonment—His Father turning His face away from Him in righteous anger. In order that God might be gracious to us in all things, Christ endured all the just punishment of our sin. In order that God might lift up His countenance on us, Jesus bore in His body the just wrath of God against our sins. In order that God might give us peace—the peace this world cannot give, the peace that surpasses all understanding, the complete and eternal shalom, actual peace with God—Christ gave Himself as the propitiation for our sins and appeased the wrath of God forever.

Do you see how much God wanted to bless His people? How far His promise of protection extended? How far He would go in His graciousness toward His poor and needy *and* sinful people? How comprehensive was the peace that He wanted to give to us? And how near He wanted to draw to us?

But the foundation of our blessing could not rest merely on the tragic end of Jesus' life. He, who died because of our sins, was raised from the dead unto eternal life and is now seated at the right hand of God as the victorious Lord of all. Our blessings flow from the heavenly throne of our resurrected Lord!

You see, His blessed Son was what God saw when He blessed the sons of Israel. Those that are blessed are blessed because they are found in the beloved Son of God. And the New Testament joyfully declares the fulfillment of God's benediction in Jesus Christ: "Blessed be the God and Father of our Lord Jesus Christ, who has blessed us *in Christ* with every spiritual blessing in the heavenly places" (Ephesians 1:3). "For God, who said, 'Let light shine out of darkness,' has shone in our hearts to give the light of the knowledge of the glory of God in the face of Jesus Christ" (2 Corinthians 4:6).

Complete Blessing In Jesus Christ

You possess every *spiritual* blessing in the *heavenly* places in Jesus Christ. Oh, how complete is God's blessing on us! God's blessings would not be complete unless they were "imperishable, undefiled, and unfading, kept in heaven" for us (1 Peter 1:4). For what does it matter if we possess all the blessings of this world, only to be stripped of them at death? What does it benefit us to be protected from all the dangers and evil men of this world if we are not kept from eternal damnation in hell? And what is so valuable in achieving some kind of inner peace through meditation or whatever if we are at enmity with God?

But if we should have peace with God, what of the trials and tribulations we face in this world? If the Lord should keep us, what of the persecutions and oppressions we suffer at the hands of the evil one and his hosts? And if the Lord should bless us with every spiritual blessing in the heavenly places, what of all the loss and bereavement in this life? If the Lord should bless us, who is to curse? As Balaam said to Balak, "Behold, I received a command to bless: he has blessed and I cannot revoke it" (Numbers 23:20). How marvelous, then, is the fact that God has blessed us with every spiritual blessing in the heavenly places! Who can revoke God's blessing upon us? "If God is for us, who can be against us?" (Romans 8:31) God promises, "I will bless those who bless you, and him who dishonors you I will curse" (Genesis 12:3). God has shone the light of His eternal love for us in the face of His Son, Jesus Christ. One of our hymns, from Edward H. Bickersteth, confesses:

One word from thee, my Lord, one smile, one look,
And I could face the cold, rough world again;
And with that treasure in my heart could brook
The wrath of devils and the scorn of men.

If one look from our Savior is enough to do this, how much more if Christ should never take His eyes off us?

Living Out Of The Abundance Of God's Blessing

Oh, you are the blessed people of God! Live out of every spiritual blessing God has bestowed upon you in Christ Jesus! Think on your election. Think on God's predestination concerning your salvation in Christ Jesus. Think on your forgiveness through the blood of Jesus Christ. Think on your adoption as sons. Think on the Holy Spirit, who is given you as the pledge of your eternal inheritance in heaven. Think upon these things especially when the dark clouds of tribulations and trials come. The dark clouds may be able to hide the sun,[29] but not the light of the knowledge of the glory of God that shines in the face of Christ!

Let us cling to Christ, then, in whom all the promises and blessings of God are yes and amen. And let us confess that Christ is all that we want and more, that Christ is sufficient for us in this life and in the life to come. Though we see it now, we see it only dimly now, for when that day of glory comes, we shall see more clearly the full extent and riches of the blessings that Christ is for us! Until then, let us hold on to God's irrevocable blessings in Christ Jesus!

---

29 See the Westminster Confession of Faith, 18.4.

They Journeyed

[1] These are the stages of the people of Israel, when they went out of the land of Egypt by their companies under the leadership of Moses and Aaron. [2] Moses wrote down their starting places, stage by stage, by command of the LORD, and these are their stages according to their starting places. [3] They set out from Rameses in the first month, on the fifteenth day of the first month. On the day after the Passover, the people of Israel went out triumphantly in the sight of all the Egyptians, [4] while the Egyptians were burying all their firstborn, whom the LORD had struck down among them. On their gods also the LORD executed judgments....

[50] And the LORD spoke to Moses in the plains of Moab by the Jordan at Jericho, saying, [51] "Speak to the people of Israel and say to them, When you pass over the Jordan into the land of Canaan, [52] then you shall drive out all the inhabitants of the land from before you and destroy all their figured stones and destroy all their metal images and demolish all their high places. [53] And you shall take possession of the land and settle in it, for I have given the land to you to possess it. [54] You shall inherit the land by lot according to your clans. To a large tribe you shall give a large inheritance, and to a small tribe you shall give a small inheritance. Wherever the lot falls for anyone, that shall be his. According to the tribes of your fathers you shall inherit. [55] But if you do not drive out the inhabitants of the land from before you, then those of them whom you let remain shall be as barbs in your eyes and thorns in your sides, and they shall trouble you in the land where you dwell. [56] And I will do to you as I thought to do to them."
Numbers 33:1-4, 50-56

It was God who commanded Moses to record Israel's wilderness journey. But why? This recitation is not the most exciting and engaging piece of literature—and not the easiest one to read, either. In fact, many of us may find it to be quite an effective sleep-inducer. So, then, why would a loving God include such a challenging passage in the

Bible? If God wanted us to read and love His word, this is not the way to do it, is it? Or did God insert these passages just to test our patience? No. God loves us too much to put us through misery just for the sake of misery. We will see that there is a big encouragement to be found even in this portion of Scripture.

Timely Encouragement

Why the recounting of Israel's journey at this point? It was to encourage the Israelites as they were about to enter the promised land, finally! They had just averted a serious national crisis (Numbers 32). The two tribes of Reuben and Gad came and said that they did not want to cross the Jordan into the promised land with the other tribes. They wanted to stay on the east side of the Jordan because the land of the Amorites was great for their livestock. Moses was enraged. He compared this to the treachery of the 10 spies who incited Israel to refuse to go into the promised land. At Moses' harsh rebuke, the two tribes repented and pledged to fight alongside their brethren as they conquer the land of Canaan.

Thus a national crisis was avoided and Israel was now poised to enter the promised land. The people were encamped by the Jordan (Numbers 33:49). Only the Jordan River stood between Israel and the promised land. Their 40-year wilderness journey was almost over. It was a good time for Israel to pause and reflect on their journey before making the actual entry into the promised land.

So, then, one of the primary purposes of this review was to show that the wilderness journey was indeed coming to an end. This meant that the period of God's wrath against the exodus generation was almost over. As you may know, the exodus generation had to wander in the wilderness for 40 years (more specifically 38 years) as God's punishment for their unbelief and rebellion, specifically in refusing to enter the promised land: "And the LORD's anger was kindled against Israel, and he made them wander in the wilderness forty years, until all the generation that had done evil in the sight of the LORD was gone" (Numbers 32:13). Notice how, among all the journeys that are recorded, only two have time markers (Numbers 33:3-5 and 33:37-40). One refers to the first year (verses 3-5) and the other to the last year of Israel's wilderness journey (verses 37-40). By marking the first and the last year, God showed that Israel had finally reached the end of its wilderness journey. The time of Israel's entrance into the promised land was imminent. So we are not surprised that this review is followed by His command concerning the conquest and the division of the promised land (verses 50-56).

You see, God is using this review to encourage Israel before it carries out its final mission to take possession of the promised land. Take a look at the things that are highlighted in this review. Each leg of the journey in most cases is recounted in a uniform way according to a standard formula: "they set out from X and camped at Y." But there are obvious deviations from this standard format. These deviations occur in the way of added comments. Just compare verse 5 and verse 6: "So the people of Israel set out from Rameses and camped at Succoth [the standard formula]. And they set out from Succoth and camped at Etham, which is on the edge of the wilderness [note the extra comment added at the end]." Such a deviation naturally draws our attention. Let us highlight some of the more notable exceptions and their significance.

God's Sovereign, Incomparable Power

God draws our attention to how it all began. In verses 3-5, the Passover is mentioned, which was the beginning of Israel's journey toward the promised land. It mentions how the Egyptians buried their firstborn after the Lord struck them with the final plague; how God executed judgments even upon the Egyptian gods; how Israel left Egypt triumphantly in the sight of the Egyptians. What a wonderful reminder of God's sovereign, incomparable power over all other gods!

How precious was this reminder as Israel was about to enter the land of Canaan and battle against the Canaanites and their many gods! God was reminding His people how the whole thing began! He was reminding them that, even as Pharaoh and the Egyptian gods were nothing to Him, the peoples and the gods of Canaan were nothing to Him.

God's Constant Faithfulness

Then God shows how He led Israel through all kinds of different places. Verse 6 mentions Etham, which is on the edge of the wilderness. Etham is mentioned to show Israel's point of entry into the wilderness. In verses 7-8 we are told that God led Israel even through the midst of the sea. At the end of verse 8 we hear of the "three days' journey" to Marah. Marah means "bitter" and the place is so called because the water there was bitter. In verse 9, we have a description of Elim as a place of 12 springs of water and 70 palm trees. In verse 14, Rephidim is mentioned as a place where the people had no water.

Do you recognize the point being made? There were difficult places (like Marah, where the water was bitter) and there were good places (like a beautiful oasis at Elim) but the faithfulness of God was constant through them all, even through the sea on dry land! Through them all God brought His people all the way to the plains of Moab where they could see the promised land beyond the Jordan! How great is His faithfulness!

Signs Of The Wanderings Coming To An End

There are other things that are mentioned for Israel's encouragement. Notice Aaron's death, which is mentioned in verses 37-40. It took place in the 40th year. Only Aaron's death is mentioned despite the fact that over 600,000 people died in the course of the whole journey. Why? Aaron was an important figure. As Israel's high priest, he was a representative of Israel. So then, he is set forth as the representative of the first generation, which was sentenced to die in the wilderness. So it was no accident that he died in the 40th year, the final year of the wilderness journey. This signals that the door was finally opening for the second generation to enter the promised land.

Also mentioned is the king of Arad (a Canaanite) hearing about the coming of the sons of Israel (verse 40). The news of Israel's approach to the land of Canaan is reaching the kings and the peoples in Canaan.

And, finally, we read in verse 49 that the Jews encamped "by the Jordan from Beth-jeshimoth as far as Abel-shittim in the plains of Moab."

This is an indication of the large size of Israel, testifying to God's faithfulness to His promise to Abraham, Isaac and Jacob to multiply their descendants.

Oh, how gracious God is to encourage His people this way! This passage cannot be reduced to boring material meant to test our patience!

Welcome Relief

But there is more. As we read this section, we cannot fail to notice the breathless, rapid succession in which the journey is recounted. Israel seems to be always on the go, traveling from one place to another constantly. The reality, of course, was not quite like that. As one rabbi says,

> The 42 stops recounted by Moses in *Mas'ei* [this particular portion in the Book of Numbers] represent 40 years of wandering. Yet Rashi calculates that "if we omit the first and last years, when the Israelites were constantly on the move, there were only 20 stations visited during 38 years" (*Etz Hayim: Torah and Commentary*, ed. David L. Lieber [New York: Rabbinical Assembly, 2001], p. 954). Thus, it is incorrect to think of Israel as constantly on the march. Rather during most of the 40 years in the desert, the Israelites were living normally at one oasis or another for years at a time.[30]

While that may be true, this rapid review must have had a profound psychological impact on Israel. The journey through the wilderness for 40 years was hardly a picnic on a verdant hill. They were living in tents; they were still in the wilderness; they were constantly affected by the unsettled feeling of a nomadic life. As they heard this rapid review, they could breathe a sigh of relief that all those years of wandering were finally behind them. We know how that is. While we go through a trying time, time seems to crawl at a snail's pace, if it does not feel completely suspended. But once we come out of it and look back, we can even cherish that time, and how quickly it went by. This was the time for Israel to look back and breathe a sigh of relief.

---

30 See http://urj.org/Articles/index.cfm?id=7277.

Particular Benefits For Readers

It is clear that this account is more than just a generic recapitulation, a simple review of Israel's wilderness journey. In fact, many of the place-names appear for the first time here in this passage (verses 13, 19-29).[31] We realize, then, that the accounts in Exodus and Numbers were some of the highlights of Israel's journey, not an exhaustive record of Israel's travels. Having gone through these places, the Jews themselves probably had some memories associated with each locality. But those associations are forever lost. For God in His wisdom did not choose to record those events in the Bible. Even so, God desired that we should be the intended readers and beneficiaries of this record as much as the Jews in the wilderness were without knowing all the specifics of Israel's journeys. What would be those benefits?

To see that, we must recognize that this summary of Israel's wilderness journey has its own points of emphasis. As we saw briefly before, these emphases come by way of certain accounts deviating from the standard format, particularly in the form of added comments. Many of these emphases are expected. But there are some surprises.

Gracious Omissions

First, we notice that some important events in Israel's journey are not given any extra comments. The most notable is the incident at Kadesh in the wilderness of Paran. It is there that Israel refused to go into the promised land because of the bad report of the 10 spies. You see, the whole reason for Israel's 38-year wilderness wandering was that event at Kadesh. But this important incident is buried almost unnoticeably in verses 17-18: "And they set out from Kibroth-hattaavah and camped at Hazeroth. And they set out from Hazeroth and camped at Rithmah." We know, according to Numbers 12:16 that the Kadesh incident occurred after Israel moved from Hazeroth and encamped in the wilderness of Paran. Rithmah may well have been the location of Israel's encampment in the wilderness of Paran. But, as you can see, Kadesh is not even mentioned. How can this be?

---

31 Dennis T. Olsen, *Numbers,* Interpretation (Louisville: John Knox Press 1996), p. 184.

And we further notice that this recounting of Israel's journey is devoid of any negative comment about Israel. There is no mention of any of Israel's numerous complaints and rebellions. Take a look at verse 8 where Marah is mentioned. Marah means "bitter" because the water there was bitter. But it was a "bitter" place also because the Israelites grumbled against Moses about the bitterness of the water there. Only when a tree was thrown into it according to God's command did the water become sweet enough to drink. But in this account of Numbers 33, there is no mention of Israel's complaint.

Also take a look at v. 14, where Rephidim is mentioned. All we read there is, "And they set out from Alush and camped at Rephidim, where there was no water for the people to drink." That's all it says! How remarkable! Rephidim is given an extra comment to draw attention to it. Yet all that the extra comment says is that there was no water for the people to drink there. But do you remember what really happened there? Israel "quarreled with Moses"; Israel "tested the LORD" (Exodus 17:2); they grumbled against Moses, "Why did you bring us up out of Egypt, to kill us and our children and our livestock with thirst" (Exodus 17:3)? And all we have here in Numbers 33 is, "Rephidim, where there was no water for the people to drink." Where is their sinful response?

Do you see? The intent of this recounting is not to rehash the shameful history of Israel's wilderness journey. What a relief! Going through the book of Numbers, you come across so many accounts of Israel's offenses and rebellions. But here in this retelling of Israel's wilderness journey, there is no mention of Israel's sins. It is as if in this retelling of Israel's journey, Israel's sins were buried in the wilderness. Isn't this every sinner's deepest longing? At least, shouldn't it be? And could it be that this was a small glimpse of that glorious day when God shall remember our sins no more?

were buried in the wilderness. Isn't this every sinner's deepest longing? At least, shouldn't it be? And could it be that this was a small glimpse of that glorious day when God shall remember our sins no more? In God's amazing grace, it indeed was!

A New Exodus In Christ

Indeed, this is exactly what Christ has done for us! At the Mount of Transfiguration, when Moses and Elijah appeared and spoke with our Lord, what did they speak about? His departure (Luke 9:31)! The original Greek word used for "departure" is literally "exodus"! His exodus refers specifically to His death and resurrection, but more generally to His entire life—His incarnation, His life and ministry, His suffering and death, and His resurrection and ascension to heaven! In this light, consider how Matthew presents Jesus' life at the beginning of his gospel. It is presented as a retracing of Israel's exodus:

- As Israel went down to Egypt to escape the life-threatening famine in Canaan, so was Jesus taken down to Egypt to escape Herod's attempt on his life.
- As God called Israel, His son, out of Egypt, so did God call Jesus His only begotten Son out of Egypt.
- As Israel was baptized as it went through the Red Sea (1 Corinthians 10:1), so was Jesus baptized at the Jordan.
- As Israel was led into the wilderness by the pillar of cloud and fire (which was a manifestation of the Holy Spirit), so was Jesus led into the wilderness by the Holy Spirit.
- As Israel wandered in the wilderness for 40 years, so did Jesus stay in the wilderness for 40 days.
- As Israel was tested by God, so was Jesus tempted by Satan in the wilderness.
- But whereas Israel failed to learn that man did not live by bread alone but by every word that proceeded out of the mouth of the Lord (Deuteronomy 8:3), Jesus demonstrated that truth in a most difficult circumstance. Even after 40 days' of fasting, our Lord resisted Satan's temptation to turn the stones into bread by saying, "Man shall not live by bread alone, but by every word that proceeds out of the mouth of the Lord."

As you can see, Jesus retraced Israel's wilderness journey, reliving it. But where Israel failed, Jesus succeeded. In thus retracing Israel's journey and in thus succeeding where Israel failed, Jesus corrected all that had gone wrong in Israel's journey and made it right.

Sin Buried Through Christ

But it would take more from Jesus to bury our sin once for all. Notice how our passage ends with a command and a warning. Having encouraged them, God commanded Israel to drive out all the inhabitants of Canaan and destroy all that was associated with pagan idol worship. There is also a warning. If they did not faithfully execute the command, "those of them whom you let remain shall be as barbs in your eyes and thorns in your sides, and they shall trouble you in the land where you dwell. And I will do to you as I thought to do to them" (verses 55-56). We know how Israel failed to carry out this command completely and how this warning came to pass. The Gentiles, who remained in Canaan, indeed became barbs in Israel's eyes and thorns in its sides. They were a painful reminder of Israel's failure and disobedience, of the covenant curses they incurred from God.

How could the thorns of God's covenant curses be removed from the people of God? They had the temple and the sacrificial system. But these things could not shield them from God's judgment for their consistent rebellion against God. In the end, they were cast out of the promised land, just like the Canaanites their forefathers chased out. And their temple was destroyed and leveled, too. They needed something better than the animal sacrifices at the temple. They needed nothing less than the Son of God bearing the thorns of the covenant curses on behalf of His people.

And that was exactly what Christ did, wasn't it? He had a crown of thorns pressed upon His head. As the barbs and thorns were but metaphors for God's covenant curses upon Israel's rebellion and failure, so was the crown of thorns a metaphor for the full wrath of God, which Jesus was made to bear on the cross. Upon the cross Jesus suffered the covenant curses for all our sins all at once. This is why Jesus is able to say, "Come to Me, all who labor and are heavy laden, and I will give you rest" (Matthew 11:28); and, "Today, you will be with Me in Paradise" (Luke 23:43). As we saw, Jesus retraced and relived Israel's wilderness journey, succeeding where Israel failed, thus correcting all that was wrong. But that was not sufficient. Jesus had to bear the punishment of our sins. He had to go all the way to the depths of hell so we don't have to go there. What is more, He went all the way to heaven on our behalf so we too can go there on the wings of Christ's righteousness! In Jesus Christ, we have the assurance of our eternal rest in the heavenly paradise! We can have a foretaste of it even now!

Journeying With Christ

Let us pause and look back. Maybe that is not very pleasant for many of us—there are too many painful memories in our past. But in Christ, all that has been changed. Because He embraced our journey of failure and died for it, because Jesus lived the life we failed to live, we have been set free from our past. You may be living the unpleasant consequences of your bad choices and sins in the past. But know that, in His life, death, and resurrection, our Lord relived your life, suffering the barbs and thorns of your sins and failures, every one of them, every step of the way! As a result, thorns and barbs are taken out of them. Bitterness is taken out of our sorrows. Punishment is taken out of our sufferings. Even our death has lost its sting!

As C.S. Lewis suggested, when we shall arrive in heaven and look back on our journey through this world, we will realize that we have been in heaven all along since the moment we came to know Jesus, since Christ became our travel Companion and Guide—yes, even through the darkest moments of our journey! If so, why should we wait until then? Let us embrace this heavenly journey by faith, now! Yes, at times, in the midst of our trials, we may not feel our heavenly life has already begun. But remember. Where was He at the end of His life on earth? At the most God-forsaken place in the whole universe—right there on the cross, being abandoned by God and men! If He took your place before the judgment seat of God, you can be sure that He is right there with you in your loneliest moment.

By faith let us affirm (and reaffirm) that we are united with Christ! So then, His journey to heaven is our journey; His abundant life is our life; His heaven is our heaven; His eternal rest is our rest! Embrace Christ! Experience His life! Walk His journey toward heaven! Enjoy His rest! As we do this, we know that even our greatest enjoyment of these things in the present cannot compare to the fullness of joy we shall receive when we finally get to our home! So then, let us not take up the journey of our old life again. Let us fix our eyes upon Christ, seated at the right hand of God. Let us seek the things that are above, not the things that are on earth. Let us walk by faith until we finish our journey, knowing that, as surely as Christ has already finished the journey, we too shall finish it someday and enter into His glory!

www.ingramcontent.com/pod-product-compliance
Lightning Source LLC
LaVergne TN
LVHW051255080426
835509LV00020B/2993